GOOD
NEWS
for
WOMEN

GOOD NEWS for WOMEN

A Biblical Picture of Gender Equality

REBECCA MERRILL GROOTHUIS

Baker Books

A Division of Baker Book House Co
Grand Rapids, Michigan 49516

Published by Baker Books
a division of Baker Book House Company
P.O. Box 6287, Grand Rapids, MI 49516-6287

Second printing, June 1997

Printed in United States of America

Library of Congress Cataloging-in-Publication Data

Groothuis, Rebecca Merrill.
    Good news for women : a biblical picture of gender equality / Rebecca Merrill Groothuis.
        p.   cm.
    Includes bibliographical references and indexes.
    ISBN 0-8010-5720-5 (pbk.)
    1. Women in the Bible. 2. Woman (Christian theology)—Biblical teaching. 3. Feminist theology. I. Title.
    BS680.W7G66 1996
    261.8'343'09015—dc21   96-45208

For current information about all releases from Baker Book House,
visit our web site:
                    http://www.bakerbooks.com

To my parents
Paul LaRose Merrill
and
Jean Northrup Merrill
with gratitude for
so many things—
especially the example
of their loving life
together,
which taught me more
than any book on marriage
ever could

Contents

Acknowledgments

 am grateful to all those who contributed their time and energy toward helping me complete this book. A number of people read and critiqued various parts of the manuscript at various stages of its development, and some suggested resources that I found useful. Their names include Craig Keener (who read and offered valuable suggestions on the entire first draft of the manuscript), Doug Groothuis, Bob Hubbard, Roger Nicole, Jean Merrill, Sulia Mason, and Nancy Johnson. Special thanks, as always, go to my husband, Doug. Without his numerous prayers, occasional pep talks, periodic scholarly counsel, and much practical assistance, this book surely would never have come into existence. I am especially grateful to those few, unnamed, but noble souls who prayed for me over the period of several years that this book was being written, rewritten, and rewritten.

Introduction

y motivation for writing this book arises from my own experiences as a Christian woman, and from the sampling of similar stories that I have heard from other Christian women. On the one hand, it has been somewhat encouraging to learn that I am not the only one who has been made to feel out of place—and has been put *in* her place—because she doesn't happen to fit the conventional mold. On the other hand, I have been saddened to learn that such experiences seem to form a pattern that is pandemic in conservative Christian circles, despite the fact that we live in a society that puts a strong emphasis on equality and liberty for everyone.

Experience is not the sole source and arbiter of truth; but it has a way of nudging one's mind into explorations of different perspectives and new alternatives. When experience is illuminated by the truth of God's Word and the guidance of the Holy Spirit, the result can be a truer understanding of how our lives may be lived more fully for the glory of God. It is my hope that the viewpoint offered in this book will help both women and men understand more clearly how their gifts may be used—with freedom and fulfillment—in obedient service to the Lord.

The general belief that God has reserved certain positions of spiritual or religious authority for men seems to prevail in one form or another in most evangelical churches and Christian ministries. As a result, women who desire to give all that they have to give to the cause of Christ (as *all* believers should desire to do) are usually met with a maze of rules and restrictions. Moreover, they often find that these rules and restrictions vary from one situation to another, usually without any compelling or consistent rationale.

The line that women are prevented from crossing may be drawn in different places at different times for different women; but always, it is drawn. And it is drawn not only in terms of official church policy and teaching, but also (and even more cruelly) in the usually inarticulated prejudices and unexamined assumptions that guide so many people's ideas about what women can and cannot do, and what the limitations of their "place" should be.

A restrictive, stereotypical view of womanhood remains entrenched in the evangelical church because it is believed to be backed up by biblical proof texts. Therefore, we need to examine the alleged basis for such thinking in Scripture. Could it be that an unprejudiced assessment of biblical teaching finds no compelling evidence of an eternal spiritual principle requiring men to occupy roles of leadership and women to assume roles of subordinate domesticity? Could it be that the traditional definition of womanhood is more cultural than biblical?

Many Christians assume that the church's traditional position on this issue is reason enough to affirm hierarchical gender roles as the only biblical option. How could so many years of church tradition be so wrong? However, the belief that women should be subordinate to male authority is neither unique to, nor original with, the Christian church. All cultures of all traditions since the beginning of recorded history have endorsed this view of gender distinctions. It is, therefore, quite possible that the church imbibed this idea from cultural assumptions, and then interpreted the Bible in light of these assumptions.

The church is far from infallible. The Bible, not tradition, is our final authority. Protestants, especially, should understand this. The Reformation cry of *sola scriptura* represented the Protestant break from the absolute authority of church tradition. In that particular case, the church's teaching on the doctrine of justification had taken a wrong turn and needed to be corrected. The church has held many wrong ideas in its long history—ideas which are disavowed by the church today. For example, early in church history women were shunned as evil, "the devil's gateway" in the words of one church father (Tertullian); and during the Middle Ages, belief in this innate female evil led to an exaggerated fear of witchcraft among women. Due to a misinterpretation of Genesis 3:16, women were denied medical relief from pain during childbirth. There is also a long history of Christians persecuting Jews as "Christ killers." When Copernicus and Galileo announced that the earth circled the sun rather than vice versa, the theory was rejected as an affront to biblical authority. Until relatively recently, many in the church condemned women's suffrage as unbiblical, proclaimed biblical support for the practice of slavery, and regarded people of nonwhite races as inferior.[1]

None of this means that tradition in itself is evil or wrong. By and large, church tradition has proven, through the grace of God, to be a fairly reliable guide on matters central to orthodox theology (such as the nature of God, Christ, and humanity, the way of salvation, the purpose of history, and so forth). But because the Bible is our ultimate authority—not tradition, not even traditional interpretations of the Bible—tradition should not automatically be accepted as true. Rather, tradition should always be examined with suspicion for evidence of its tendency to take sinful patterns of human behavior and enshrine them as normative. Jesus spoke of this tendency when he upbraided the Pharisees, saying, "You have let go of the commands of God and are holding on to the traditions of men" (Mark 7:8). Blaise Pascal also had some wise words on the subject: "Whatever the weight of antiquity, truth should always have the advantage, even when newly discovered, since it is always older than every opinion men have held about it."[2]

Sadly, church tradition has often denied women the opportunity to use whatever gifts they might possess, and to serve in whatever ways God calls them, for the good of the church and the glory of God. The traditional view that men and women differ radically from each other, and thus should have gender-specific roles of unequal status in the home and the church, needs to be replaced with a view of individual gifts and ministries that affirms the fundamental equality of women and men in Christ.

The purpose of this book is to show that the broad sweep of biblical thought aligns more readily with gender equality than gender hierarchy, and that the biblical proof texts used to support traditionalist gender roles fail to present an open-and-shut case for the position. Rather, the assertion of a universalized and spiritualized gender hierarchy in the home and church seems to go beyond—and against—what is clearly stated in Scripture.

Before examining the biblical texts that refer specifically to women and men (or to wives and husbands), we need to look at the overall outline of biblical teaching and its implications for relationships between men and women. Toward this end, the first part of the book will present a biblical case for gender equality and examine some of the logical and theological problems with the traditionalist position. These four chapters are foundational to an understanding of the subject, and provide the framework within which the material in the following chapters should be understood. The second part of the book will assess the biblical texts that traditionalists regard as universally mandating women's subordination to the spiritual authority of men. The final chapter will bring together various strands of the issue, and suggest ways to proceed toward a resolution of the conflict.

The argument for traditionalist gender roles, however, does not actually begin with the standard set of biblical proof texts. Rather, it begins with a set of assumptions about feminism and modern culture. The argument seems to goes like this: Any challenge to "traditional" gender roles is "feminist," and anything feminist is entirely a product of modern culture, and modern culture stands in total opposition to biblical values. Therefore, any interpretation of the Bible that questions traditional gender roles could only arise not out of a genuine respect for the authority of Scripture, but out of a desire to use the Bible to justify an agenda that the church has imported from modern culture.

Because this viewpoint is taught by many evangelicals today, it needs to be dealt with before the biblical case for gender equality can receive a fair hearing. Otherwise, Bible-believing Christians who know nothing more about feminism and modern culture than what they hear from traditionalists will be reluctant to entertain any ideas labelled "feminist," for fear they will find themselves slipping unwittingly into apostasy.

For this reason I wrote my first book, *Women Caught in the Conflict: The Culture War between Traditionalism and Feminism*. In it I place both evangelical feminism and traditionalism in their cultural and historical contexts, in order to show how they stand in relation to previous and present perspectives on gender roles. I offer a clear and careful definition of evangelical feminism (or biblical equality) and explain how its premises, goals, theology, and history differ fundamentally from that of other types of feminism today. I also discuss the basic tenets and background of the position variously termed traditionalist, antifeminist, hierarchical, and complementarian. I probably should note, however, that I do not use the term "complementarian" in either book because I believe its meaning is ambiguous. Discussion of gender roles is so easily obfuscated, overheated, and sidetracked, it is important that our terminology be as precise as possible. Unlike the other terms for the nonegalitarian position, "complementarian" does not point to the distinctive beliefs that are at issue in this debate. It could just as easily be used to describe a position of biblical equality; certainly no one is claiming that men and women do not complement one another.

Before beginning a biblical study of the gender issue, it is essential to understand that the debate between traditionalism and biblical equality is not—as some suggest—a titanic struggle between the orthodox and the heretical, or the biblical and the secular. It is, rather, a theological and hermeneutical disagreement over what the Bible teaches about gender roles.

When the ground has been cleared of assorted preconceptions and misconceptions, then this debate can be cut down to scale; the feminist bogeywoman will cease to terrify, and an open-minded, Spirit-guided, Bible-based critique of both positions can commence. It is at this point, I hope, that *Good News for Women* will enter the picture. But I would like to suggest, if I may, that those Christians who have concerns about how the idea of biblical equality fits into the modern cultural and conceptual landscape begin a study of this issue by reading *Women Caught in the Conflict*.

PART 1

The Biblical Case for Gender Equality

1

One in Christ and Heirs of God

ecause the concept of equality is employed in so many ways to mean so many different things, confusion and consternation typically attend any discussion of the subject. Biblical equality refers to the fundamental biblical principle that every human being stands on equal ground before God; there is no group of persons that is inherently more or less worthy than another. It follows from this principle that there is no moral or theological justification for permanently granting or denying a person status, privilege, or prerogative solely on the basis of that person's race, class, or gender.

A biblical view of gender equality does not mean that gender makes no difference in a person's identity or behavior, but that gender ought not, in and of itself, limit a person's status or ministry opportunities. The appropriate outworking of the biblical ideal of equality is for women and men to have equal opportunity for ministry in the church, and shared authority with mutual submission within marriage. The positing of a universal spiritual principle of female subordination to male authority within the home and the church runs contrary to the principle of biblical equality.

The truth of the equality of all persons under God is grounded in creation. Genesis 1:26–27 and 5:1–2 state that both male and female humans bear God's image equally and without distinction. Both have been commanded equally and without distinction to take dominion, not one over the other but both together, over the rest of God's creation for the glory of the Creator. The essential equality of all people is foundational to the message of Jesus Christ, who insisted that the concern of his disciples be the exercise of submission and servanthood, rather than the effort to claim or attain status and authority (Matt. 20:25–28; Mark 10:42–45; Luke 22:25–27).

In the new covenant, God shows no favoritism for one group of people over another (Acts 10:34–35; Rom. 2:11; James 2:8–9), and believers are filled with the Holy Spirit and gifted in prophetic ministry without respect to age, gender, or social status (Acts 2:17–18). According to Galatians 3:26–28, all believers are "sons," or heirs, in Christ; there is no longer any distinction in spiritual privilege or status between either Jew or Gentile, slave or free, male or female. First Peter 3:7 states that husband and wife are equal heirs of God's gift of life, and Romans 8:15–17 declares that all believers are adopted sons of God, and hence "heirs of God and co-heirs with Christ."

Biblical equality is reflected in the doctrine of the priesthood of all believers (1 Peter 2:5, 9; Rev. 1:6; 5:10), and in repeated New Testament exhortations to believers to honor one another and to be humble and submissive toward one another (Matt. 23:8–12; Rom. 12:3, 10; Eph. 5:21; Phil. 2:3; 1 Peter 5:5). Equality will be fully realized in the new heaven and the new earth when all believers (regardless of gender or any other classification) will reign together with Christ (Dan. 7:18, 27; 1 Cor. 6:2–3; 2 Tim. 2:12; Rev. 2:26–27; 3:21; 5:10; 22:5).

The Word of God is bracketed at its beginning and its end by a clear message of equality: all persons are made by God in the image of God, and all the saints will reign together with Christ forever.[1] These fundamental truths concerning our creation and re-creation by God in Christ leave no room for any permanent and universal stratification of spiritual authority based on gender.

God's Plan for Equality

The biblical truth of women's equality with men is not a new idea imported into the church from secular culture. It is rooted in the first chapters of the Bible, where we find the statement that male and female humans alike are made in God's image (Gen. 1:27; 5:1–2), as well as a very nonpatriarchal description of God's original intent for marriage (Gen. 2:24). But, as Genesis 3:16 indicates, the entrance of sin into God's created order destroyed the equality and mutuality between woman and man. Before the fall, marriage consisted of two equal partners serving God together in a common mission, the cultural mandate to have dominion (Gen. 1:28). Since the fall, men and women have perverted God's command to exercise responsible dominion over creation. Men have been inclined to exert authoritarian domination of other people, especially of women, while women's sin patterns have tended more toward dependency, passivity, and manipulation.[2] This perversion of God's original order has resulted in cultural patriarchy.

God revealed himself and his plan for his people by means of patriarchal cultures, adapting his revealed Word to fit the understanding and limitations of its original recipients. It is, therefore, necessary to distinguish between those biblical statements that are universal, normative commands and those that are concessions to ancient patriarchal culture. As Craig Keener observes, "The culture defined different roles for men and women, roles that changed from time to time and from culture to culture, and God worked with this aspect of the culture. But there is never any indication in the Old Testament that God mandated that men have sole authority over the home."[3] Nor, for that matter, does God ever directly authorize a husband's rule of his wife anywhere in the New Testament.[4]

Jesus explained that God allowed divorce because people's "hearts were hard," but that it was not God's original intention (Matt. 19:8). In the same way, it seems, God allowed the subjugation of women and other social groups because people's hearts were not ready to receive the fullness of God's good news with all its sociocultural implications. But throughout biblical revelation God progressively made known his redemptive plan, whereby the essential equality of all people would ultimately be restored and the practice of gender hierarchy brought to an end.

The Old Testament, unlike the New, has nary a verse enjoining women to be submissive. It was simply accepted as part of the cultures of that time. Old Testament Law safeguarded women from certain abuses, but it did not challenge the cultural patriarchal norm of female subordination to male rule. Deviations from this social norm did occur occasionally, when God would raise up female prophets who exercised spiritual and even civil leadership, thus indicating that women's normally subordinate role was a cultural matter and not a result of divine decree or of any inherent deficiency in femaleness per se.[5] By and large, however, the old covenant was directed toward a very select group of people, namely, free Jewish males. Other groups of people were not permitted to participate fully in the religious life of the community. This stratification of religious status had become even more rigid in the Jewish law current at the time of Christ.[6]

Jesus, the Messiah, was born under the Law; he himself was a free Jewish male, and he chose free Jewish males for his closest disciples. Jesus knew the Law, and that he had come under the Law to fulfill the Law; but he also knew what was coming—a new covenant in which the male/female, Jew/Gentile, free/slave distinctions no longer would entail superior/inferior relationships in terms of spiritual status. The message of Jesus Christ and the new covenant that he instituted make it clear that the patriarchal values in Old Testament Law and custom were due to the influence of human culture rather than divine command. This aspect of Old Testament Law is most accurately seen as an accommodation to cultural patriarchy, not as an affirmation of it.

Jesus' interaction with people outside the favored class of free Jewish males clearly pointed toward the new ethic of biblical equality. Jesus broke a number of the patriarchal norms in the culture of his time. He spoke to women in public (Luke 13:10–13; John 4:7–27), though women of that time had no place in public discourse. He taught women theology, both in private and in public, much to the surprise of his disciples (Luke 10:38–42; John 4:7–27; 11:21–27) and contrary to the rabbinic belief that women and theology should have nothing to do with each other. He was unconcerned about the touch of an "unclean," hemorrhaging woman, whom he healed (Mark 5:25–34). He sent a woman as a witness to history's greatest event, the resurrection (John 20:17), and this in a society where a woman's word was so devalued her testimony counted for nothing in a court of law. He

pointed out that a man's lust for a woman is due to the man's sinful-
ness (Matt. 5:28), when the religious mind of the time blamed male
lust on the sexual impurity of the woman. And he stated that woman's
primary purpose in life is not motherhood or domestic work, but knowing God's Word and obeying God's will—as was true for any man as
well (Luke 10:38–42; 11:27–28).

Some of Jesus' most theologically rich statements were spoken
only to women. He talked with the Samaritan woman at the well about
his messiahship, the nature of God, and how God should be worshiped
(John 4:21–26). After Lazarus's death, Jesus told Martha that he was
the resurrection and the life, and that whoever believes on him would
never die (John 11:25). Jesus did not just throw the women a few theological tidbits. Uneducated and socially undervalued though they
were, he gave to women the real meat of his word.[7] In all these things,
"the equality of woman before God and the created solidarity of man
and woman is dealt with in real earnest over against the contemporary cultic and social degradation of woman."[8]

After Christ's death and resurrection and the establishing of the new
covenant, there arose for the first time a need for church leaders to
exhort women to be properly submissive. Why? Did Christian women
need to be told to submit because they were picking up some egalitarian notions from secular society? No, the dominant cultural mentality
at this time was still that a woman should stay out of public leadership
roles and be submissive to her husband's authority. The idea of gender equality came not from society, but from the gospel of Jesus
Christ—wherein there is "no longer male and female" but all are "sons"
(or heirs) of God in Christ. Religious patriarchy had been vanquished
by the redemptive work of Jesus Christ. Societal patriarchy, however,
remained intact. W. Ward Gasque explains why the leaders of the young
church needed to remind believers to refrain from allowing their newfound spiritual freedom to lead to unseemly social behavior.

> The danger for the church in Paul's day lay in the exact opposite direc-
> tion from the church in our day; that is, there was the danger that it might
> press the principle of Christian freedom too far. Rather than defending
> the status quo (as is often the case with the church in our day), the first-
> century church called into question many of the fundamental structures
> of contemporary society. First-century Christians might—and many

did—push their newfound freedom to extremes. . . . Our precious heritage of freedom in Christ, says Paul, should not become a stumbling block in the way of anyone's coming to faith or to Christian maturity. There is a law higher than the law of liberty: it is the law of love.[9]

In ancient Greco-Roman culture, only men were educated in the Scriptures; women generally were not allowed a public voice, but were expected to work primarily in their homes. Men were regarded as morally and intellectually superior to women, and women were obligated (both culturally and legally) to obey their husbands' civil authority over them.[10] The presence of such laws and customs—in combination with the hostility and persecution that the church faced from the outside society—naturally affected the appropriate application of Christian principles for righteous living at that time.

Because the New Testament church was intent on gaining as wide a hearing as possible for the gospel message, it was necessary for the church to put first things first, and for the principle of biblical equality to be exercised with some restraint. The apostle Paul's emphasis was on the need for Jews and Gentiles to be reconciled into one body. Outside of this important social and religious change, believers were encouraged to conform to existing customs (within the limits of godly behavior). Christian women and slaves were to submit to their husbands and masters, as were all Christians to the governing authorities. New Testament church leaders did not want Christianity to be perceived as a subversive social movement intent on overthrowing traditional moral values and social structures, for this would only have brought more persecution, as well as public reproach on the name of Christ.[11] As Klyne Snodgrass explains:

That Paul did not spell out the implications for slaves and women more than he did is not too surprising if one allows for his concern for missions. Other factors, no doubt, were the fear of social upheaval and the fear that the Christian movement would be seen as a political force and, as a result, would be stamped out. . . . Another obvious reason . . . is that there was no one saying "You must be a free person or a male to become a Christian." . . . The categories of slave/free and male/female were not a threat to the understanding of the gospel, as the Jew/Gentile issue was.[12]

Women's exercise of their new liberty in Christ was necessarily limited not only because of the prevailing social laws and customs, but also because women's prior experience had not prepared them for the religious roles held by men. Most women were ill-equipped for public discourse and needed to become educated before they could become teachers and leaders in the church. However, as we will see in chapter 8, the New Testament church did encourage the service of those women who had been equipped and called by God to pastoral and teaching ministries.

In short, the strategy of the New Testament church was to tolerate the social subordination of slaves and women so as not to risk alienating non-Christians from the gospel, and yet to modulate and moderate these customs, and ultimately to point beyond them to God's original intention for human relations. Today, however, when non-Christians are not likely to be offended by an equalitarian gospel, but *are* likely to find a hierarchical gospel offensive, we have no reason to perpetuate the cultural practices that were initially intended for Christians living in patriarchal societies.

Indications of the essential equality of all people glimmer throughout the pages of Scripture and serve as intimations or signs that God did not endorse the established patriarchal order, but had a better plan in mind. God's plan for establishing a new order through Christ, however, did not point toward a sudden cultural revolution, but toward a gradual outworking of the principles of life and liberty through all those who are heirs of God.

It is important to remember that the political structures for peaceful reform that are taken for granted in democratic societies today did not exist in the highly stratified, authoritarian societies of ancient times.[13] The early Christians did not have at their disposal the means to effect broad social reformation. Social reform, of course, should never be the *primary* goal of the church; but in ancient society it was not feasible for Christians even to attempt such a thing.

Male and Female: Equal Heirs and One in Christ

Of all the texts that support biblical equality, Galatians 3:26–28 is probably the most important. Unlike the New Testament proof texts traditionalists use to support hierarchical gender roles, this text is not a specific command directed toward a specific cultural situation. Rather, it is a broadly applicable statement of the inclusive nature of the new covenant, whereby all groups of people, regardless of their previous religious status under the law, have now become one in Christ. "There is neither Jew nor Greek, slave nor free, male nor female" (v. 28). The old distinctions have become irrelevant. All are equally "sons," or heirs, of God. F. F. Bruce declares that "Paul states the basic principle here; if restrictions on it are found elsewhere in the Pauline corpus, as in 1 Corinthians 14:34f. . . . or 1 Timothy 2:11f., they are to be understood in relation to Galatians 3:28, and not *vice versa.*"[14]

In order to understand the meaning of any biblical text, it is necessary to understand the author's intent in writing it. It is apparent that Paul wrote this letter to the Galatians in order to refute the Judaizers, the Jewish Christians who maintained that Gentile Christians must follow the law of Moses—specifically, that the men must be circumcised—in order to be fully accepted in the Christian church. The larger context of 3:26–28 concerns the radical change that resulted from the old covenant being replaced by the new. Paul is, as usual, particularly eager to explain the redeemed relationship of Jew and Gentile. In verse 28, however, he points out that the old inequalities under Old Testament Law have been nullified with respect not only to Jew and Gentile, but also slave and free, male and female. F. F. Bruce explains:

> The breaking down of the middle wall of partition between [Jew and Greek] was fundamental to Paul's gospel (Ephesians 2:14f.). By similarly excluding the religious distinction between slaves and the free-born, and between male and female, Paul makes a threefold affirmation which corresponds to a number of Jewish formulas in which the threefold distinction is maintained, as in the morning prayer in which the male Jew thanks God that he was not made a Gentile, a slave or a woman. . . . The reason for the threefold thanksgiving was not any positive disparagement of Gentiles, slaves or women as persons but the fact that they were disqualified from several religious privileges which were open to free Jewish males. . . . [Paul] takes up each of these three distinctions which had considerable importance in Judaism and affirms that in Christ they are all irrelevant.[15]

The issue addressed in this text concerns how exclusive the church ought to be. What should be its terms of full membership? Were the old categories—gender, ethnicity, and social status—to continue to determine the limits of a person's status in the religious community? Or was there a new insight, God's view of humanity, whereby anyone who accepts Christ becomes a full and equal member of the church with no permanent, built-in limitations of status or religious privilege, thus rendering obsolete the earlier categories that had excluded from full participation all who were not free Jewish males?

Galatians 3:26–28 speaks of the spiritual equality and unity that all believers enjoy under the new covenant; thus, it is not specifically a Magna Charta, freeing various social underclasses from their positions of servitude in society. However, it does not seem unreasonable to conclude that if people are equal before God, they are equal with respect to one another and ought to treat one another accordingly. If neither race, gender, nor social class determines a person's status in God's eyes, then what right have members of any society to grant persons of one gender the opportunity to prove themselves qualified for a particular role or status, but to deny that opportunity to persons of the other gender? The social implications of spiritual equality seem clear enough.[16] Nevertheless, in order to stay as close as possible to Paul's purpose in writing these words, this discussion will focus primarily on equality of spiritual and religious status rather than of social status.

Role Distinctions and Galatians 3:26–28

In arguing against an egalitarian interpretation of this text, traditionalists frequently point out that Galatians 3:28 does not provide grounds for the obliteration of all role distinctions between the various groups mentioned. This certainly seems to be an accurate observation. But it does not lead to the conclusion that this text has *nothing* to say about appropriate roles for women and men. If women and men enjoy spiritual equality under the new covenant, then this equality is fundamentally contradicted by an exclusively male prerogative to interpret and determine the Word and the will of God authoritatively in the home and in the church. Galatians 3:28 does require the obliteration of this gender role distinction.

Certainly, people will have different roles because every individual is different from every other. There will also be role differentiation pertaining to differences in sexual/reproductive function, and differences in class standing as determined by the social structures of the time. Paul was not advocating sexual sameness, nor was he demanding immediate social change. These issues are not the point of the text—nor, for that matter, of the debate between traditionalist and egalitarian interpretations of this text. Rather, the spirit and intent of Galatians 3:26–28 is that differences of race, social class, and gender should no longer determine differences of status and privilege within the religious community. As F. F. Bruce succinctly states, "It is not their distinctiveness, but their inequality of religious role, that is abolished 'in Christ Jesus.' . . . In other spheres, indeed, the distinctions which ceased to be relevant in church fellowship might continue to be observed."[17]

When traditionalists attempt to defend gender hierarchy by noting that role distinctions do not negate the essential spiritual equality of women and men, they often point to the numerous New Testament references to the variety of gifts and offices that are distributed among believers. If all these role distinctions—many entailing different levels of authority—exist with no loss of spiritual equality, why, traditionalists ask, should biblical feminists object to delineating male and female roles?[18] Such an argument sidesteps the point that is expressed so clearly in Galatians 3:28. This text is not saying that there is no longer any distinction in spiritual roles and ministries between individuals, but that there is no longer any distinction in spiritual roles and ministries between classes of people.

In other words, a person's membership in a particular race, class, or gender is not to be regarded as automatically and permanently disqualifying that person from certain roles and ministries in the spiritual body of Christ. Clarence Boomsma describes the equality between social groups that follows from unity in Christ:

> The equality of people's potential for worth, function, responsibility, and authority lies in their unity with Christ, which is not restricted by their ethnicity, social status, or gender. Of course, equality does not mean that the capacities of all are the same, that all are biologically alike, that there are no dissimilarities in character and personality, in

intellectual, emotional, and physical endowments, in spiritual gifts and talents. All such differences in individuals have a bearing on a person's suitability for particular service in the church as is taught in 1 Corinthians 12. But the point of Galatians 3:28 is that no person is unsuitable because of his or her nationality, social status, or gender.[19]

Because people are not all the same when it comes to spiritual gifts and maturity, some individuals are unfit to exercise spiritual leadership. However, unlike the exclusion of women, the exclusion of a person from leadership on account of spiritual unfitness is not a permanent and arbitrary exclusion. In time, this person could grow in knowledge of God and the Bible and become qualified to fill such a position.

Spiritual Equality?

When many of the roles that require higher levels of spiritual maturity, understanding, and giftedness are the roles from which women are excluded—as is the case in the traditionalist agenda—it is something of a stretch to insist that the essential spiritual equality of women is not being violated thereby. The implication that femaleness is spiritually inferior to maleness cannot be avoided when femaleness alone provides sufficient grounds to deny a person the opportunity even to earn the right to fill certain spiritual roles, and when maleness does not restrict a person from performing any ministry he may be qualified to do.

Nowhere are unequal spiritual roles for men and women more clearly delineated than in the traditional Anglican and Catholic teaching about the priesthood requiring the "masculine uniform," as C. S. Lewis put it.[20] But the spiritual inequality of men and women is implicit even in the traditional Protestant prescription for unequal gender roles, whereby positions of spiritual authority in the church are reserved for men, and every married man is deemed the spiritual leader, or "priest," of his home, the representative of God to his family.

To circumvent the evident contradiction between traditionalist gender roles and Galatians 3:26–28, advocates of gender hierarchy maintain that this text's declaration of the spiritual equality of all believers refers only to an equality of salvific status. In other words, Galatians

3:26–28 says nothing more than that all believers are equally saved, and so does not negate the requirement that roles of spiritual authority be reserved for men. But is it biblically justifiable, or even meaningful, to understand spiritual status only in terms of salvific status, and to insist that being spiritually equal simply means being "equally saved"?

The central point of this passage is that things under the new covenant are different than the way they were under the old covenant. Something has changed; there is a new unity and equality between believers. The old religious categories of Jew and Gentile, slave and free, male and female, have been rendered irrelevant. Therefore, the question at stake in understanding Paul's words accurately is this: In what respect were these group distinctions once relevant, but now are no longer relevant?

Is the difference simply that people who would have been unequally saved under the Law are now equally saved? But what does equal or unequal have to do with being saved? There are no gradations of justification. One either has been forgiven of sin through faith in God or one has not; one is either in the covenant community, or one is outside it. Why should Paul belabor the obvious by saying all are equally justified? In the old covenant, women, slaves, and Gentile proselytes belonged in the community of the redeemed along with free Jewish males. Gentiles were, of course, more likely to be ignorant of and, therefore, disobedient to Old Testament Law. But "the Hebrews did not teach that people were redeemed on the basis of being born a Jew, a nonslave, or a male."[21]

Moreover, "Christianity did not suddenly grant women access to God that they did not have in Judaism. Women belonged to the covenant in Israel, and . . . neither the Old Testament nor Judaism saw the categories slave/free or male/female as significant for salvation."[22] Why should Paul have made a point of assuring women that they were not excluded from the new covenant if they had not been excluded from the old? "The salvation of Jews and Gentiles, slaves and free, men and women was not in question when Paul wrote Galatians."[23] If Paul is speaking here only of salvation, then he is not telling the Galatians anything they don't already know. The claim that this text means only that members of these different groups are "equally saved" renders Paul's words superfluous and redundant.

It seems clear that Galatians 3:26–28 is saying that women are now equal with men (and slaves with free persons, and Gentiles with Jews) in a way that they were not under Old Testament Law. Distinctions in religious status between certain groups of people have been nullified under the terms of the new covenant. In order to grasp Paul's intent in this passage, we must identify what has changed with respect to women, slaves, and Gentiles in the transition from the old covenant to the new.

The Old Covenant Versus the New

In the Old Testament, a person's spiritual and social inheritance depended largely upon that person's natural lines of heredity, whether national or familial. Jonathan, who was a better man than Saul, was denied the throne because of his father's sins (1 Sam. 13:13–14). The sins of Korah and of Achan were punished not only by their own deaths, but also the deaths of everyone in their respective households (Num. 16; Josh. 7). Entire Canaanite tribes—including newborn babies—were slaughtered because of their national heritage. The people of Israel were blessed or cursed, depending on the moral status of their king.

The idea that a person's circumstances of birth (gender, nationality, and so forth) should determine his place in life—including his religious place—was foundational to the patriarchal societies of biblical times. Old Testament Law accommodated and incorporated many of these patriarchal precepts of traditional society. It is difficult for us to appreciate how vastly different this way of life was from the democratic, individualistic culture in which we live today.

In the New Testament era, persons are either in or out of the family of God by virtue of their individual standing before God. Branches remain, are lopped off, or are grafted in (John 15:1–8; Rom. 11:17–24), depending on the presence or absence of saving, trusting, obedient faith in each person. Stephen Clark explains that the Jewish people

> were structured along the lines of kinship and racial purity. Someone became an Israelite primarily by birth. One was born into God's people. Proselytes were received into the people, but even the full proselyte could not achieve the status of the full Israelite. . . . However, the coming of Christ replaced the principle of natural birth with the principle

of spiritual birth. Ancestry and racial purity played no role in either spiritual or social status among Christians.[24]

In the Old Testament, women had membership in the covenant community through their male family members because male circumcision was the sign of the covenant. While women were members of the covenant community, their status was derived from and secondary to that of the men. There was a corresponding inequality in the degree to which women could participate in the religious life of the community. Women participated, but not fully; they were members of the covenant community, but not equal members. Certain religious privileges were limited to free Jewish males. In the temple that was rebuilt during Herod's reign, Jewish women were not permitted to enter past the court of the women, which was one court past the court of the Gentiles.[25] This architectural arrangement aptly illustrated the religious place that Jewish women held with respect to Jewish men.

Women, of course, could not serve as priests under the old covenant. But neither could most men. In order to be accepted into the priesthood, a man had to be a descendant of Aaron, he had to be physically perfect (without blemish or defect), and the woman he married had to be a virgin (Lev. 21:13–23). Further restrictions were imposed on priestly service in the innermost sanctuary, which could be entered only once a year by the high priest. Eileen Vennum explains that

> The Old Covenant priestly qualifications were tied to what human beings valued in each other. They were related to accident of birth, or station in life, or visible physical characteristics that had nothing to do with the heart or the character of a person. However, God, the Great Teacher, used human ideas of specialness to teach us about God's own specialness.[26]

Paul points out in Galatians 3:6–18 that the Old Testament provided glimpses of the grace of a God who looks on the heart of a person and does not judge according to human values but justifies a person by faith (Hab. 2:4). However, the old covenant served primarily to teach God's people elementary lessons about God's glory and moral perfection by means of concrete illustrations derived from the things that were valued in human culture. Therefore, priests were required to be males without physical defect. As Paul explains in Galatians 3:23–25 and 4:1–7, those under the law did not have all the rights, liberties, and privileges of sons, because they "were in slavery under the basic principles of the world" (4:3). With its emphasis on human effort and human values, the Law—especially the ceremonial aspect of Old Testament Law—provided a very concrete and detailed picture of human sin, of God's holiness, and of the need for that gap to be bridged (see Gal. 3:19–22). The Law served as a tutor that taught a limited view of God's truth, in very human terms.

But with the redemption offered by Christ, all believers are to be recognized as having full spiritual status without regard to human distinctions and values. Paul explains the nature of this new status by analogy with the concept of the "son," the free Jewish male who comes into his full inheritance upon passing from childhood to manhood (Gal. 3:26, 29; 4:1–7). In the new order in Christ, the external restrictions and legal requirements pertaining to the priesthood and other aspects of the ceremonial law have been set aside. Just as applicants for pastoral ministries are no longer judged according to their ancestry, or inspected for physical flaws, spots, and blemishes, so there is no longer any warrant to disqualify a person from such a ministry because of gender. "Under the New Covenant, God qualifies us as priests because of our heart's response of love to Christ's substitutional sacrifice for our guilt (1 Peter 2:9)."[27]

Under Old Testament Law, a woman not only was barred from priestly service, but also had less spiritual authority than her father or husband. She could pray to God directly and even make vows to God. But her husband or father had the spiritual authority to nullify any vow she made. In some cases, by nullifying the woman's vow, the man actually bore her guilt for not keeping the vow. He was responsible to God for her (Num. 30:3–15). In this we hear echoes of today's traditionalist teaching on the man as the "priest of the home." Some advocates of gender hierarchy have even used this Old Testament vow-breaking procedure as illustrative of how male headship is to work within marriage today.[28]

The new covenant has made priests of each member of the covenant community. Even the women, the slaves, and the Gentiles are accountable directly to God for their actions. This is exemplified in the New Testament account of the sin and punishment of Ananias and Sapphira, each of whom was held individually accountable for each one's part in their act of deception (Acts 5:1–11). First Ananias was questioned, pronounced guilty, and punished; then his wife Sapphira was questioned and judged for her own guilt before God. There was no chain of command at work here. The husband was not held responsible to God for his wife's sin, but only for his own sin. And the wife was held directly responsible to God; she was punished only for her sin, not for her husband's sin (as were the wives of Korah and of Achan). As Klyne Snodgrass explains:

> The standing of a woman in the Christian community is not linked to a man; she, like every man, has her standing only because of Christ and, like every man, she as an individual partakes of the new unity in Christ. Being in Christ does not change a woman into a man any more than it changes Gentiles into Jews, but it changes the way that men and women relate to each other just as it changed the way that Jews and Gentiles relate. The differences are not denied, but valuation or status based on the difference is rejected.[29]

The sign of full membership with full privileges in the covenant community has changed from male circumcision to baptism, which is equally applicable to both men and women. In fact, many scholars believe the early Christians proclaimed their unity and equality in Christ by reciting Galatians 3:28 as they were baptized.[30] In baptism, each believer dies to himself—along with whatever privileges he might claim by virtue of his religious, social, or sexual status—and is raised to new life in Christ, clothed solely with the righteousness, value, and dignity of Christ. "For all of you who were baptized into Christ have clothed yourselves with Christ," Paul declares (Gal. 3:27). Women, no less than men, wear the uniform of Christlikeness, which alone qualifies a person for spiritual service.

Contra C. S. Lewis, it is *this* uniform—not the "masculine uniform"—that indicates a person's suitability to be an emissary or representative of Christ. Christlikeness is to be appropriated as fully by female believers as by male believers. Christ is no more a model for men than he is for women, and men are no more like Christ than are women.[31] Women, as well as men, may "receive the full rights of sons" (Gal. 4:5), that is, the full inheritance of the Father's estate. This can only mean equal religious status and impartial dispensing of spiritual gifts and callings by God to all believers. F. F. Bruce notes that baptism sacramentally affirms the equality of all within the church fellowship. "If a Gentile may exercise spiritual leadership in church as freely as a Jew, or a slave as freely as a citizen, why not a woman as freely as a man?"[32]

In the new covenant, all members are equal members, with full privileges of membership in the spiritual body of Christ. Men and women are not just "equally saved" (whatever that means). Rather, men and women have equal status in the community into which their salvation has secured their membership. All are not simply equally *in* the community of believers, but all enjoy equal opportunity to participate in the spiritual and religious life of the community. This is what Galatians 3:26–28 is all about. First Corinthians 12:12–13 and Colossians 3:9–11 also stress the equality in value and importance of every believer, as each serves the Lord and others through individually distinct gifts and functions. Gilbert Bilezikian notes that "in both context and substance, those statements (including Galatians 3:28) make it crystal clear that they were intended to provide a basic definition of the church as the human community where categoric distinctions are superseded and where all members receive an equal standing before God and before each other."[33]

The idea of a religious pecking order along lines of race, class, or gender is alien to the new order in Christ. Special spiritual prerogatives no longer belong only to males (or Jews, or freeborn citizens). No particular ethnic, sexual, or social class of believers has the intrinsic right to exercise spiritual authority over or assume spiritual responsibility for believers outside the privileged class. All are equal members and full participants. Anyone can enter the Holy of Holies and minister before the Lord as a priest. Anyone can make a vow to God and no one may break it or bear the guilt of it on her behalf.

Free Jewish male believers no longer have special religious status and privilege; they no longer have cause to recite the ancient Jewish prayer in which they gave thanks to God that they were not born a slave, a Gentile, or a woman. This is the difference grace has wrought. We are all free from the religious restrictions that were placed on non-free, non-Jewish, nonmale believers under the Law. "If God has poured out his Spirit on both the sons and the daughters (Acts 2:17ff.), it will not do for us to erect a modern-day 'court of the women' for our churches."[34] The old covenant has passed away, and with it the old religious valuations based on social and sexual differences.[35]

Traditionalism and Galatians 3:26-28

Since God does not find spiritual significance in a person's gender, then it can only be the distorting effects of sin that cause so many Christians to feel so strongly that different spiritual roles necessarily accompany different sexual roles, and that those differences entail limitations for women and privileges for men.

The most plausible, straightforward reading of Galatians 3:26–28 is that it is an acknowledgment of the fundamental spiritual equality of all categories of people, and a denial of the relevance of gender, race, or social class to the assignment of spiritual roles and privileges. The message of this text, however, is evidently easy to miss—if one is constrained by a desire to retain hierarchical gender roles. For example, Wayne Grudem states that, according to Galatians 3:27–28, there is an "equality in status among God's people," whereby "no class of people . . . could claim special status or privilege in the church." But he evidently understands "equality in status" simply in terms of Christians' attitudes toward themselves and one another; for he goes on to explain that freedmen, Jews, and men ought not "think themselves superior," and slaves, Greeks, and women should not "think themselves inferior."[36]

Similarly, Lewis Johnson explains that in the Old Testament, the Gentiles, slaves, and women were "limited in certain spiritual privileges open to Jewish males," and that the distinctions between these groups "are declared by Paul to be invalid in Christ."[37] Johnson concludes that Galatians 3:28 "does plainly teach an egalitarianism of privilege in the covenantal union of believers in Christ."[38] But he apparently sees no contradiction between this egalitarianism of privilege and the traditionalist gender agenda—which denies women a number of spiritual privileges, and then calls it spiritual equality!

Stephen Clark also points out, with respect to Galatians 3:28, that

> The Mosaic law and the teaching of the rabbis portray the Israelite nation as a people with, in religious terms, first-class and second-class members. The free adult male Israelites were the first-class members.

Women, [Gentile] proselytes, slaves, and others participated less fully and were religiously dependent on the free male Israelites. The free adult males were obligated to worship the Lord and represent the people before the Lord. . . . Through faith in Christ, Jew and Greek, slave and free, male and female are all one people in Christ, all fully part of the worship of God, all alike in their relationship with him.[39]

Clark's discussion of the Old Testament religious status of Gentiles, slaves, and women vis-à-vis free Jewish men is one of the best I have found on this text. However, he seems not to grasp the significance of the information he presents, concluding only that "Galatians 3:28 changes Christian relationships, but does not abolish role differences."[40]

Of course equality can coexist with role differentiation, and of course "equality does not require sameness," as so many traditionalists repeatedly affirm;[41] but these assertions sidestep the challenge that Galatians 3:26–28 presents to the hierarchical gender agenda. Despite traditionalist insistence to the contrary, there *is* a contradiction between the essential, spiritual equality taught in Galatians 3:26–28 and the universal principle of female subordination to male spiritual authority that traditionalists believe is taught elsewhere in the New Testament. The effort to describe female subordination as simply a "role differentiation" that has no bearing on a woman's "spiritual equality" may camouflage the contradiction, but it does not resolve it.

Even granting the contention that Galatians 3:28 refers only to spiritual and not social equality, this text still refutes traditionalist teaching. The idea of spiritual authority as unearned and intrinsic to maleness logically entails the spiritual inferiority of women. In the traditionalist system, the male is considered, solely by virtue of his maleness, to be better suited to represent God to his family and to the church congregation. He is, by implication, more like God and better equipped spiritually to access God directly. Such beliefs are incompatible with the clear teaching in Galatians 3:26–28 and elsewhere, that women and men relate to God and participate in the worship of God in the same way, with no difference in spiritual status or role.

The disagreement between egalitarian and traditionalist interpretations of Galatians 3:28 is not over the existence and validity of role

differentiation per se—despite the traditionalist effort to cast the debate
in those terms. Rather, the disagreement concerns what the male/
female role differentiation should entail and what it should not entail.

It ought to be clear from Galatians 3:26–28 and related passages
that, at the very least, role differences between men and women should
not entail any implications of spiritual inequality. But the gender roles
traditionalists prescribe *do* violate the fundamental spiritual equality
of women and men in Christ. They also violate the intent of the New
Testament texts to which traditionalists appeal for validation of their
position. These texts were written to Christians living in situations of
social inequality; yet traditionalists read them as though they were
direct statements of a spiritual principle of gender hierarchy literally
applicable to modern-day Christians who do *not* live in situations of
social inequality. Thus, the New Testament's instructions to the early
church, which were intended to show believers how to exercise Christlike mutual submission in the context of an authoritarian, hierarchical society, are taken (or mistaken) to be statements of a universal
principle of unilateral female submission to male spiritual authority.

The submission exhorted of women in the New Testament was not
a spiritual subordination necessitated solely by reason of their essential female nature. It was, depending on the particular text, either an
expression of one aspect of the mutual submission that exists between
equals in Christ, or a social subordination that followed from what
women were able and expected to do in the cultures of that time.[42] By
contrast, the gender roles advocated by traditionalists entail women's
permanent subordination to the *spiritual* leadership of men; yet this
subordination is defended as merely a difference in social "function"
that coexists with a spiritual equality in "being."[43]

Because the social subordination of women in New Testament times
was not advanced by the biblical writers as a universal principle of
women's subordination to the spiritual authority of men, but as a temporary accommodation to certain functional differences between men
and women in ancient patriarchal cultures, it *is* legitimate to invoke
a distinction between equality in being and difference in function in
order to reconcile such texts as Galatians 3:26–28 with such texts as
1 Peter 3:1–6. But today's traditionalists go much farther than the
apostles Paul and Peter, and as a result women are subordinated not
merely in their social function, but in their spiritual role. The tradi-

tionalist agenda does not consist simply of spiritual equality coupled with social inequality. Rather, it consists of the assertion of spiritual equality along with a strong prescription for spiritually unequal roles.

Traditionalist gender roles cannot be defended against Galatians 3:28 simply by pointing out that spiritual equality can coexist with different, or unequal, social roles. *That* describes the cultural situation of the New Testament church. It does not describe the roles of spiritual hierarchy that traditionalists prescribe for Christian women and men living in democratic societies today.

In traditionalism, the theoretically equal spiritual status of all believers in Christ does not translate into an equality of spiritual gifts, spiritual authority and responsibility, opportunity for spiritual ministry, or access to knowledge of God's will. The traditionalist agenda, whereby a man in some sense mediates his wife's relationship with God, is more akin to the old covenant under Mosaic Law than the new covenant described in Galatians 3:26–28.

Unless we perceive how the new-covenant relationship among men, women, and God radically differs from that which held sway under Old Testament Law, then our understanding of grace will fall far short of its reality.

2

Equal in Being, Unequal in Function?

espite the clear note of equality on which the Bible begins and ends, and which is sounded again and again throughout its pages, many believe that this message of equality should be modified and qualified in light of a handful of biblical texts that advocate or are taken to advocate women's submission.[1] In other words, evangelicals disagree concerning which biblical texts should be considered universally normative and which should be limited in terms of their direct applicability to our religious and cultural situation today.

Traditionalists take as normative the texts that they believe teach gender hierarchy (e.g., 1 Tim. 2:12), and limit the applicability of the texts that teach the equality of all believers (e.g., Gal. 3:28). Biblical egalitarians consider the equality texts to be normative, and believe that the applicability of the hierarchy texts are limited in large part by their historical and cultural contexts. These texts, therefore, ought not be regarded as direct statements of a universal principle of male authority, but as culturally specific applications of such general moral principles as civil obedience, respect for others, and social propriety.

Traditionalists have responded to the biblical equalitarian hermeneutic by denying either the reality or the influence of these historical and cultural considerations, and by upholding the hierarchy proof texts as directly applicable statements of a timeless spiritual principle of female subordination to male authority. In order to interpret the equality texts according to the "norm" of the hierarchy texts, traditionalists rely heavily on the "equal in being but different in function" explanatory device. Armed with this device, traditionalists maintain that the texts believed by equalitarians to set forth a fundamental principle of equality among all believers really refer only to an equality of "being" that has no bearing on "function." It is a spiritual not a social equality, and this spiritual equality means nothing more than that men and women are "equally saved."

Biblical equalitarians usually have responded to the traditionalist argument by attempting to defend their culturally sensitive interpretations of the hierarchy texts. The problem with such a response is that it is easier for a hierarchalist simply to quote a proof text and then say "period" than it is for an egalitarian to explain the biblical and cultural contexts of the text, to explain the biblical author's intent in writing the text (that is, the universally normative principle that prompted him to give the instructions that he gave to his particular audience at that particular time), and finally to explain how and why we should apply that biblical principle in our culture differently than it was applied in the cultures of New Testament times. This extra interpretive burden has put the case for equality at a rhetorical disadvantage in the debate—especially since many Christians today want answers in the form of simple, direct, "how to" formulas, and do not have the inclination to try to understand and apply the basic principles of biblical interpretation for themselves.[2]

In view of these things, it seems that advocates of biblical equality should not simply argue defensively against traditionalist interpretations, but should also critique the central premise of the traditionalist argument, namely, the notion that women, though "functionally" unequal, are nonetheless "essentially" equal to men. This explanatory construct needs to be looked at carefully and critically. The question that must be addressed is not whether it is *possible* to be equal in being but different in role or rank (for it *is* possible), but whether it is logically and theologically appropriate to describe and defend the traditionalist understanding of women's subordination in these terms. Does the concept of equality in being and inequality in function validly explain how gender equality and hierarchy can coexist without contradiction? Is there a meaningful distinction between "being" and "function" in the subordination prescribed by traditionalists for women?

The question of whether a being/function distinction is logically applicable to a defense of gender hierarchy is a crucial one, because this distinction is foundational to every traditionalist argument today. When traditionalists affirm in theory the essential, spiritual equality of women and men, but feel no obligation to advocate the full practical ramifications of such equality, they invoke as their rationale the notion that woman's subordination is only "functional" and has nothing to do with her essential being.

If this rationale is flawed, then the entire case for gender hierarchy is flawed. The traditionalist proof texts would then need to be interpreted in conformity with the fundamental biblical principle of women's essential equality with men. The hierarchy texts could no longer be regarded as mandating a universal and unilateral female submission to male authority.

Can woman's subordination to male authority be harmonized with her biblical equality by describing her subordination as merely functional? Normally, functional subordination exists for the purpose of accomplishing a particular task or function, and applies only to a specific area of life for a limited period of time. It is determined on the basis of either the subordinated person's inferior ability in a particular area or his or her willingness to submit to leadership in order that a particular job be accomplished efficiently. Female subordination, on the other hand, is not limited to any one area of life, nor is it merely temporary. It is automatically assigned to every woman simply because she is a woman, and it cannot be justified on the basis of inferior ability, nor can it be explained as a mere expedient useful in dealing with a specific situation. It is, rather, a way of life, a definition of a woman's personhood.

Traditionalists, however, persist in attempting to rationalize female subordination on grounds related to either ability or expediency. Reasons given for why male authority is necessary include maintaining "God's order," preserving the family and traditional moral values, avoiding heresy and apostasy, and keeping men in the church or attracting men to the church. Reasons such as these seem to be grounded in a concern for expediency (that is, accomplishing a worthy goal through the means of subordinating women to men). Other purported reasons for gender hierarchy seem to be rooted in the implicit idea that a woman's innate "difference" suits her to occupy the lower-status positions (thus strongly implying woman's innate inferiority to man). Traditionalist gender roles are said to be necessary if we are to steer clear of homosexuality and be true to the God-ordained nature of masculinity and femininity.

Nearly everyone who maintains that universal female subordination is biblically mandated attempts to reinforce this biblical interpretation with one or more of these commonly purported reasons for it. Whether or not female subordination actually accomplishes, or is required in order to accomplish, any of these purposes is open to debate. One purpose that it clearly accomplishes, however, is the allocation of upper-level positions of social and spiritual authority to men, which, in turn, leads to assorted assumptions and attitudes about the "God-ordained" differences between women and men.

The critical differences between functional subordination and female subordination—as summarized on the following chart—demonstrate why functional subordination can coexist with equality, but female subordination cannot. When a woman's subordination to male authority is both permanent and comprehensive, and when it is imposed solely by reason of an essential aspect of her being (i.e., her femaleness), then it cannot be explained as merely "functional." It necessarily implies an inequality of woman's essential "being."

	Functional Subordination	Female Subordination
Purpose	To perform a function; to facilitate getting a particular job done	To reserve upper-level positions of social and spiritual authority for men

	Functional Subordination	Female Subordination
Criteria	Determined according to an individual's abilities, or for the sake of expediency	Determined entirely on the basis of one aspect of a woman's intrinsic nature, namely, her female sexuality
Duration	Continues until the individual's abilities "outgrow" the position, or until the particular function has been completed	Endures for the entirety of a woman's life, regardless of her competencies
Scope	Pertains only to those areas related to the function for which the individual has been subordinated	There is no area of a married woman's life that is not ultimately under the absolute rule of her husband
Nature and Significance	Limited and justifiable	Unlimited and unjustifiable

Different Types of Equality

The concept of equality is problematic in that both traditionalists and feminists tend to use the term in whatever way it suits them—yet without stipulating its clear meaning. There are a number of ways in which a person or group of persons can be said to be equal to another person or group: (1) equal human worth, (2) equal ability, (3) equal maturity, (4) equal rights and opportunities, (5) equal status, (6) equal social value, and (7) equal identity (being the same, thus interchangeable in any role).

Traditionalists affirm women's equality with men, but it seems that by it they mean only equal human worth; that is, the truth that all human beings—male or female, old or young, rich or poor, wise or foolish, extremely gifted or extremely disabled—are equal in human value before God. Wayne Grudem seeks to show that because women have equal value before God, they are not "second class citizens in the church. Whether someone is a man or woman, employer or employee . . . strong or weak, attractive or unattractive, extremely intelligent or slow to learn, all are equally valuable to God and should be equally valuable to one another as well."[3] However, for women to be assured that they are no more secondary or inferior to men than employees are to their employer, or a dull-witted person to a quick-witted person, is likely to provide scant comfort. In fact, it rather misses the point.

Of course God values everyone equally, regardless of one's skills or social position. This is a wonderful biblical truth that we should never forget. But the question at stake in this debate does not pertain merely to how God views people, but to how people should treat other people. It won't do simply to assert that we must value women equally because they are equal in God's eyes. We must be more specific: Given that women and men stand on equal ground before God, is it biblically warranted for men to claim exclusive access to higher-status positions solely on the basis of their gender? What are the ethical, social, and theological implications that follow from our basic human equality of worth before God?

According to the classical liberal thought of the eighteenth and nineteenth centuries, the equality of the individual entails equal rights under the law. In a society of equals in this sense, there is no legal basis for granting or denying social status on the basis of race, class, or gender. Everyone has equal opportunity to earn—by virtue of one's individual qualifications—equality of status with any individual of any social group, whereby the standard of achievement is the same for each member of each social group. This clearly is not the sort of equality traditionalists are thinking of when they insist that they value women equally. In reserving leadership positions for men, traditionalists deny women the opportunity to demonstrate their equality of ability and maturity, and thereby to earn equality of status and social value.

The classical feminism of the nineteenth century applied the principle of equality under the law to women, as well as to men.[4] The equal human worth and dignity of all persons under God was seen to lead, by logical and ethical necessity, to a social recognition of the equal right of each man and woman to acquire and demonstrate a level of maturity or ability by which he or she may earn the social status appropriate to his or her individual characteristics.

The practice of equality in this sense would seem to be the most consistent and just application of the biblical truth of God's equal valuation of each human life. Richard Mouw points out that the Dutch theologian Abraham Kuyper

> insisted that Calvinism is profoundly democratic. The proclamation that God alone is sovereign has an important social-political corollary: no human power or office can claim the kind of authority that belongs only to God. Totalitarianism, whether civic or ecclesiastical, is unacceptable. Every human being is directly responsible to the Creator.[5]

Biblically, both men and women are directly responsible to God, and both are privileged to hear directly from God, whether through Scripture or prayer. God's kingdom does not leave room for the totalitarian (absolute and unearned) authority of one person over another, whereby one person "stands in the place of God" for the other.[6]

However, many hierarchalists see an antithesis between God's order and a democratic social order. This may arise from the common misbelief that any idea found in secular culture could not possibly be consistent with biblical teaching,[7] as well as from a strong penchant for confusing the various types of social and political equality with an equality of identity or sameness. Equality in the classically liberal/biblical egalitarian sense, however, does not deny the many differences between individuals or the sexual differences between women and men. It merely claims that generalized or stereotyped differences between groups of people should not be seen as a reasonable cause to deny opportunities to members of some groups and grant those opportunities to members of other groups.

Nonetheless, traditionalists tend to direct much of their criticism of biblical equality toward what they falsely perceive to be the common denominator of all types of feminism, namely, the belief that women and men are alike, undifferentiated, the same. Wayne House, for example, describes egalitarianism as "identical roles for both sexes."[8] It seems that when traditionalists look at the egalitarian rejection of those gender role distinctions that have nothing to do with sexuality (but which concern generic human activities such as teaching, serving, and making decisions), they see a rejection of the entire idea of sexual differentiation. But why should an acknowledgment of a general equality in rights and intellectual ability between the sexes be seen as tantamount to a complete breakdown of all sexual differentiation? Such a conclusion can follow only from the (false) premise that status differences are inherent to sexual differences, and so to deny gender hierarchy is to deny the very essence of sexual differentiation.

In reality, evangelical egalitarians affirm all types of equality between women and men *except* the equality of identity or sameness. No one is saying that all sexual roles are reversible or that sexual differences make no difference at all. The disagreement in the evangelical gender debate does not concern the existence of differences between women and men, but rather the extent and the effect of these differences. The question to which egalitarians and traditionalists offer divergent answers is this: In what areas of human behavior is sexuality relevant to, or determinative of, that behavior, and in what areas is sexuality not especially relevant? The answer to this question will determine which roles are deemed interchangeable between women and men and which are not.

The traditionalist maintains that gender differences are fairly extensive, pervading virtually every aspect of the personality, and that these differences determine to a large degree what is and what is not appropriate behavior for men and women, not simply within a sexual relationship, but in general social interaction. The biblical egalitarian is more likely to say that gender differences flavor, but do not determine, an individual's behavior in areas of general social interaction.

Sexuality, by definition, pertains to the ways in which men and women differ. Obviously, male and female are not identical, nor are male and female sexual roles interchangeable. Sexually differentiated roles follow from the differences that exist between men and women. However, the sexually based differences in abilities that do exist between men and women—the most notable of which are the different roles in reproduction—do not justify the subordination of one gender to the other. Moreover, there are many roles and activities for which these differences are largely irrelevant or not determinative.

Status and roles pertaining to nonsexual activities should be determined according to actual abilities of individuals rather than average abilities of gender groups. For example, although men on average have greater size and upper body strength, some women are larger or stronger than some men; and, generally speaking, these women should be given opportunity to fill the roles for which they can meet the physical requirements. However, differences in physical strength mean a great deal less today than they did in preindustrial societies. In modern societies, intellectual ability is far more relevant than physical ability in determining an individual's qualifications for the higher-status social roles. Compared to average differences in physical abilities, average differences in intellectual abilities between women and men are fairly inconsistent and insignificant.

Different Ways to Have Different Roles

Traditionalists can often be heard saying that difference doesn't necessarily mean inferiority; therefore, it is not unreasonable to say that although women are different in function from men, they are not inferior to men. The problem with this argument is its disregard of the fact that role differentiation can occur in many different ways, with very different consequences. The fact that role differentiation does not *necessarily* indicate inequality does not mean that it *never* does. A difference in role may be either justifiable or unjustifiable, and it may or may not entail inferiority.

Just as equality can have various meanings, so there are various ways in which people can have different roles or functions in life. One way is for people to perform different tasks, yet have comparable ability and the same level of status. For instance, when two people wash the dishes together, one may scrub and the other rinse and stack; the next night they could switch roles, with no implication of either one being inferior to the other in general dishwashing status or skill.

There can also be a difference in ability and, hence, in function, yet without any inequality in status. When a man and a woman have a child, they necessarily perform very different functions initially. Like the different dishwashing roles, male and female reproductive roles are equal in value and status (whether or not they are always recognized as such). Unlike the dishwashing roles, however, sexual reproductive roles are not reversible because they follow from innately differing abilities.

Sometimes people of equal ability will assume roles of unequal status temporarily. For example, persons who are of generally equal status and ability in an organization may choose one of their number to serve as their leader or chairperson for the purpose of getting a particular job done. Here the inequality in status between the person in charge and the other persons is a temporary and limited arrangement devised for the sake of expediency.

Another possibility is for a person to have a role that is inferior in status because of that person's inferiority in ability. There are two types of inequality in ability that justify an inequality in function. A person may have the sort of inferior ability that can be overcome through further education or experience. For example, a music student is inferior to her teacher in ability and status in the musical world, although she may be superior to her teacher in another area of endeavor. If the student continues her musical training and becomes an acclaimed concert artist, she may become superior to her former teacher in musical ability and status.

Another type of inferior ability is that which is intrinsic to a person's nature and, therefore, entails a permanently subordinate function in whatever area the person's inferior ability is pertinent. For example, a blind person should always be subordinate to and never in authority over a sighted person when it comes to negotiating unfamiliar territory. Such subordination, although permanent (assuming the blindness is permanent), is not comprehensive. If the blind person possesses greater intelligence than his sighted guide, then in any situation requiring the function of logical thought, the judgments of the sighted person should normally be subordinated to those of the blind person.

Egalitarian enthusiasts sometimes fail to recognize that functional inferiority arising from inferior ability is not necessarily unjust. For example, when the FAA instituted the perfectly sensible rule that only those people who are able to open emergency exit doors on airplanes should be allowed to sit in the seats next to these exits, the National Federation of the Blind

> launched a "civil-rights struggle" dedicated to the proposition that blind people have an inalienable right to sit next to emergency doors that they are unlikely to be able to open. Preposterously comparing themselves with Rosa Parks, who refused to move to the back of the bus

because of her color, blind demonstrators have squatted in exit-window seats and refused to move, causing cancellation of several flights.[9]

Such bizarre goings-on also indicate that traditionalists are not the only ones who confuse equality of rights with equality of sameness. Just because everyone should have an equal right to prove himself qualified to sit next to an emergency exit does not mean that everyone *is* qualified to so do. The question at issue is whether or not a particular difference should make a difference. The color of Rosa Parks' skin was completely irrelevant to where she should have been allowed to sit on a bus, but the condition of a person's eyesight *is* relevant to where he should be allowed to sit on a plane.

The final category of role differentiation occurs in a social system in which roles and status are determined by inborn characteristics (accidents of birth) that are unrelated to a person's qualifications for the role or status to which she is assigned. In other words, various versions of a caste system may permanently consign individuals of a certain race, sex, nationality, or socioeconomic class to limited roles and a subordinate status in society, regardless of each individual's abilities. Unlike the other types of role differentiation, the absence of equal rights in a caste system leads to an inequality of status that is unjustifiable and unlimited in both scope and duration.

Traditionalists insist that the "functional" differences they prescribe for men and women are comparable to the functional differences that normally occur in contemporary society. Similarly, the traditionalist relationship of authority and subordination between men and women is presented as comparable to the various structures of authority in a modern democracy. Consequently, when equalitarians object to hierarchical gender roles, traditionalists often see this as an objection to *any* role differentiation and *all* types of authority structures.[10]

Although traditionalists do not acknowledge it, their prescribed gender roles belong in the final category of the "caste system," while the differences in roles and status that normally occur in society today fall into the other categories—in which there is either no inferiority in status or justifiable reason for a limited inferiority in status. Analogies that liken the traditionalist subordination of women to ordinary instances of functional subordination are, therefore, inappropriate and inaccurate.

Traditionalists often seem heedless of the radically different ways in which functional differences can be socially determined. On the one hand, there is the way of free societies, whereby individuals move in and out of leadership roles according to their experience and expertise. On the other hand, there is the way of the caste system, in which certain people are born into a permanently lower status and have no opportunity even to earn a higher-status position, regardless of their experience or expertise. The former is compatible with a belief in the equality of every individual before God; the latter is not. The disagreement between traditionalists and equalitarians does not concern the legitimacy of status differences per se, but the means by which status differences are rightfully determined.

The Best One for the Job

The primary differences between normal social occurrences of functional inequality and the "functional" inequality of traditionalist gender roles are in the areas of criteria, duration, and scope. Say, for example, that Person A and Person B both wish to model for a shampoo commercial but A's hair doesn't equal the beauty of B's hair. So B gets the job. In this case, the functional inequality is deserved and fair. It is only right for the person with the best hair to get the job. However, in the traditionalist system, a woman who is well qualified for a leadership position is quite likely to be passed over in favor of a less qualified man, simply on account of the gender difference—a difference which, as a criterion for determining leadership status, is irrelevant and unjust.

Person A (with the bad hair) could choose to take a lot of vitamins, use expensive hair potions, obtain professional assistance, and then come to the next modeling opportunity with hair even better than Person B's. Thus, the duration of Person A's functional inferiority need not be permanent. A woman, however, cannot change her femaleness. Because female is something a woman cannot help but be, the inferiority in status to which she is relegated on account of her femaleness continues for the duration of her life. Of course, if Person A's inferior hair was the result of inferior hair genes, she may be unable to improve the condition of her hair sufficiently to qualify as a model for a shampoo commercial. But at least her permanent inferiority in function would reflect an actual inferiority in nature, and would, therefore, be fair and appropriate.

Hair quality, however, is only one small aspect of a person. Someone with bad hair could excel in more important areas in life and not feel fundamentally inferior to all persons with good hair. But the question of whether someone is fit to govern or is in need of being governed covers a significant and sizable area of personal worth and identity.

Subordinating a woman solely by reason of her femaleness can be deemed fair and appropriate only if all females are, without exception, inferior to all males in their ability to perform the particular function for which they have been subordinated. If that function is the government of one's own life and the lives of others, then femaleness must consistently render a person less wise, less mature, less responsible, and less rational than those persons who are males.

Of course, some people *are* intellectually or emotionally "challenged," and it may be appropriate for them to be governed by a responsible adult. But the determination to place such a person under supervision is normally based on observation of his actual behavior and competencies. Moreover, such a person often can learn to be more mature and responsible, and thereby earn a degree of autonomy over his own life. But because a woman's subordination is determined by her gender and not her abilities, not even this option is open to women in the traditionalist system.

Being and Function

Because a woman's traditionally inferior status follows necessarily from the single fact of her essential, female nature, her status is itself a function of her "being"; it is determined by what she is, not by what she can do. A woman's inequality, therefore, pertains not merely to her "function," but to her essential "being." The insistence of traditionalists that a woman's inferior function has no bearing on the valuation of her essential nature contradicts the clear implications of the woman's role.

It stands to reason that anyone who is deemed permanently unfit to occupy the superior position must be inherently incapable of performing that function satisfactorily. And certainly, someone who *is* inferior should occupy only the inferior or subordinate position. Because inferiority in function follows logically and necessarily from inferiority in being, it seems unreasonable to maintain—as traditionalists do—that inferiority in function can also follow necessarily from an equality in being.

To deflect attention from entailments of female inferiority, traditionalists often will make the juxtaposition of equality and subordination appear more congenial by referring to the respective roles of women and men as "different" rather than unequal, and "complementary" rather than hierarchical. Traditional male privilege and authority will be spoken of as a man's "responsibility" to "serve" his wife and his church, and to "provide" spiritual leadership and instruction. John Piper and Wayne Grudem illustrate this euphemistic tendency when they say that men "bear the responsibility for the overall pattern of life."[11] This makes it sound as though men are saddled with an onerous obligation, of which women are fortunately free. What is meant, however, is that men and not women have the exclusive right to decide and determine the direction of things in both the home and the church.

The employment of euphemisms cannot entirely camouflage the fact that the traditionalist gender assignments are *not* "different but equal" functions. Despite the effort to emphasize the element of responsibility inherent to any position of authority, there is no denying that the central question concerns who has the ultimate "right to direct the actions of others"; nor can it be denied that the traditionalist answer to this question is that men have this right and women do not.[12] Such a demarcation of roles is not value neutral. The male role entails having control over one's own life, as well as the lives of others. The female role entails placing the control of one's own life into the hands of another.

When authority of this nature is reserved for men and denied to women, it is meaningless and misleading to talk of it as not being a privilege but a responsibility, and not a position of superiority but of servanthood. The normal, commonsensical understanding is that this sort of role differentiation is what distinguishes the privileged (or ruling) class from the underprivileged (or disempowered) class. To construe such a power inequity in any other way is to engage in word games.

Regardless of how hierarchalists try to explain the situation, the idea that women are equal *in* their being, yet unequal *by virtue of* their being, is contradictory and ultimately nonsensical. If you cannot help but be what you are, and if inferiority in function follows inexorably from what you are, then you are inferior in your essential being.

Raymond Ortlund Jr. complains that feminism admits no distinction between subordination of position and subordination of person.[13] However, when positional subordination is assigned solely on the basis of what a person is (i.e., female), it *is* personal; it cannot be otherwise. A permanent and comprehensive subordination based on a person's essence is an essential (not merely a functional) subordination. In the final analysis, gender hierarchy allows for no meaningful distinction between the person and the position.

Functional Subordination and the Godhead

In functional subordination, an inferior function does not necessarily reflect an essentially inferior being, because the subordination can be transcended when the subordinated person's abilities have outgrown the limitations of the role, or when the particular function has been accomplished. In other words, when there is a change in what needs to be done or in what the person can do, then the functional subordination is no longer applicable. Female subordination, on the other hand, is not based on what a person can do, but solely on what a person is; it is not temporary, but permanent; it is not limited to the task at hand, but comprehensively covers all areas of a woman's life. Therefore, it is not a functional but an ontological subordination, and necessarily indicates an inequality not merely of a woman's function, but of her essential female being.

One type of functional subordination (as discussed earlier) occurs when someone subordinates himself to another person of equal rank in order to accomplish a particular purpose. For example, an individual may serve on a committee under the direction of a co-worker who is otherwise her equal in the organization. The time of subordination for the committee member will come to an end when the committee has completed its assigned task. Such functional subordination occurs not only in human experience, but also among the members of the Trinity. In the incarnation, God the Son gave up some of his divine privileges and subordinated himself to God the Father during his earthly life, in order to accomplish the work necessary for the redemption of humanity (see Phil. 2:6–7). Millard Erickson reminds us that this subordination "is to be understood as a temporary role for the purpose of accomplishing a given end, not a change in his status or essence."[14]

Functional subordination was necessarily entailed by the nature of the work Jesus came to earth to do, because he came specifically as God's representative—more than that, as God Incarnate. By definition, someone who serves as a representative must be sent, delegated, and authorized by the sender. A person is not a delegate or representative unless that person is subject to the authority of the person or group that he represents. But the delegate's subordination to that authority is purely functional; it pertains to and exists for the purpose of accomplishing a particular function in the capacity of "official representative." As long as, and to the extent that, a person is performing this particular function, he is under the authority of the one whom he represents. But in other areas of enterprise, he is not under this authority. And, when the function is accomplished, the subordination ends. This is the nature of functional subordination. It describes well the subordination of the Son to the Father, but clearly does not describe the permanent and comprehensive subordination to which traditionalists assign women.

Aware of the disanalogy between female subordination and a temporary, functional subordination of the Son to the Father, traditionalists typically maintain that the Son is eternally subordinate to the Father—but also eternally equal. This is then employed as an illustration—even a justification—for how men and women can be essentially equal, yet functionally unequal.[15] Wayne Grudem goes so far as to claim that the doctrine of an eternally hierarchical structure of the Godhead is a "truth" that is "clearly" an "essential" element of orthodox trinitarian theology, and he professes surprise that not all evangelical scholars see it this way.[16]

The doctrine of an eternal hierarchy within the Trinity is a necessary corollary to the doctrine of gender hierarchy. If being the "head"

of woman is to be understood as man's permanent position of authority over woman, then God being the head of Christ must be understood as the eternal subordination of the Son to the authority of the
Father. Otherwise, 1 Corinthians 11:3 cannot be used as the proof text
for the "chain of command," and "head" cannot be said to refer to the
husband's authority over the wife.[17]

To invoke an eternal subordination of the Son to the Father in an
attempt to demonstrate the legitimacy of male authority is a questionable strategy for at least three reasons. First, it is by no means clear
from Scripture that the members of the Godhead are related to one
another in terms of an eternal structure of rule and submission. This
is a debatable point of theology on which conservative scholars disagree. Second, as Stanley Grenz observes, Christ's obedience and submission to the Father during his time on earth is presented in the Bible
as an example of how believers in Christ ought to relate to the Father;
it is not intended to illustrate the subordination of one group of persons
(women) to another group of persons (men).[18] Third, if the coexistence of equality in being and subordination in function is not logically possible with respect to the permanent and comprehensive subordination of woman to man, then neither would it seem to be viable
with respect to an eternal subordination of the Son to the Father.

Unlike functional subordination, eternal subordination cannot be
described as the subordination of one equal to another for the purpose
of accomplishing a particular function; rather, it is built into the very
nature of the subordinated person. If Christ's subordination is not limited to a specific project or function but characterizes his eternal relationship with God, then Christ is not merely functionally subordinate;
he is by nature subordinate. Subordinate is what he is, what he always
has been, what he always will be. It is a matter of ontology (i.e., being),
not merely of function.

In Robert Letham's attempt to ground the permanent subordination of woman to man in an eternal subordination of the Son to the
Father, he begins by stating the necessity of recognizing "full equality in terms of essence" between Christ and God.[19] Two paragraphs
later, however, he asserts that the subordination of the Son to the Father
is not merely economic but ontological. "The revelation of the economic Trinity truly indicates the ontological Trinity," he declares,
apparently unaware that ontological equality and ontological subor-

dination are mutually exclusive.[20] It is significant that an ontological aspect to Christ's subordination enters Letham's discussion at the point where he attempts to establish that the Son is *eternally* subordinate to the Father, and not merely subordinate in the capacity of his work as Redeemer.

Similarly, if a woman is under a man's authority for the length and breadth of her life, she is not merely functionally subordinate but ontologically subordinate. It is the *nature* of femininity to be subordinate, and the *nature* of masculinity to be in authority. In fact, it is precisely in these terms that traditionalists tend to define the meaning of manhood and womanhood, and on these grounds that they reject gender equality.[21] And when this essential gender inequality is grounded in and justified by a supposed eternal hierarchy of authority and subordination within the Trinity, it easily becomes cosmic, universal, and eternal in its scope. Letham, in fact, is enthusiastic about the idea of gender hierarchy continuing in the afterlife as an eternal imaging of the hierarchy at the heart of the Godhead.[22]

Royce Gruenler offers a corrective to such grandiose notions of eternal trinitarian subordination, pointing out that if we take "Jesus' language about always listening to and obeying the Father and being less than the Father" as a literal statement of the "interrelationship of the eternal divine Family," we are led to the absurd conclusion that only the Father has authority to speak while the Son may only passively listen. Rather than being taken as "absolutes that describe the eternal relationship" of Christ and God, "the sent/listen/obey sayings of Jesus . . . are to be exegeted as a genre of language by which Jesus dramatically and ironically describes his voluntary servanthood on behalf of the divine Family in the redemptive program."[23] "One must not mistake voluntary submission for necessary submission," Gruenler observes. Indeed, this confusion points to the heart of the subordinationist error. Gruenler adds that "it would not be good exegesis to reintroduce such subordinationism into the Trinity in order to sanction unequal roles of authority and obedience within the believing community."[24]

If subordination can coexist with equality only when the subordination is functional and temporary, then it follows that the persons of the Godhead are eternally equal not only in essence, but also in status and authority. Indeed, Millard Erickson's discussion of the internal relations of the members of the Trinity concludes with just such an observation. "A temporal, functional subordination without inferiority of essence seems possible, but not an eternal subordination."[25]

Even if it could be demonstrated somehow that the Son *is* eternally subordinate to the Father, this would neither illustrate nor prove viable the notion of woman being essentially equal, yet functionally subordinate, to man. No matter how extensive Christ's subordination is understood to be, the very nature of the relations of the members of the Trinity renders any subordination of one member to another very *un*like the sort of subordination traditionalists prescribe for women.

We know from Scripture that Christ chose, in mutual agreement with the Father and the Spirit, to take upon himself human flesh and the punishment for human sin, and that in performing this function of redemption Christ subordinated himself to the Father voluntarily (John 6:38; Phil. 2:6–8; Heb. 10:7). Jesus did not come to earth simply because God told him to do so. He came because God the Son, God the Father, and God the Holy Spirit were equally desirous of providing redemption for fallen humanity, and equally in agreement that, in his redemptive role, the Son should be functionally subordinate to the Father.[26]

If, as traditionalists would have it, Christ's subordination within the redemptive program—which was a voluntary subordination—is to be considered indicative of his eternal subordination to the Father, then his eternal subordination must also be regarded as voluntary. It must not be seen as the kind of subordination that is automatically assigned to or imposed upon a person regardless of that person's interests, inclinations, or abilities. Nor can it imply any need for one person to cast the deciding vote in case of disagreement, for there is always a perfect relational oneness among all three persons of the Godhead. Disagreements between humans are caused by sin (self-centeredness) and ignorance. The persons of the Trinity, however, are always perfectly loving, righteous, wise, and knowledgeable.[27] Among such persons, there can be no occasion for discord or disagreement and hence no need for any "chain of command" or structure of authority that would ever require the subordinate person to act against his own judgment or preference.

Therefore, the defining features of the traditionalist subordination of woman to man, namely, the routine imposition of a subordinate status upon the woman and the supposed need for one partner in a marriage to have the right to make the "final decision" in case of disagreement, are necessarily absent from the interpersonal relations in the Trinity, regardless of how Christ's subordination is conceived.[28] Although the eternal subordination of the Son to the Father is a necessary corollary to the doctrine of female subordination, it cannot be invoked as a sufficient demonstration of the legitimacy of gender hierarchy. Voluntary submission (as in Christ's submission to the Father) is not of the same order as the necessary and unilateral submission that the traditionalist agenda requires of women to men.

Subordination With and Without Inequality

Traditionalists frequently attempt to justify gender hierarchy by claiming that women's subordination to men is no more demeaning or inappropriate than the subordination of children to their parents, church members to their pastors, or the Son to the Father when he came to do the Father's will. In Ortlund's statement of this argument, he even likens women's subordinate helping role to the assistance he renders his children when they are doing their homework, and to the help God offers us in our needs. He then states that feminists arbitrarily and fallaciously equate subordination with denigration and dehumanization.[29]

The fallacy, however, lies in Ortlund's equivocation concerning the concept of subordination. The argument assumes that all forms of subordination are alike, and that if in some instances subordination is not denigrating, then it never is. In reality, however, the instances of subordination to which traditionalists compare female subordination are all fundamentally different from the subordination of women to men. In these other instances, the subordination is not lifelong but temporary; it is not determined by the subordinated person's essential and unchangeable nature, but by the respective abilities of the persons involved; and it is not fundamental to the very principle and purpose of the subordinated person's existence. This contrasts sharply with the traditionalist agenda, wherein woman's chief purpose in life is to serve as man's subordinate assistant. She is born into this position; she did not choose it and she cannot change it. Her subordinate placement does not follow from her personal abilities; it defines her identity as a woman.

Children are subordinate to adult authority for a very good reason: they are children. (Women, incidentally, are not children.) Moreover, children grow up and leave the sphere of their parents' authority when they have matured sufficiently to require it no longer. Church members who do not like their pastor's leadership may leave the church or try to find a new pastor; those who are of the acceptable gender may even enter the pastorate themselves. And the Son has returned to the Father, to the glory he had with him before the world began (John 1:1; 17:5). As for Ortlund helping his children, and God helping *his* children, in these cases the "subordinated" persons actually retain their higher status throughout the time of their "subordination," thus making these instances dubious illustrations of subordination of any sort, let alone of the traditionalist subordination of women.[30]

A more appropriate analogy for women's subordination than the ones today's traditionalists use would be the enslavement of African Americans in this country prior to the Emancipation Proclamation in 1863 or, for that matter, their systematic social subjugation and oppression, especially in the South, that followed their emancipation from slavery. Although this certainly was a more extreme and oppressive subordination than that which traditionalists advocate for women today, its underlying structure and rationale bears a greater resemblance to female subordination than do illustrations along the lines of a father helping his children with their homework.

As is true with the traditionalist subordination of women today, African Americans were subordinated by white people solely because of an unchangeable aspect of their nature (i.e., their race), with no regard for the intellectual or leadership abilities that individual persons within the subordinated group may possess. Their subordination was comprehensive and permanent (everywhere and always applicable) and entirely unjust (grounded in an essential personal attribute that was irrelevant to the functions required of them or denied them).

As discussed earlier, unequal or different treatment is not objectionable when it is limited to its justifiable context. But the permanent and comprehensive subordination of an entire group of people (such as women or blacks) to another group of people (such as men or whites) is fundamentally unjust and unjustifiable—unless, of course, the subordinated group is inferior by nature.

Southern supporters of slavery attempted to justify the system by claiming that African Americans *were* inferior. They insisted that God had created all black people for menial labor and subordinate helping tasks, and had made them needful of being governed and provided for by white people. As one proponent of slavery explained:

> In all social systems there must be a class to do the menial duties, to perform the drudgery of life. That is, a class requiring but a low order of intellect and but little skill. . . . Fortunately for the South, she found a race adapted to that purpose to her hand. A race inferior to her own. . . . We use them for our purpose, and call them slaves.[31]

Some proslavery spokesmen defended slavery by comparing blacks to women and children. George Fitzhugh, for example, opined that "We do not set children and women free because they are not capable of taking care of themselves, not equal to the struggle of society. . . . But half of mankind are but grown-up children, and liberty is as fatal to them as it would be to children."[32] Charles Hodge followed a similar line of argument, stating that "the general good requires us to deprive the whole female sex of the rights of self-government."[33] As with woman to man, the relationship of black to white was that of child to adult.

The belief that people of African descent are inferior persons (not fit to be free) was slavery's logical concomitant. Likewise, the consensus of those who have advocated the subordination of women to men has historically been that women are inferior to men and hence not fit to be free. The current traditionalist notion of a lifelong subordination that is determined by a person's inherent nature, but which does not imply inherent inferiority, is a historical, as well as a logical, anomaly. However, the insistence of today's traditionalists that women are somehow "equal," in spite of their inferior status, at least has had the effect of eliminating much of the blatantly insulting sexist rhetoric that was commonplace in earlier centuries.

In conclusion, the subordination that traditionalists prescribe for women is not properly described by the term "functional subordination." There *is* such a thing as a functional subordination that does not entail the inferiority of a person's entire being; but it differs at every point from the traditional subordination of women. Unlike female subordination, which is determined on the basis of an innate, unchangeable, necessary aspect of a woman's being, namely, her female sexuality, functional subordination is determined on the basis of expedience; roles and responsibilities are assigned and accepted according to the most efficient division of labor, and according to individuals' differing abilities to perform particular tasks.

Because functional subordination is defined and determined by functional considerations rather than a person's essential being, it also differs from the subordination of women in that it is limited in scope to the specific function that is at issue, and is limited in duration to the time it takes for the function to be accomplished or for the subordinated person to "outgrow" his limitations. Such a subordination is radically different from that of the traditionalist woman, whose subordination to her husband's authority comprehensively covers all her activities, and endures throughout all her life. She never outgrows it; it never ends.

3

Issues in Inequality

he idea that women are essentially equal but functionally unequal raises some important questions. What are the implications of this "equal yet unequal" status for a woman's personal identity, vocation, self-worth, and social value? How does it affect her relationship with her husband, with God, and with people in general? And how does a woman's subordination to male spiritual authority square with the biblical truth of the fundamental spiritual equality of all women and men?

Role, Identity, and Personal Worth

Raymond Ortlund Jr. describes a feminist as someone who believes that "my personal significance is measured according to my rung on the ladder."[1] He claims that "feminism loses its logical power and moral attractiveness if one's personal worth and one's role are allowed to be registered independently of one another."[2] It should be noted, first of all, that these statements entail a tacit admission that the traditionalist woman's role *is* inferior to the man's role. If it were not, there would be no need to insist so vigorously that woman's worth is nonetheless equal to man's.

It is true that a woman's personal worth is unaffected by her role—if personal worth is defined in terms of God's view, which is, after all, the ultimately true point of view. Since nothing can affect God's view of people, certainly a person's place in the social order cannot. However, it is not true that a feminist can be defined as someone who believes her personal worth is determined by the social status of her role (from which it would seem to follow that no person should ever be obliged to function in a low-status role). Although such a misguided notion may be held by some people (feminist or otherwise), the central tenet of classical feminism is not that everyone must have the same status in order to be equal, but that everyone should have equal opportunity to *earn* his or her status, and that the high-status positions should not be dispensed to some and denied to others on the basis of factors (such as gender) that are unrelated to a person's ability to function in those roles.

The point of any reasonable feminist position is not that personal worth is determined by a person's role, but that personal worth is established when a person's role is determined by a person's identity (that is, a person's unique set of abilities, interests, and experiences). When personal identity is *not* allowed to determine a person's role, as often happens in the traditionalist system, then one's role *does* end up determining both personal worth and identity. Ortlund wants a person's worth and a person's role to be completely independent of each other. But personal worth, role, and identity are unavoidably interactive—even in traditionalism.

A sense of personal worth and significance comes from doing one's best at the work for which one is best suited, regardless of where that work is ranked on the ladder of social status. For traditionalists, a person's female gender means that the work to which that person is called and best suited will always be on the lower rungs of the ladder. This thesis is rejected by egalitarians, who believe that, as with a man, a woman's individual identity could lead her to a position on any rung of the ladder; as with a man, she will serve God worthily in her position if, and only if, she is humble and not self-seeking or power hungry.

While no function or role, no matter how lowly, can detract from a person's basic, God-given human worth, a person's worth *is* denigrated when she is prohibited from using the abilities that distinguish her as a unique individual, for she is thereby unable to fulfill the purpose for which she was created. A woman who is a "born leader" but is not allowed to lead will never actualize her purpose and worth as a leader or (because her leadership gift is part of her personal identity) as a person. The abilities of an individual's "being" are rendered distinct from a person's function only at the risk of doing the person a great injustice.

Someone who, simply on the basis of her womanhood, is denied access to a position for which she is qualified may readily and reasonably conclude that womanhood is of less worth than manhood. It is likely, as well, that she will not be the only one to draw this conclusion. Does not her femaleness limit her opportunities and does not maleness render a man fit to do that which she is not allowed to do? After all, a man is permitted to prove himself worthy of any rank, but a woman is worthy only of the lower-status positions. It is no wonder that women—especially Christian women—have, in general, lower self-esteem than men.[3]

Traditionalists typically claim that hierarchical gender roles follow from the different natures of men and women, and that gender equality violates the natural male/female distinction. However, they seem to arrive at their understanding of the male and female natures by reasoning backwards from their belief that the man's role is to lead and the woman's role is to obey. Hence, masculinity is seen essentially as leadership, and femininity as submission to male leadership.[4] A man and woman are perceived as having forsaken their respective gender identities if they function as equals rather than as leader and subordinate. In other words, the denial of a person's function within a hierarchy is seen as tantamount to a denial of the "being" from which the function necessarily proceeds. But this is to define one's personal identity according to the status of one's role—which comes a lot closer to the error Ortlund sees in feminism than the actual feminist belief that a person's role should be determined by, and not determinative of, personal identity.

Sexual Identity

In their efforts to refute gender equality, traditionalists often appear not to be arguing against any ideas actually held or expressed by evangelical feminists, but against the common caricature of feminism as the denial of all sexual differences. Ortlund, for example, states "that male–female equality does not constitute an undifferentiated sameness," and he illustrates "the importance of distinct sexual identity" by referring to the perverse and repulsive sight of a transvestite. He concludes that "sexual confusion is a significant, not a slight, personal problem."[5] All of this is true enough, but fails to address the point of disagreement between traditionalists and biblical equalitarians. From whence comes this recurring traditionalist fear that if people of different sexes have equal rights and equal vocational opportunities they will melt into an undifferentiated sameness with the sexual identity confusion of the transvestite?

This is a red herring that pops up repeatedly in antifeminist writings. Refutations of gender equality frequently will commence with the observation that because men and women are different, sexual role differentiation is a natural and necessary consequence that does not entail inequality of value. Next will come the assertion that any and all feminism is a dangerous threat to the God-ordained sexual difference, and that the inevitable end of gender equality is the legitimation of homosexuality—which, of course, follows from a denial of *all* sexual role differences. Such a line of argumentation, however, neither proves traditionalism nor disproves biblical equality. The matter in question is neither sexual differentiation nor the different sexual roles that follow necessarily from it. Rather, the issue concerns the status difference that does not necessarily follow from the sexual difference.

Worried as traditionalists are about gender equality leading to homosexuality, it should be noted that an understanding of sexual difference as status difference can easily be seen as a reason to prefer homosexuality over heterosexuality. The belief that the status of womanhood is inferior to that of manhood could lead some men to feel such contempt for women that they prefer males for sexual partners.[6] The prevalence of this belief can also lead some women to conclude that heterosexuality is inevitably oppressive and that the only possibility of an egalitarian sexual relationship is with another woman.[7] By contrast, far from leading a woman *into* homosexuality, a biblical egalitarian perspective can prove helpful in leading a woman *out* of homosexuality; for it clearly establishes without equivocation or qualification the equal value and status of womanhood in God's loving plan for human sexual relationships.[8]

The equation of sexual difference with status difference undermines the traditionalist's insistence that "one's personal worth and one's role . . . be registered independently of one another."[9] When inferior status is considered intrinsic to and definitive of female sexuality, a woman's essential (female) nature is not independent of, but fundamentally expressed by, her subordinate role.

This points to the sticking point of the entire debate, namely, the deeply entrenched, but often inarticulated, traditionalist premise that the right to command is uniquely definitive of masculinity. For those who hold this view, the fundamental meaning of sexuality inheres in male authority and female submission to male authority. As long as this belief holds sway, women will never be allowed equal opportunity to earn positions of authority, for this would allow women to be "masculine," and would destroy what is perceived to be the essential difference between the sexes.

Because traditionalists perceive a challenge to gender hierarchy as a threat to the very meaning of sexuality, many respond to this perceived threat by placing sexuality (and the hierarchy they believe it entails) at the very center of a person's identity, role, and calling in life. Hence, Ortlund states that "our distinct sexual identity defines who we are and why we are here and how God calls us to serve Him."[10] In the same vein, John Piper refers to sexuality as "an all-pervasive and all-conditioning dimension of personhood."[11] Elisabeth Elliot declares that "our sexual differences are the terms of our life," and for this reason she does not want to be regarded simply as a "person" but rather as a woman first and foremost.[12]

The traditionalist belief in the profoundly determinative force of sexuality in virtually every area of social interaction can create some strange dilemmas. Piper, for example, is concerned that if a woman should have occasion to direct or instruct a man that she do so in a feminine way, and that a man receive her directions or instructions in a masculine way. Because Piper regards the sexual difference as animating and permeating everything a man or woman does, he endeavors to point out that a "housewife in her backyard [who] may be asked by a man how to get to the freeway" should offer the man directions in such a way "that neither of them feels their mature femininity or masculinity compromised."[13] For Piper, such a situation is rife with risk; it requires that great care be taken, lest a man or woman end up with a case of compromised masculinity or femininity. However, this is not a problem for the egalitarian, who believes that giving and receiving directions to the freeway are not sexual activities, and that these roles, therefore, are easily interchangeable between male and female persons without risk of violating anyone's masculinity or femininity.

When one's sexuality determines one's place and purpose in all of life, it also determines one's identity. Ironically, the fallacy that sexual identity is equivalent to personal identity is at the root of radical homosexual-rights thinking. Gay-rights activists argue that if they are required to deny their sexual preference for any reason (whether religious or legal), they are being required to deny their very personhood, their core identity. Any stricture against homosexual behavior is, therefore, an unjust assault on the very essence of the homosexual person. In commenting on the homosexual-rights activists' view that sexuality is "the most fundamental thing about us as human beings," David Neff aptly observes that "for any of us to claim that the meaning of life is primarily about sexuality is a cruel narrowing of vision. . . . True freedom is found in growing toward what God, not biology, calls us to be."[14] The equating of sexual identity with personal identity seems to characterize the gender ideology at both the conservative and the liberal ends of the spectrum.

When this observation is compared with the well-worn traditionalist objection that biblical egalitarians have presuppositionally committed themselves to an advocacy of homosexual rights, the irony is apparent.[15] Generally speaking, evangelicals believe that a practicing homosexual should be denied the right to exercise spiritual leadership because his persistent disobedience to God's Word renders him spiritually unfit for such a role.[16] A woman, however, is not committing a sin merely by being a woman. Sinful behavior has nothing to do with why women are denied equality of spiritual status. Clearly, the issue of equal rights for women in the church is entirely disanalogous to the issue with respect to homosexuals.

The logic of biblical equality—far from entailing the legitimation of homosexuality—allows spiritually qualified women to exercise authority for the same reason it disallows practicing homosexuals.

When the relevant criterion for spiritual leadership is not sexuality but spiritual integrity, then granting women the opportunity to exercise spiritual leadership in no way leads to granting this opportunity to practicing homosexuals.

However, for traditionalists, sexuality *is* a primary criterion for allocating spiritual leadership. Traditionalists, therefore, regard equal status for women as a product of denying the sexual difference (which they believe entails a status difference). They then conclude that equal rights for homosexuals in the church must go hand in hand with equal rights for women; for both follow from a denial of sexual differences. But when status difference is rightly separated from sexual difference, it becomes clear that gender equality neither presupposes a denial of sexual difference nor leads to the legitimation of homosexuality that follows from such a denial.

Evangelical egalitarians believe that where sexuality is relevant, sexual difference *should* determine a person's behavior or role (such as whether one marries a man or a woman, the sort of clothing one wears in a particular culture, and so forth). But they do not believe that status differences are inherent to sexual differences, or that gender identity is the primary determinant of a person's calling and vocation. Gender may color the style in which a person does a particular job, but gender ought not be seen as a reason to deny a woman access to a position if she is, in fact, qualified to perform the work.

It is, after all, in their sexuality that men and women differ, and these differences must not be dismissed. On the other hand, it is in their common humanity (which makes people more alike than different) that men and women are equally deserving of the opportunity to express their humanness.

Social Status and Social Value

Traditionalists frequently observe—and it is quite true—that a difference in role does not necessarily imply a difference in value. However, when a role difference entails a status difference, the person with the higher status will be considered to be of more value in connection with the particular situation over which he has authority. Normally, the work involved in a higher-status position requires more skill, and the person performing it is more difficult to replace. This is why, for example, generals and heads of state do not serve on the front lines of battle during war time; they have greater political and military value than the foot soldier.

Of course, the higher social value that accompanies a higher-status role does not alter the intrinsic human value in which all persons share equally. A general and a sergeant are not unequal in human worth. If they each are serving in roles appropriate to their individual abilities, then neither are they unequal in personal worth, for each is faithfully fulfilling the purpose for which he is best equipped. But the general and the sergeant are of unequal social status in the military, and their interaction with one another will be marked by their awareness that the general has the right to command and the sergeant has the obligation to obey him. They will not relate to one another as equals. The inequality in their military relationship will be a logical and appropriate outworking of their unequal military rank—despite the fact that, because their respective ranks could change, or either one could leave the service, their inequality is not necessarily permanent.

In the husband–wife relationship, however, there is no discharge from service (outside of divorce) and, according to traditionalists, no change of rank in the marital hierarchy. Nevertheless, the husband is instructed by traditionalists to treat his wife as an "equal." But if a general is not expected to treat a sergeant as his equal within the context of their military relationship, how realistic or reasonable is it to expect a man to regard as his equal a person over whom he has comprehensive and permanent authority? He may govern her with kindness and consideration; but if it is *he* who must always govern *her,* she simply is not his equal within the marriage relationship.

Because higher status normally entails greater ability and greater social value in areas pertaining to the high-status position, it goes against the grain of common sense to insist that the husband's permanently higher status does not entail a higher valuation of his place in the family. As Royce Gruenler observes, "It is logically difficult to hold to a command/obey relationship on the one hand and on the other to deny that in some important sense one party is superior and the other inferior."[17]

Theoretically, the traditionalist model allows for women's ideas to be taken respectfully into consideration by the men who are in authority. But in practical reality, a person whose essential nature disqualifies her from all high-level decision-making responsibilities is probably not going to be regarded as seriously or as respectfully as the person whose essential nature does not so disqualify him. In all likelihood, her voice will not be heard, her views will be disregarded, her ideas and analyses will be patronizingly dismissed—regardless of how much she may be appreciated for keeping a clean home, raising well-behaved children, and cooking a fine meal.

Unfortunately, an observation of this sort is likely to be misconstrued by traditionalists, who tend to regard any sort of feminism as nothing other than the female lust for power. Ortlund asserts that "the absurdity of feminism lies in its irrational demand that a woman cannot be 'a serious person' unless she occupies a position of headship [i.e., authority]."[18] This caricature of feminism could become an accurate description of most types of feminism, including evangelical feminism, if it were altered to read that a woman will not be considered a serious person unless she has equal opportunity with men to earn positions of authority. As long as men know that a woman's voice in any matter will never be definitive and can always be vetoed, they are not likely to take her views as seriously as they would a man's.

Because traditionalists insist that they do grant women equality despite their subordinate role, any complaint women make about inequality is usually regarded as evidence of a desire for power, not for equality. The idea seems to be that men who seek high-status positions do so because God has called them to such roles, whereas women who seek such positions do so out of their own pride and sense of self-importance—which, of course, makes it wrong. This is a rather unfair conclusion to draw, given that egalitarian women are merely defending their *equal* right to prove themselves qualified for higher-ranking positions, while hierarchalist men are defending their *exclusive* right to occupy these positions. If any gender should be accused of being power hungry, it does not seem that it should be the female gender in this case.

A Function That Is Fitting, Permanent, and God-Ordained

The imposition of a radical disjunct between one's vocation (i.e., "function") and one's interests and abilities as a unique person (i.e., "being") runs counter to both biblical teaching and the most rudimentary principles of social justice. Yet this is precisely the traditionalist position. A woman's "being" is deemed fundamentally equal, and her "function" fundamentally unequal. Her gifts may well equip her for a calling she is not permitted to pursue. Her permanently subordinate function is, nonetheless, God-ordained and befitting of her essential female nature.

The basic idea behind biblical teaching on God's gifts and callings is that one's calling follows naturally from one's gifts. A lifelong calling, therefore, ought not specifically deny the exercise of a person's most salient gifts or require a significant use of gifts a person does not have. God is not likely to ordain a permanent misfit between what he has equipped a person to do and what he has called a person to do. As Stephen Lowe observes, "the obvious emphasis" in Paul's listing of gifts in Romans 12:3–8 "is that whatever one's gift, he is to perform the ministry function that the gift enables him to do ('if serving, let him serve; . . . if teaching, let him teach,' 12:7)."[19] The same emphasis is evident in 1 Peter 4:10–11.

Therefore, any function that requires a significant part of a person's identity to remain untouched and unutilized, or requires the use of abilities that are lacking in a person, cannot justifiably be deemed permanent, fitting, and God-ordained. Such a role may be fitting for a limited period of time, if circumstances call for it. But as a permanent and unalterable calling, it would be neither fitting nor in keeping with the character of God to ordain such a thing.

Because everyone does not possess the same array of innate talents and potentialities, situations of permanent subordination in certain areas of function *can* be warranted. If a person's inferior function in a particular area follows from his innately inferior ability to perform that function, then that person's subordinate role can be said to be justifiable. However, it cannot be said that the person in the subordinate role is nonetheless equal to his superior in terms of the particular function at issue.

If a person is permanently subordinated to another person in everything that she does, and if, in fact, her abilities are in every area permanently inferior to the abilities of the one to whom she is subordinated, then her role is a fitting reflection of her being. Her inferiority in function follows justly and logically from her inferiority in being.

But the idea of a person being inferior in all her abilities, in every area of life, for her entire life, is purely hypothetical. Except, perhaps, for some who are severely handicapped in a number of functions, every person has superior ability in some areas and inferior ability in other areas, and many of these areas of superior and inferior abilities will change over time as new skills are developed and old skills abandoned. If function is to follow from being—that is, if roles are to be considered justifiable—then many of a person's roles will be in flux throughout the course of her life.

If, as traditionalists maintain, the female role of subordination to male authority in the church and home is fitting, permanent, and God-ordained, then the female nature must be inferior to the male nature. Up until fairly recently in church history, women's subordination was seen clearly not only to imply, but to be justified by, women's inferiority.

Traditionalists today, however, deny that women's permanent subjection to the spiritual leadership of men has anything to do with women being morally incompetent to provide such leadership themselves.[20] According to John Piper and Wayne Grudem, the rationale for gender hierarchy is rooted in "God's created order for manhood and womanhood," "the underlying nature," "the true meaning," and "the deeper differences of manhood and womanhood."[21] But what, in Piper and Grudem's view, is the essence of the nature, meaning, divine order, and deeper differences of manhood and womanhood? It is precisely that men are meant to lead and women are meant to support and submit to the leadership of men. These differences in status reflect the deep differences between men and women, and are definitive of the very meaning and nature of masculinity and femininity. Men are leaders by nature; women are not.

If masculinity is expressed in the exercise of authority while femininity is expressed in subordination to that authority, then it is inherently fitting for a man to lead a woman and inherently unfitting for a woman to lead a man. What determines the fittingness of male authority and female subordination? Nothing less than the "underlying nature" of the male and the female. A man is fit to lead by virtue of his male nature. A woman, by virtue of her female nature, is not. Yet, traditionalists insist, a woman is perfectly competent to lead a man; nonetheless, for her to do so is for her to act in opposition to her true nature. It seems that a woman is, by nature, at the same time fit to lead and unfit to lead. She has the natural ability to do so, yet it is somehow unnatural for her to do so.

How can these two propositions be reconciled with one another? Woman's naturally inferior position is not due to any incompetence or inferiority in her nature; yet her subordination is grounded in her nature. What in a person's nature could possibly demand her permanent assignment to an inferior status and function? What, indeed, other than a natural incompetence to do the thing that her subordinate position denies her opportunity to do?

The distinction between saying that women are unfit to lead men, and saying that it is contrary to a woman's nature for her to lead a man, seems purely semantic. Either gender hierarchy follows from and is justifiable on the basis of ontological inequities between males and females, or it has nothing to do with ontology and is, therefore, completely arbitrary. And if the rationale for women's permanently inferior status is rooted in the ontological difference of womanhood, then such a difference is necessarily a difference of inferiority. The middle ground that traditionalists seek simply does not exist.

Traditionalists today deviate from both tradition and logic in their attempt to deny that women are inferior to men, and yet to insist that the permanent subjection of women to male authority follows necessarily from the essential nature and meaning of manhood and womanhood. Such thinking does not begin to have the logical consistency of, say, the viewpoint of Protestant Reformer John Knox, who maintained that women should be subordinate to men because the female nature is stupid, weak, unstable, and cruel.[22] As Nicholas Wolterstorff observes:

> In earlier days, men in the church insisted that women were not equal. They were inferior—made inferior by God. . . . But notice: If we do in fact believe that women are inferior, we also believe that there is a difference between men and women that is relevant to the unequal distribution of benefits and deprivations. Such a way of thinking at least makes sense. But nowadays we are in the strange position where those who insist that women must be kept out of the offices of the church insist that they are fully equal with men.[23]

When traditionalists assert that women are "equal in being," they equivocate on the meaning of both "being" and "equality." They invest each term with a virtually meaningless meaning ("being" = "human being"; "equal" = "equally human"), then use the terms without indicating that their meanings have been eviscerated of meaningful content. There is no such thing as being inferior in the sense of being less human; but one *can* be inferior in the sense of being less competent. When a person's function or role is deemed permanent, fitting, and God-ordained, and when it is determined solely on the basis of an intrinsic aspect of that person's nature, then its imposition upon a person is a clear statement about that person's being—not in the generic sense of "human being," but in the particular sense of being a unique individual with a personal identity and a specific set of abilities.

If the female nature alone is sufficient to render a person unfit for leadership—and even for the governance of her own life under God— then it follows that the female nature is indecisive, irrational, lacking in wisdom and moral discernment, perpetually childlike in the need for guidance and governance (implying an unstable emotional nature), and, in the case of spiritual leadership, less able to access God directly in order to understand his Word and to know his will.

The idea that women are spiritually inferior to men is clearly denied by the Bible.[24] Yet the current traditionalist exclusion of women from leadership pertains primarily to spiritual leadership. Women's "functional subordination" in areas of spiritual authority implies more than women's essential inferiority in those intellectual and temperamental abilities requisite to good leadership; it implies that women are also inferior spiritually. Yet this is precisely what traditionalists deny. Men and women are "spiritually equal," they claim repeatedly and insistently.

Why, then, is a male believer, solely by virtue of his maleness, deemed fit to act as the "priest" or spiritual leader in his home and church? Does not God make his will and Word known to women as well as to men? And if so, why must a woman subordinate her understanding of God's will to a man's understanding of God's will? How can it be said that women and men stand on equal ground before God, and that in Christ there is no distinction between male and female, if persons of one gender are obliged to obey and hear from God by hearing from and obeying persons of the other gender?

"Servant Leadership"

A corollary concept to the being/function distinction is that of the husband's "servant leadership." This term is employed by traditionalists in order to reconcile the doctrine of male authority with the actual biblical instructions to the husband—which do not command him to rule, lead, or make decisions on behalf of his wife, but do instruct him to regard his wife as his equal in Christ and to love, respect, serve, care for, and lay down his life for her.[25]

If the doctrine of a universal, God-ordained hierarchy in marriage is not to contradict the clear biblical admonition for a husband to be a servant to his wife, then a man's leadership of his wife must be construed as a service to her. But if a husband and wife are spiritually equal, how could the husband's spiritual leadership of his wife be a service to her? In what way does a woman need her husband to exercise spiritual authority over her?

A servant, by definition, does for someone what that person needs or desires to have done for her. Unless a woman is spiritually in need of a man's governance in every area of her life, its imposition upon her is of no service to her. A woman cannot be served by a man's spiritual rule unless *her* ability to discern the will and understand the Word of God is inferior to the ability God has given men in this regard. In other words, the husband's spiritual leadership of his wife is a service to her only if she is in fact spiritually inferior to him.

In order for male authority in marriage to be considered "servant leadership," women must also be presumed to be more childish than men. Thus, a husband would serve his wife by overriding her desires or choices whenever he believes they are wrong or harmful to her or to the family. After all, a child's desires and decisions *are* more likely to be foolish and harmful than an adult's. A child does need and benefit from a parent's guidance and governance when it is exercised with a view to the child's best interests, which a parent, from the vantage point of maturity, should know better than the child knows herself. In describing what he calls "considerate leadership," Grudem states that "there will be times in every marriage when a godly husband simply will have to make decisions that affect the whole family, that go against his wife's desires and preferences and that he nonetheless is convinced, before God, are right."[26] This sort of paternal governance describes the proper relationship of parents to their children. According to traditionalists, this is also the proper relationship of a husband to his wife.

If, however, a wife is not more childish than her husband, and if she is not spiritually inferior to her husband, then as an adult she has as much need to achieve spiritual maturity through learning to discern God's will and make right decisions as does any grown man. In this case, a man who makes final decisions for his wife is not acting as one who serves her, but as one who represses her spiritual growth and personal maturity. Rather than laying down his life for her sake, he may instead be sacrificing her maturity and ministry for the sake of his own male right (or "responsibility") to lead.

True servant leadership requires that the leader be qualified and deserving, and that those who are led by him benefit from the service his leadership offers. When one person exercises leadership over another for a reason unrelated to either the leader's qualifications for leadership or the subordinate's need for leadership, and when there is no area of life in which the leader does not have the right to command and the subordinate the obligation to obey, then such leadership is not "servant leadership."

The ideal of servant leadership among competent adults is apropos only for situations in which: (a) a group of people need a leader in order to act in a united and effective way, and (b) the leader has earned his authority and is accountable to the people for his leadership. In the traditionalist model, a man has authority over a woman who is no more in need of someone to govern her life than is the man. Moreover, his leadership of her is not accountable to her. Only God has the right to overrule what the husband deems to be God's will for his wife and family.

But, traditionalists say, the authority of a loving husband is not tyrannical. A man who practices servant leadership respects and solicits his wife's views and takes them into consideration in making his decisions. In fact, a husband's love and respect for his wife as an "equal" would normally prohibit the exercise of his right to command her obedience. Admittedly, this constitutes a more humane exercise of authority than the historically traditional model in which the wife and children were obliged to submit passively to the decisions of the household patriarch. But if the ideal is for husband and wife to make decisions together, why shouldn't they always do so?[27] Why must the husband be reserved the right to make the "final decision"? How could he ever exercise this right without violating his wife's equality with him?

Simply having the right to command obedience whenever he so chooses accords a man absolute authority over his wife. No matter how sensitively a husband may wield it, his authority has all the essential elements of authoritarianism; it requires complete obedience, its jurisdiction covers the entirety of a person's life, and it is not accountable to those who are governed. Whether a husband exercises his authority tyranically or benevolently depends entirely on the condition of his moral character. Since there are no qualifications of character by which a man earns his male authority, and no established methods of redress to which he is held accountable, a husband's benevolent exercise of authority can be neither relied upon nor enforced. It is commendable that today's traditionalists are exhorting men to lead with consideration and kindness, but the nature of the husband's authority does not demand or even encourage benevolent rule.

Unearned, Unaccountable, and God-Ordained

In the nineteenth century, the absolute authority of a man over his wife was backed up by civil law and not simply by the opinion of traditionalist church leaders. John Stuart Mill observed that the "almost unlimited power" granted a husband by such law "evokes the latent germs of selfishness in the remotest corners of his nature—fans its faintest sparks and smoldering embers—offers to him a license for the indulgence of those points of his original character which in all other relations he would have found it necessary to repress and conceal." Mill did not mean by this that most husbands were cruel despots; on the contrary, most men tempered the exercise of their authority out of affection for their wives. Mill's point, rather, was that "laws and institutions require to be adapted, not to good men, but to bad."[28]

Because it is not the good men or the good marriages that need the regulation the law provides, the law ought to be designed for the bad marriages and the bad men. The fatal flaw of nineteenth-century marital law is the same as that of the spiritualized chain of command taught today; the law is harmless only if the husband is wise, kind, and loving, and the marriage characterized by mutual respect and affection—if, in other words, the law is not needed and, therefore, not implemented. As long as the husband is good and the marriage is healthy, the husband will be unlikely to enforce his authority, and he and his wife will live in a practical (if not a theoretical) equality. It is when the husband or the marriage begins to fall short of this standard of righteousness that the law of male authority is most likely to be implemented—at the precise point at which it is capable of doing the most harm.

Advocates of male authority insist that if men exercise "godly" leadership, it will always bless and never demean women. But it is unwise and unrealistic to assume that if men are given absolute authority they will never use it abusively. Granting someone the opportunity to indulge the selfish desire for control is never a good idea—the human sin nature being what it is. Mandating a relationship of rule and submission between husband and wife can be a risky business. "Hierarchical marriage . . . constantly teeters on the edge of God's boundary. . . . It operates too close to where temptation is difficult to resist."[29] The rationale for male rule in marriage becomes even more dubious when traditionalists insist that women are naturally more spiritually inclined than men.[30] Why should men have the spiritual authority if women are better equipped than men to handle it wisely and righteously? (Of course, there is no biblical evidence that either gender is better qualified to exercise spiritual authority.)

Although the stern patriarchal authority of truly traditional social custom has been modernized and mollified by today's traditionalists, its absolute nature remains intact.[31] In nineteenth-century law, the husband's authority was unearned, unaccountable, and, in religious circles, considered God-ordained. These elements still characterize the nature of the authority granted men by traditionalists today.

Because the husband's authority is not earned, it cannot be taken away. Regardless of how cruel or stupid a man might be, he retains the right of "final say" in the family. Some traditionalists today do acknowledge that a woman should not stay with a man who physically abuses her, or obey a man who commands her to do something that is sinful. Although this is a welcome modification of the truly traditional view of a husband's authority, the basic principle remains: The husband does not need to prove himself worthy to rule. Being male is the only qualification. Undeniably and inexcusably evil behavior is the only possible disqualification.

The husband is also unaccountable to anyone for his decisions. He is, of course, considered accountable to God; but when God's will is determined for a woman by her husband, this is of no practical use for her. To whom can a woman appeal if her husband makes a decision that, though he thinks it best, she firmly believes will be injurious to her, to the children, or even to him? There is no board of directors, no court of appeals, no impeachment process available. Outside of appealing to the law or to her church in the case of physical abuse (experience has shown neither option to be particularly satisfactory), the wife is granted no biblically sanctioned recourse. Her only option is to try her best to persuade, and then to submit to whatever he decides. In the final analysis, her voice, her view, her understanding of what is right and wrong—while it may be heard and even sometimes heeded—nonetheless always counts for less than his. Theoretically, she is completely at his mercy, and he is completely in control.

Adding to the force of the husband's unearned and unaccountable authority is its spiritual nature. The husband is not only the leader, he is the spiritual leader, the God-ordained leader. He does not speak only with his own authority, but with the authority of God. He has been vested by God with the responsibility to discern God's will on behalf of himself and his wife and children. Whether he does this with or without his wife's input, with or without any consideration for his wife's interests or expertise, his "final decision" has the stamp of divine authority. For a wife to question whether her husband's "final decision" really *is* God's will for their lives is for her to question God's wisdom in ordaining him as the spiritual leader and decision maker of the family.

If, in fact, the man has been uniquely vested by God with the spiritual authority "to decide, in the light of Holy Scripture, what courses of action will most glorify God" for his household,[32] to be "the finally responsible member of the partnership" for both his and his wife's moral and spiritual health,[33] to "act *as* Christ" and "*for* Christ" with respect to his wife;[34] if the man's role in the family entails his "standing in the place of Christ" for his wife, and if it obligates him to "protect [his family] from the greatest enemies of all, Satan and sin,"[35] and if women have been excluded from this spiritual responsibility and authority, then men and women are not on the same spiritual level at all.

Why should the tasks of discerning the will of God, taking responsibility for someone else's spiritual condition, and protecting others from Satan and sin be solely a man's job? Where does the Bible say that God has made these things a distinctly male calling? If Christ is a female believer's Lord and Master as much as he is a male believer's, then why should a woman need a man to stand in the place of Christ for her? If we all stand on equal ground before God, and if all believers are priests (1 Peter 2:5, 9), for what reason should anyone take spiritual responsibility for anyone else?

The spiritual authority of the male over the female would rightly exist as a spiritual principle only if, in theological truth, the male qua male were better equipped to discern God's will and to provide spiritual direction, and the female qua female were more in need of spiritual guidance and governance. But if such were the case, then man and woman would not be spiritually equal. Although traditionalists repeatedly deny that they regard women as spiritually inferior to men, they insist on women occupying roles that entail clear implications of women's spiritual inferiority.

Sexual Differences: Physical or Metaphysical?

If a person's gender alone determines whether that person is to exercise or submit to spiritual leadership, then it follows that there is some spiritual or metaphysical component to sexuality that mandates such a difference in spiritual roles. Those who hold to a metaphysical view of sexuality typically reverse the usual approach to understanding gender differences. Instead of beginning with the physical differences (in reproductive organs, hormone levels, and so on) and then determining the social and psychological ramifications of these differences, metaphysical sexual differences are posited at the outset; then physical differences are regarded as mere reflections of this greater cosmic reality. When sexuality becomes a metaphysical affair, masculinity and femininity come to be regarded as cosmic polarities—rule and submission, initiation and response, creativity and receptivity, objectivity and subjectivity—which pervade the spiritual essence of the universe.

C. S. Lewis declares that in the matter of sexuality, "we are dealing with male and female not merely as facts of nature but as the live and awful shadows of realities utterly beyond our control and largely beyond our direct knowledge."[36] Drawing on what he believes to be "celebrated in all mythologies and assumed in Scripture," Thomas Howard states that the sexual "distinction is assumed to run down to the root of the world and up to the top of things. Nothing is sexless."[37] Elisabeth Elliot follows suit, appealing to "ancient truth which mankind has always recognized. God created male and female, the male to call forth, to lead, initiate and rule, and the female to respond, follow, adapt, submit. Even if we held to a different theory of origin, the physical structure of the female would tell us that woman was made to receive, to bear, to be acted upon, to complement, to nourish." The differing bodies of men and women signify such universal polarities as masculinity and femininity, power and passivity, rule and submission—which, Elliot believes, are described by the Chinese religious concept of the polar principles of *yin* (the feminine) and *yang* (the masculine). Archetypal femininity is defined by submission, self-giving, suffering, and sacrifice; and since this is also the role of the church, the church is feminine with respect to God.[38]

Larry Crabb, likewise, believes that the physical aspect of sexuality is merely the tip of a metaphysical iceberg. "Our distinctively shaped bodies reflect distinctively shaped souls," he says, for the deepest natures of men and women have equipped them for fundamentally different modes of relating to their worlds and to each other.[39] Sexual function is symbolic of a person's *every* function: "Men were designed to enter their worlds strongly, providing for their families, leading them . . . toward God, moving toward others with sacrificing, powerful love. Women were designed to courageously give all they have . . . to others in warm vulnerability, allowing themselves to be entered and wrapping themselves with supportive strength around those with whom they relate."[40] If, in fact, these sexualized personal traits are not merely generally applicable to male and female behavior, but are essential to the very natures of men and women, then they should characterize *every* woman and man. The reality, however, is that they simply do not. How, then, can the "deviant" men and women be accounted for? Evidently, those men and women whose social behavior does not typically reflect their sexual behavior have somehow missed out on their essential natures as males and females.

Crabb cites Emil Brunner as saying that "our sexuality penetrates to the deepest metaphysical ground of our personality. As a result, the physical differences between the man and the woman are a parable of the psychical and spiritual differences of a more ultimate nature."[41] Piper and Grudem also invoke this statement of Brunner in support of their belief that "there is a profound female or male personhood portrayed in our differing bodies," and that these profound differences between the psychological and spiritual natures of men and women ordain that men should lead and that women should submit to male leadership.[42] Indeed, if the sexual difference alone determines a person's qualification (or lack thereof) for spiritual leadership (as it does in the traditionalist marriage relationship), then there *must* be some "deeper" element to sexuality that would be relevant to such a determination.

Brunner, however, qualifies the metaphysical difference between the sexes by noting that "it recedes in exact proportion to the measure in which the spirit, and the personal spirit in particular, becomes strong."[43] In other words, the sexual demarcation in the spiritual and psychological dimensions is by no means as clear-cut as in the physical realm, and becomes increasingly obscure and irrelevant the more spirituality is emphasized and the less physicality is emphasized. Conversely, the less a person's spiritual nature is developed, the more that person's sexuality will dominate and determine her personal/psychological nature.

It seems a shame that today's Christian proponents of spiritualized sexuality do not share Brunner's circumspection in this highly speculative area of thought. They probably would not as readily cite Brunner's compelling observation that

man, as the actually dominating shaper of history, culture, the conditions of the law and of public education . . . has artificially riveted woman to her natural destiny, and has hindered the free development of her mind and spirit, to which she, as well as the man, as one who has been made in the image of God, has been called. . . . Even at the present day, and to a far greater degree than we usually realize, woman is still the slave of man, even the woman in the higher classes, even the educated woman. Hence her real nature cannot yet be clearly discerned. It is still concealed behind the picture of woman as man wants her to be. . . . The man has had every opportunity to show what he really is; he has indeed—and this is a part of his self-manifestation—shown what he is in the very fact that he has deprived woman of the same possibility.[44]

The metaphysical, spiritualized view of sexuality is not usually emphasized in evangelical arguments for female subordination to male authority. Indeed, such a view lacks adequate biblical support, and bears an alarming resemblance to pagan religious ideas that tie in sexuality with gods, goddesses, and cosmic spiritual forces. However, the spiritualization of sexuality does seem to be logically and theologically entailed by the doctrine that men have been authorized by God to exercise spiritual authority over women for the entire scope and duration of their lives. If different spiritual roles arise necessarily from sexual differences, then the sexual nature in some sense defines and determines the spiritual nature. Sexuality, therefore, is not merely physical, but ultimately metaphysical.

The only way to circumvent the implication of spiritualized sexuality is to assert that hierarchical gender role assignments are completely arbitrary, and that there is nothing inherent to maleness that makes roles of spiritual authority any more suitable for men than for women. This position is rarely taken by traditionalists, although it probably is more likely to be held by female advocates of gender hierarchy.[45] The arbitrary assignment explanation, however, runs aground ethically, logically, and theologically. It fails to account for why an entire class of humans should be subject to the spiritual authority of another class of humans if there is no inequality in spiritual status, maturity, or understanding between the two classes. The entire proposition must be deemed absurd, unjust, and antithetical to the character of God as revealed in the Bible.

If, however, one is to maintain that the assignment of spiritual roles along lines of gender is not arbitrary, then one must posit something about maleness that is more suited than femaleness to assuming the place of Christ and representing him authoritatively, or something about femaleness that is more in need of spiritual guidance and governance. In short, there must be a spiritual element to sexuality that mandates an inequality in the spiritual roles, rights, and obligations of men and women.

Such thinking about sexual and spiritual differences cannot be reconciled logically or theologically with the traditionalist insistence that despite their "different" roles, men and women are nonetheless "spiritually equal." Nor can such fundamental spiritual inequality be reconciled with what the Bible teaches about the divine image in both male and female humans, the priesthood of all believers, and Christ as the *one* mediator between God and humanity. Moreover, the idea that maleness singularly qualifies a person for leadership (whether spiritual or otherwise) is at odds with our experience of men and women in society, where we find many women who are qualified to lead (spiritually or otherwise), as well as many men who are not.

Despite—or perhaps in ignorance of—these problems and inconsistencies, most traditionalists maintain that men and women are spiritually equal *and* that the mandated role differences between men and women reflect and are justified by the inherent differences between the sexes.[46]

In Search of a Definition

John Piper upbraids evangelical feminists for not clearly defining masculinity and femininity. Yet he is unable to claim any biblically based knowledge about essential differences between men and women other than what he can infer from a traditionalist interpretation of biblical teaching on gender roles. Thus, if a man's role is to lead and a woman's role is to submit, then the essence of masculinity is leadership and the essence of femininity is submission to male leadership.[47] A biblical defense of gender hierarchy cannot be grounded in propositions about the essential nature of masculinity and femininity because the Bible does not contain the raw material for such propositions. The Bible does not define or regard masculinity and femininity as separate and opposite ways of being; in fact, it does not even address the subject.

The attempt to define metaphysical differences between men and women raises many troubling questions. Susan Foh asks some of these questions in her critique of Piper's approach to gender differences:

Are these definitions or any definitions of manhood and womanhood
found in the Scripture? Is the emphasis of the biblical texts (such as
Eph. 4:22–24; Gal. 5:22–23; Col. 3:9–15) on becoming Christlike in
two different modes (blue and pink)? . . . If man and woman are essentially different in being (though equal), do they reflect God's image
equally, differently? . . . If our sexuality colors our whole being and
was intended to do so before the Fall, what happens to it after the Resurrection (Matt. 22:30)?[48]

Although she is a traditionalist, Foh recognizes that "the Bible does
not even hint at any mysterious, metaphysical differences between
men and women; God's word is mainly concerned with persons." And,
if men and women are basically persons, we ought "to cease thinking
of certain traits as being masculine or feminine and to advocate that
each person develop into a *godly* individual."[49] The Christian hagiog-
rapher, Theodoret of Cyrus, expressed a similar sentiment some fifteen centuries ago: "Virtue cannot be separated into male and female.
. . . For the difference is one of bodies not of souls. As St. Paul says,
'in Christ Jesus . . . there is neither male nor female.'"[50]

In exploring the question of whether women and men experience
God differently, Christian philosopher Elizabeth Morelli concludes
that spirituality must be considered gender neutral, for our spiritual
capacity resides in our common human nature, which transcends sexual differences. "Insofar as we understand our access to God [i.e., our
spirituality] to be the very ground or core of the human spirit, then we
cannot attribute to woman *qua* woman a specific conscious access to
God. To do so would be to assert that woman is not quite human, or
that there are two distinct human natures."[51]

Masculinity and femininity are not spiritual archetypes or personality profiles, but simply aspects of male sexuality and female sexuality. Men can differ greatly from other men in terms of their spiritual
gifts and personality traits; yet these differences do not necessarily
make some men any more or less masculine than other men. Because
of these differences, however, masculinity will be expressed differently in different men. The same, of course, is true with respect to the
femininity of women.

The traditionalist tendency is to ascribe to sexuality the power to
determine both personality and spirituality, and thereby to inflate the

matter of sexuality to cosmic proportions. But there is no biblical basis for this, and there are many theological problems entailed by it, as we will see in the next chapter. It is better to extricate the concept of sexuality from implications and intimations of spirituality, for then women and men are not obliged to conform to metaphysical archetypes and cosmic hierarchies, but are set free to be the unique human persons God made each one to be.

4

Sexuality in God and in the Image of God

erhaps the biggest problem with the spiritualization of sexuality lies in its implications concerning the gender of God. If masculinity and femininity describe universal spiritual polarities inherent to the nature of ultimate reality (as proponents of metaphysical sexuality would have it), then it is difficult, if not impossible, to regard the Bible's gendered imagery for God as anything other than statements of God's essentially masculine (and perhaps also feminine) spiritual nature. Once the gendered imagery for God is reified, such that it is seen as literally describing God's essential nature, a great deal of confusion develops in the ensuing effort to avoid actually imputing sexuality to God.

Donald Bloesch's discourse on the subject is illustrative:

> God . . . cannot be subsumed under either masculine or feminine categories. At the same time, this God is the ground of both the masculine and the feminine . . . . God includes masculinity and femininity within himself, though not human sexuality; yet the God of the Bible is not androgynous, half male and half female. He includes masculinity and femininity as

movements within himself . . . . In one respect he appears to be alto-
gether masculine, and in another predominantly feminine. The *masculine* and *feminine* are ontological categories which are not absolutely
transcended in God, but which arise out of God.[1]

Later, however, Bloesch declares that the masculine terms "Father"
and "Lord" carry a "univocal meaning" with respect to the nature of
God—a meaning that "embraces the element of omnipotent or
absolute power which is a masculine, not a feminine, attribute." God
as Father goes beyond metaphor; it is "an archetypal or foundational
analogy," which does not merely resemble fatherhood but defines it.[2]

It seems that, for Bloesch, God's nature is not sexual nor can it be
identified as masculine or feminine; nonetheless, God is alternately
characterized by masculinity and femininity as "movements" within
his nature. Masculinity and femininity are included in, grounded in,
and almost transcended by God's nature. Yet, God is more masculine
than feminine, in that certain traits deemed essentially masculine are
foundational to God's own nature.

C. S. Lewis does not attribute femininity to God in any sense, but
asserts the absolute masculinity of God as an essential element of the
Christian religion. He maintains that those who deny what he perceives to be the significance of the Bible's masculine imagery for God
"are really implying that sex is something superficial, irrelevant to the
spiritual life. To say that men and women are equally eligible for a
certain profession is to say that for the purposes of that profession
their sex is irrelevant."[3] Lewis is correct enough on this point, and he
would see the "irrelevance" of sex to the spiritual life and ministerial
profession himself, if it were not for his entrenched belief that metaphysical sexuality defines and determines God's nature, human nature,
our relationship to God, our relationships to one another, and, of
course, those who may and those who may not represent God in the
priesthood.

For Lewis, God is not merely masculine, but so masculine that both
men and women are feminine by comparison. Men are, however, masculine in relation to women, while women are not masculine in any
sense; therefore, men should be granted sole access to the spiritually
masculine roles—that is, the roles that represent God. Compared to
the masculinity of God, Lewis declares, "we are all, corporately and

individually, feminine to Him. We men may often make very bad priests. That is because we are insufficiently masculine. It is no cure to call in those who are not masculine at all [i.e., women]."[4] Craig Keener observes that this type of argument "reads like something out of Philo, who saw men as feminine before God, just as women were feminine before men, masculinity being the ideal spiritual state."[5]

According to Lewis, masculinity is an essential property of God's nature—which God possesses in totality; men, by virtue of their male sexuality, possess it in small measure; women, by virtue of their female sexuality, lack it entirely. Clearly, masculinity in humans is a property of maleness and not of femaleness. But, Lewis insists, "God is in fact not a biological being and has no sex."[6] God's masculinity evidently does not derive from maleness, as it does in male humans. God, therefore, is not male exactly, but male-like, as it were. This distinction is technical at best. If God has the spirituality of maleness, what does it matter if he hasn't the biology? If the spiritual nature of men is similar to God's nature—and, conversely, the spiritual nature of women is dissimilar (or, at least, less similar) to God's nature—then God is in effect, if not in fact, male; and men are more like God than women are. If, on the cosmic spectrum, humans are feminine and God is masculine, and, on the human spectrum, women are feminine and men are masculine, then women are to men as humanity is to God: dependent, derivative, and deficient. Femininity (the female nature) is inferior to masculinity (the male nature), even as humans are inferior to God.

An interesting complication in viewing men as less masculine than God arises from the fact that the Bible also refers to God in feminine categories—even biologically feminine categories involving such activities as giving birth and nursing at the breast (Deut. 32:18; Isa. 42:14; 46:3–4; 49:15; 66:13; James 1:18). If God's nature includes the motherly characteristics typically associated exclusively with women, God must be not only more masculine than any human male, but also more feminine than any human male.[7]

Reifying the gendered imagery for God results in a God who suffers from some gender identity confusion. In two of the biblical references to God giving birth to his people, God is also spoken of as being our father (Deut. 32:18; James 1:17–18)![8] It seems the biblical descriptions of God simply are not intended to be taken as indicators of God's gender.

The Image of a Masculine God

What does it mean for male and female to be created in God's image, if God possesses gendered characteristics, and if human sexuality, therefore, is somehow a part of the image of God? Does the male most fully and directly, and the female only secondarily and indirectly, reflect God's fundamentally masculine nature? Or do males image God's predominantly masculine attributes and females image God's less prominent feminine attributes? Either way, it is inevitable that the divine image in woman be regarded as less complete than the divine image in man.

Those who assert that God is masculine, and humanity feminine in relation to him, are obliged to deny the logical implications of this belief. Generally speaking, they maintain that despite God's masculinity, men are not more like God than women are, and women are equally in God's image. J. I. Packer and Thomas Howard put it thus:

> Does the consistently masculine presentation of God in Scripture mean that men bear more of God's image than women do? No; the declaration that God made humanity, male and female, in his own image shows that just as all authentically masculine characteristics find their source in God, so do all authentically feminine characteristics. Women bear God's image as truly and fully as men do. What we should learn, as it seems, from the fact that God is "he" in Scripture and that the Word was incarnated as a human male is not that men are more like God than women, but that we are all, men and women alike, feminine (so to speak) in relation to our Maker and Redeemer.[9]

Let's see what we have here. If even the most masculine man is so deficient in masculinity that he is feminine compared to God's masculinity, then masculinity is an attribute that characterizes God and distinguishes God from what is not God. This is also C. S. Lewis's position. To be masculine is to be like God; to be feminine (i.e., not masculine) is to be unlike God. Yet, Packer and Howard tell us, God is also feminine, such that he is himself the source of all femininity.

God, apparently, is the source of that which is the antithesis of his essential nature. Moreover, men, who possess masculinity (which is both definitive and representative of God's nature), are no more like God than women, who do not possess masculinity.

There is, in this type of thinking, the bizarre juxtaposition of several logically incompatible assertions: (1) God has in himself (he is the source of) all masculinity and all femininity. (2) God's nature is essentially masculine; in fact, his masculinity is so pure and total that in contrast with him even the most masculine male human is merely feminine. (3) Men are, nonetheless, somewhat masculine; women are not masculine at all; this renders men uniquely qualified to represent God as priests. (4) Men are not more like God than women are. (5) Women do not image God any less than men do.

Traditionalist theologian Werner Neuer further exemplifies the dilemmas entailed by the spiritualization of sexuality and the sexualization of God. He poses the question, "Are men and women the image of God only in regard to their common human nature, or do they also reflect God's nature through their sexual distinctiveness?"[10] He then sets the stage for answering this question by asserting that "the biblical view of man and woman is rooted in the nature of God. . . . For since in the Old and New Testaments God is depicted exclusively in male terms (as 'Father,' 'Lord,' 'King,' etc.), it is natural that he must be represented by men and not by women."[11] Moreover, Neuer claims, God's essential masculinity is conclusively demonstrated by Jesus' consistent reference to God as Father rather than as Mother.

In explaining why Jesus could not have called God "Mother," Neuer appeals to what he perceives to be "the nature of fatherhood and motherhood. Fatherhood involves the active procreation of new life, whereas motherhood is characterized by the overwhelmingly passive acts of conceiving, carrying, and bearing new life."[12] This observation proves nothing other than the extent to which androcentrism can twist perception. It seems that a good deal of imagination and determination is required in order to characterize the strenuous effort required of a woman's body in nourishing, growing, and delivering a child as "overwhelmingly passive," while depicting the male role of standing around watching it happen as "active"!

Actually, much less mental gyration than this is required in order to understand why Jesus referred to God as his Father. It is fairly obvious that Jesus already had a mother; yet, being born of a virgin, he had no earthly father. God, therefore, was the Father of Jesus—but not in the sense that a man becomes a father by means of begetting offspring; for God the Son is eternally coexistent with God the Father. The Father/Son language of Scripture is primarily expressive of the Son's similarity to and equality with—rather than his derivation from and subordination to—God the Father.[13]

In calling God "Father," Jesus demonstrated their intimate personal relationship—a relationship he was making available (in a lesser sense) to his disciples as well. It is this relationship between God and Christ—not any divine masculinity—that is emphasized and illustrated by Jesus' referring to God as his Father.[14] The personal, relational picture that the New Testament presents of God the Father constitutes a significant change from the Old Testament, in which God's fatherhood was considered relevant on the national rather than the personal level, and in which reference to God as a Father occurs a mere fifteen times. With Jesus, the image of God as a Father is augmented and transformed. The somewhat distant patriarch of a nation becomes the Abba Father personally and lovingly known by each believer in Christ. This fundamental change in God's relationship to his people through Christ is reflected in the frequency (245 times) with which God is called "Father" in the New Testament.[15]

Neuer, however, insists that Jesus called God "Father" because the essential nature of fatherhood (active, self-sufficient, and so forth) properly characterizes God's essential nature, whereas the attributes distinguishing motherhood "are completely foreign to his nature."[16] Finally, in view of what he has presented as "the masculine-shaped picture of God in Scripture," Neuer answers his original question about human sexuality imaging God: "So up to a point the man may be said to reflect God or Christ more completely than the woman does, whereas she more clearly portrays creation and the church. . . . But this statement must not be misunderstood to mean that the woman is in only a limited sense the image of God." Nonetheless, it is "possible to differentiate slightly how man and woman reflect God through their sex. . . . The male reflects God in a special way and the female reflects creation."[17]

By way of summary, Neuer declares that "the biblical view of God entails with consistent logic the headship of the man over the woman, for the man is in a special way the representative of the God revealed in Scripture."[18] In other words, because the male images God in a "special" way that the female does not, he is divinely fitted to represent God as the woman's "head" in creation, marriage, and the church—although, of course, the woman does not image God in any lesser sense than the man. Alas, the "consistent logic" that Neuer sees in this rationale is not apparent.

Neuer's case of equivocation concerning the divine image in woman and man is not unique among traditionalists. James Hurley and John Frame both state that the man, in his position of authority over his wife, images God's authority or lordship in a way that the woman does not. Frame, however, allows that the woman images God in her helpful submissiveness to her husband, whereas Hurley, like Neuer, sees woman's submission as imaging creation and the church, rather than God.[19]

Once masculinity is posited as an essential attribute of God's nature, and authority as an essential attribute of masculinity that is shared by men and God (but not by women), any effort to deny that male humans are more godlike than female humans is fundamentally unconvincing. As Faith Martin observes, such arguments are attempting "something that cannot be done—speaking of masculinity in some disembodied sense. No matter how perfectly the distinction between masculinity and male might possibly be maintained, the root question remains: Why bother talking about masculinity at all if it is not going to be tied, in the end, to persons with male bodies?"[20]

If it is because of their maleness that men have the spiritual authority to act as representatives of God, then there must be something about maleness that is more godlike than femaleness. Correspondingly, God must be more male-like than female-like. Ultimately, the masculinity—the spiritual essence of maleness—inherent to God's nature must be seen as imaged in men and not women, thus rendering women spiritually deficient, lesser image bearers.

Neutralizing the Gender of God

Some Christian feminists endeavor to redress the gender imbalance in traditionalist thought by emphasizing the Bible's feminine imagery for God and asserting that God possesses both feminine and masculine attributes. But this solves nothing. For one thing, as Faith Martin points out, this strategy entails the same errors that are employed by those in the traditionalist camp:

> (1) they understand the male and female anthropomorphic images used to describe God in the Bible to be literal truths, (2) they label Christian graces as either masculine or feminine, and (3) they take spiritual truths and identify them as either masculine or feminine in nature.[21]

For another thing, "*any* attribution of sexuality to God is a reversion to paganism," whether it is an attribution of masculinity or of femininity. "Many people harbour illusory views about the importance of recovering and appreciating feminine theological vocabulary in the Old Testament," Mary Hayter observes. "Not only is the methodology adopted for such a task often semantically confusing and exegetically unsound, but most approaches to feminine imagery exaggerate the significance of their subject matter."[22] Indeed, if the Bible's gendered imagery for God is to be taken literally, it is inevitable that God be regarded as more masculine than feminine. Tallying up the number of times the Bible uses masculine and feminine imagery for God not only fails to "balance out" God's "gender," but retains all the fallacy and confusion that attend the imputation of gender to God in the first place.

The view that God is both masculine and feminine confuses and distorts the image of God in humanity. It requires that the divine image be divided between women and men, such that women image God's feminine aspects and men image God's masculine aspects. This sexualizing of spiritual attributes renders men and women spiritual "opposites," creating a need to compartmentalize aspects of spiritual life and ministry into separate masculine and feminine quarters.

Characterizing God's nature in terms of masculine and feminine attributes also renders impossible the fundamental biblical doctrine that "Jesus alone, without a female partner, is the complete (perfect) image of God, and the *only* image to which we, men and women, are to be conformed (2 Corinthians 3:18; 4:10; Romans 8:29; Galatians 4:19)."[23] If sexual characteristics are inherent to the divine nature, and if Jesus (a male) is the "exact representation" of God (Heb. 1:3), then

God must be fundamentally masculine; God cannot be both feminine and masculine. If, on the other hand, categories of sexuality are rightly deemed irrelevant to God's spiritual nature, then the divine image may be seen to reside in essential humanness and not essential sexuality, thus eliminating any problem with seeing Jesus as the perfect image of God to which male and female believers alike are to be conformed.

Only when sexuality is de-spiritualized, God de-sexualized, and the basic human spiritual qualities allotted to both men *and* women, will these theological dilemmas melt away. But when sexuality is used as a cosmic knife, dividing each personal trait from its polarity, and male roles from female roles along lines of status and authority, inequity inevitably intrudes into the ways in which women and men are viewed as imaging, relating to, and ministering on behalf of Christ. As Mary Evans points out,

> The more the distinction between the sexes is stressed, the greater the tendency to assume that men relate to God in a different way from women. This is accentuated if one starts arguing that man as a male can be a representative of Christ in a way that a woman can never be and the image of God in a way that a woman is not. How then can a woman be identified with Christ? If we stress Christ's maleness rather than his humanity, how can a woman be sure that he can stand as her representative?[24]

It seems that many people feel strongly compelled to spiritualize the nature of sexuality in order to make sure that human sexuality is taken seriously, and that Christians don't fall into the sexual irresponsibility of promiscuity and unfaithfulness that so plagues contemporary culture. However, this danger can be avoided without imputing sexuality to the nature of God and injecting it into the divine image in humanity. While human sexuality does not directly reflect God's nature, it has the capacity—unlike sexuality in animals—to reflect the uniquely spiritual nature and moral consciousness (i.e., the divine image) that humans possess. That is to say, sexuality in humans can and should serve as a means through which the image of God in the human spirit is expressed. Thus, with humans, such activities as mating and rearing young become more than the instinct-driven, rather haphazard affair that they are in the animal kingdom. Human sexuality can and should be ennobled by its conjunction with, and reflection of, the divine image. It is not, however, an essential aspect of the divine image, for there is no sexuality in God to be imaged.

The Feminist Backlash

With so much talk of sexualizing the nature of God—from which it is generally concluded that God is masculine—it is no wonder that many thoughtful women who yearn for a knowledge of spiritual reality feel drawn to goddess religions. Such women see the theological consequences of a religion with a "male" God. However, they do not reject the false notion that the biblical God has a gender. They simply reject any God with a masculine gender, and turn instead to a female deity in order that their relationship with *their* deity may be as full and unimpeded as a man's relationship can be with the supposedly male God of the Bible.

These women do not know that the Bible teaches that because men and women equally image God, they equally resemble God, and that God, therefore, should not be deemed more male-like than female-like. They do not understand that women and men image God, who is spirit (John 4:24), in their shared human spirituality and not in their sexuality; that God created sexuality so his creatures might reproduce themselves and have families, not so they may reflect God's nature in their own sexual nature.

Women in feminist religions do not know that the Bible teaches that God does not show favoritism for certain groups of people (Acts 10:34–35; James 2:9), and that the new covenant inaugurated religious equality between women and men, who now are one in Christ and equal heirs of God's gift of life (Gal. 3:26–28; 1 Peter 3:7). Nor do they know that in the new covenant all are priests before God (1 Peter 2:5, 9), and that because Christ is the only mediator between God and humanity (1 Tim. 2:5), he requires no submediators in the form of males who claim special spiritual prerogatives on the basis of their gender.

These feminists do not understand that the biblical God is sexless. God is not a gendered being. Deuteronomy 4:16 states clearly that neither maleness nor femaleness represents God's image: "Do not become corrupt and make for yourselves an idol, an image of any shape, whether formed like a man or a woman." God is not to be imagined as either male or female, because God is neither male-like nor female-like. Carl Henry, who is not an egalitarian, delineates the orthodox position: "The God of the Bible is a sexless God. When Scripture speaks of God as 'he' the pronoun is primarily personal (generic) rather than masculine (specific); it emphasizes God's personality . . . in contrast to impersonal entities."[25] The proof of divine masculinity that many people see in biblical references to God as "he" results in large part from confusing a grammatical category with an imputation of sexuality.[26]

Nowhere in the Bible is God referred to as a sexual being. Rather, especially in Old Testament Law, sexuality is kept meticulously separate from religious worship and other spiritual concerns. Completely absent from biblical religion is any hint of sexuality as a spiritual force, or of masculinity and femininity as spiritual principles in the Godhead or the cosmos. Biblical religion stands distinct and apart from the pagan fertility religions in its strictly nonsexualized concept of spiritual reality and the nature of God. The nations surrounding ancient Israel believed that the fertility deities created and perpetuated human, plant, and animal life through their own divine sexual activity. "But Israel did not share in the 'divinization' of sex; it was a phenomenon of the creature," not of the deity.[27]

To be sure, God is often portrayed in the Bible in masculine imagery—such as Father or King—but this does not make God male in any sense. In biblical times, "Father" was a more apt description for God than "Mother," not merely because a Mother-God would have been confused with the pagan fertility deities of the surrounding cultures, but primarily because fatherhood presented a picture of God as a person with power and authority—which, in ancient patriarchal societies, was possessed almost exclusively by men. Alister McGrath explains that

> To speak of God as father is to say that the role of the father in ancient Israel allows us insights into the nature of God, not that God is a male. . . . Neither male nor female sexuality is to be attributed to God. Indeed, sexuality is an attribute of the created order that cannot be assumed to correspond directly to any such polarity within the creator God himself.[28]

Sadly, goddess feminists do not understand that the biblical Father-God is a person not only of great power, but also of everlasting love, tender care, and unfailing faithfulness. The God of the Bible has all power, but never uses it abusively. The picture of the authoritarian human patriarch who rules from a cruel emotional distance does not fit the biblical picture of God.

"Father" is a divinely inspired description of God, a central term used by God in revealing his character to his people. It cannot be dismissed as merely an androcentric invention of men who have sought to make God in their own masculine image. Neither, however, can we disregard the metaphorical element in this designation. "Father" is an important biblical metaphor for God, because fatherhood in many ways describes God's relationship to his people. In order to understand the meaning of this metaphor, we must ask: In what ways is God *like* a father, and in what ways is God *un*like a father?

Fatherhood on the human level has two constituents, the biological and the cultural. God is not our Father in the biological sense of having created us through sexual reproduction. However, God did create us; therefore, we belong to God and are under his authority. In this sense God is like a human parent.[29] God performs many of the non-sexual acts of a father. God provides, protects, loves, guides, governs, and disciplines. Just as a father in ancient times ruled over his own property and then passed on to his sons the property under his jurisdiction, so the father–son relationship of God to his people entails the rule of God and the spiritual inheritance of those who become "sons" by putting their trust in the Lord.[30] God is called our Father because God is *like* a father to us in the limited, metaphorical sense of filling many of the cultural roles of a father.

The relationship of Father and Son within the Trinity is also in some ways like and in other ways unlike that of a human father and son. It is unlike the human relationship in that God does not pre-exist Christ, nor is Christ a product of God having reproduced himself; yet this is the primary understanding that we have today of the father–son relationship. In ancient cultures, however, there was between a father and his firstborn son a strong sense of family bonding, oneness, continuity of name and identity, and equality of position through inheritance; and this is the sense in which God and Christ are Father and Son.

The only completely non-metaphorical name for God in the Bible is the one by which he identified himself to Moses: I AM WHO I AM or I WILL BE WHO I WILL BE (Exod. 3:14).[31] But this leaves us asking "am *what?*" and "will be *what?*" So we turn to the metaphorical language for God in the Bible and, through exegesis that takes into consideration the biblical author's intent within the cultural contexts of the time, we discern what this language reveals God to be like—and what it does *not* reveal God to be like.

Clearly, the biblical language does not reveal God to be like a male. Tikva Frymer-Kensky, a scholar of ancient religions, points out that when the Bible speaks of God in masculine terms,

> these masculine qualities of God are social male-gender characteristics. The monotheist God is not sexually a male. He is not at all phallic, and does not represent male virility. Biblical anthropomorphic language uses corporeal images of the arm of God, the right hand of God, God's back, and God's tears. God is not imagined below the waist.[32]

Any implication that the nature of the Deity participates in or corresponds to human sexuality confuses the Creator with the creation. This pantheistic proclivity does not result simply from imputing femaleness to the Deity (although, in androcentric cultures, female images imply sexuality more than do male images), but rather in imputing sexuality of *any* sort to the Deity. "Thus," Hayter notes, "both the feminists who venerate a female deity and those who react against this by stressing the maleness of God are revitalizing the unhealthy emphases of the fertility cults which the Old Testament roundly condemns. They are departing from faith in a transcendent Creator and Redeemer and re-mythologizing—even re-magicalizing—religion."[33]

Unfortunately, many people today—including some Christians—fall eagerly into this error. In Thomas Howard's effort to deny women ordination on account of God being masculine, he turns to the message of the ancient mythologies, which he regards as compatible with "Jewish and Christian Scriptures."

Everything and everyone divides itself up into male and female. The creator, the demiurge, the sun, the titans, the chief gods—they commonly appear as male. (There are some titanesses—Rhea, for example.) There has been, obviously, some notion rooted deeply in human consciousness, of an initiating or generating office attached to the masculine image. The myths are of a piece with the cloth of human sexual anatomy on this point. The creator begets life upon the earth. The sun pours energy into the earth and things spring up. The god begets offspring from the goddess. For Jews and Christians, the Creator is spoken of as "he."[34]

Contemporary neopagan religions also draw a connection between sexuality and spirituality. In these religions, sexuality is believed to modify and energize spirituality, and to delineate the inherent nature of spiritual reality. For many neopagan feminists, worship of a goddess "is often coupled with worship of a god, and their gender polarity is frequently seen as expressing an important truth about the cosmos." Most feminist religions, however, give primacy to the goddess and to the spiritual leadership of women in ritual worship.[35] This is the "flip side" of the traditionalist error of masculinizing God and making men the leaders in worship.

When women are led to believe that God's fatherhood bespeaks God's male sexuality in some sense, they understandably will feel marginalized and alienated by Christianity, and may even respond by constructing a feminist mother-goddess of their own. But when God's fatherhood is rightly understood as a figurative description of what God is like (a personal, powerful, and protective provider) rather than as a literal description of what God is (a male parent), then there is no reason to replace one error (the spiritual superiority of masculinity) with another (the spiritual superiority of femininity). Women may instead enter readily into a trusting relationship with their Father God, without fear of male domination or implications of female inferiority. Susan Foh points out that when sexuality is rightly regarded as physical and not metaphysical, it

> removes the need to try to find so-called feminine attributes or aspects in the Godhead, and it even removes (or should remove) any slight or offense women might feel because of God's Fatherhood or Christ's incarnation as a man. Since men and women are fundamentally persons

. . . women are unquestionably in the image of God just as men are and, if believers, will be fully conformed to Christ's image just as Christian men will be.[36]

Sadly, however, feminists involved in goddess religions do not understand these fundamental biblical truths; so they turn from the true God to a feminized counterpart of what they perceive to be the male God of the Bible. Why do they not understand the inclusive, gender-free nature of Christianity and the biblical God? It is because so many Christians for so many years have failed to understand it themselves, and instead have advanced a sexualized religion that deifies masculinity and masculinizes the Deity, and they have called it Christianity.

Defending Gender Hierarchy Theologically

Any doctrine that links sexuality and spirituality so fundamentally and intrinsically, and in such antithesis to the spirit of biblical religion, would seem to require a firmer foundation and a more persuasive defense than four or five texts largely plagued by translational ambiguities and hermeneutical loopholes. In other words, it seems unwarranted to derive separate and unequal spiritual roles for men and women from selected biblical proof texts, when the idea of a universal, God-ordained male hierarchy of spiritual authority is absent from and alien to the overall message of Scripture.

Those who would assert a universal, spiritual principle of male rule need more than a handful of proof texts. They need a systematic, theological defense of their position. Catholic and Anglican traditionalists understand this. Michael Novak observes that those who reject the Catholic view of the priesthood have no theological reason to object to the ordination of women; and without a theological defense, the only grounds for opposition are custom, habit, and psychological resistance to change.[37]

Is it possible to set forth a theological defense of male hierarchy without positing a masculine God, imputing spiritual significance to a male Christ, and defining the ordained ministry as Catholics define the priesthood—that is, as a role of divine representation (a stand-in for God, as it were)? I do not think so. For, as discussed earlier, the idea that men have the spiritual authority and prerogative to discern the will and the Word of God on behalf of women leads logically to the idea that femaleness disqualifies and maleness qualifies a person to stand in the place of God. Maleness, therefore, must be more like God than femaleness. And if maleness is godlike, then God is somehow male-like; that is, masculinity or male-likeness is an integral aspect of who God is as God. These concepts seem to be necessary components of any systematic, theological defense of gender hierarchy. Such thinking, however, runs counter to the clear biblical teaching on the equality of women and men as image bearers of God (Gen. 1:26–27; 5:1–2), as "sons," or equal heirs, of God in Christ (Gal. 3:28; 1 Peter 3:7), and as priests unto God (1 Peter 2: 5, 9; Rev. 1:6; 5:10).

Other difficulties in a theological defense of male authority are entailed by its supposition of fundamental spiritual differences between men and women. If Christlikeness comes in two shades (pink and blue), then what is morally right for a man to do may well be morally wrong for a woman to do. This concept may sound odd (as it should)! Indeed, there is nothing in the Bible on which to ground a fundamental differentiation of moral virtue along lines of gender. As Sarah Grimke, foremother of evangelical feminism, observed in 1838, both men and women should be bound by the same set of moral values.

> According to the principle . . . that man and woman were created equal, and endowed by their beneficent Creator with the same intellectual powers and the same moral responsibilities, and that consequently whatever is *morally* right for a man to do, is *morally* right for a woman, it follows as a necessary corollary, that if it is the duty of a man to preach . . . it is the duty also of a woman.[38]

The theological problems inherent to gender hierarchy have gone largely undetected and unchallenged—probably in part because the concept of male authority fits so neatly with what androcentrically oriented people "naturally" believe about the "nature" of men and women. But it is also due in large part to the traditionalist teaching that unequal gender roles are merely a difference in "function" and have nothing to do with essential "being" or the spiritual dimension.

At any rate, most evangelical traditionalists do not have a systematic theological defense for their beliefs about gender. Most argue from their interpretations of the proof text passages, and from a set of assumptions about feminism and modern culture.[39] Yet, although it was perhaps surprising to proof text-minded traditionalists, when evangelical Anglican J. I. Packer argued in *Christianity Today* for an all-male presbytery, he relied primarily on a theological, rather than an exegetical, defense of his position.[40]

Let's take a look, then, at the argument for male hierarchy from high church tradition. How well does it comport with orthodox doctrine about the nature of God and of humanity? How coherent is its rationale for assigning men and women to positions of unequal spiritual status solely on the basis of their gender?

The Priestly Role

The traditional theological argument, which Packer articulates, asserts that because presbyters (or priests, or pastors and elders) represent God to the people, they ought to be male as Christ is male. But is this the primary function of the priestly office? The priest's role in the Old Testament seems to be focused more on representing the people to God than on representing God to the people.[41] In biblical times, it was primarily the prophet who represented God to the people. Gilbert Bilezikian notes that "the people spoke to God through the priest, but God spoke to the people through the prophet. The mantle of authority was worn by the prophet more than by the priest."[42] Given that women did minister as prophets in both the Old and New Testaments, it could not be true that God requires male representatives of himself.[43] Moreover, as Paul Jewett points out, "Since the church is the bride of Christ and therefore feminine to him, one could just as well reason that the universal priesthood of all believers should find its individual expression in the woman *rather than* in the man, an inference which the theologians, as males, have never drawn."[44]

According to Catholic and other high church ecclesiastical traditions, the one who serves as priest (or presbyter) must be male, because his role is to act "in the person of Christ." Even apart from the assumption that Christ's maleness is theologically necessary, this understanding of the priest's office is highly questionable. By no means is the smallest point of confusion the tendency to speak of Christ's representative in the sense of a representation, an onto-logical image, whereby the minister somehow embodies the very nature and person of Christ. Biblically, a priest represents God to the people and the people to God in the sense that an ambassador serves as a representative. An ambassador speaks and acts on behalf of the one who sent him; but he does not impersonate the one who sent him. In the new covenant *all* believers—as members of Christ's body and as priests unto God—are representatives, or ambassadors, of Christ.[45]

The idea that the priest is an "icon" of Christ and that maleness is an essential aspect of Christ's nature that priests *must* image "arrived rather late on the scene in Christian history."[46] It is a doctrine that assumes for the minister of God a ministry that belongs to the Spirit of God. The Holy Spirit, not the priest, makes the person of Christ present in the midst of his worshipers.[47]

It is interesting to note that the distinction between being and function is not only irrelevant but anathema in the theological defense of a male-only clergy. Traditionalists argue that because the priest's role is to represent a male Christ, a priest must have the male nature. On the other hand, they contend that the woman's role is to be subordinate (inferior in rank) even though the woman's nature is not inferior. In the one case, function *must* correspond to being; in the other, function must *not* correspond to being. If being and function can so easily and completely be dissociated in the case of woman's status, why is their dissociation in the case of the priestly role deemed a violation of the very nature of God and the Christian faith?[48] Why is it divinely required that the role of representing Christ be filled only by those persons whose male nature most closely corresponds to the role, when the mismatch between women's equal being and inferior status is perfectly fitting, even divinely mandated?

The presumed inseparability of being and function with respect to the priestly role serves as the connecting link between the premise that maleness is essential to who Christ is as Christ, and the conclusion that any role of representing Christ must be filled by one whose nature includes the attribute of maleness. But this link entails a denial of the fundamental traditionalist conviction that being and function need not correspond, but can—and, in the case of woman's role, *should*—be utterly unrelated and independent of one another.[49]

The Spiritual Significance of Jesus' Maleness

Regardless of how Christ is understood to be represented by his ordained minister, the notion that a male Christ must be represented by a man hinges on the theological supposition that, as Packer puts it, "Jesus' maleness is basic to his role as our incarnate Savior."[50] One must wonder why maleness should be deemed the one aspect of Christ's biological nature that is "basic" to his essential identity and which, therefore, *must* be duplicated in his ordained representatives. Jesus was not only male but also Jewish, which was at least as theologically important to his messiahship as his maleness. Shouldn't we, likewise, require that pastoral candidates be of Hebraic descent because they would represent Christ more accurately than non-Jewish pastors? Cornelius Plantinga also questions the assumption that maleness is integral to who Christ is as Christ.

> The New Testament authors knew that God incarnate was a male. They needed no inspiration to see that male titles and offices were therefore the apt ones. How does it follow in any way that Jesus' maleness is basic to his role as our incarnate Savior? One might as well argue that because God incarnate was Jewish, single, and an inhabitant of a pastoral setting, that Jewishness, bachelorhood, and thorough knowledge of sheep are all basic to Jesus' saving us.[51]

Ruth Tucker points out that "Jesus offered the gospel of the kingdom to the Jews in the person of a rabbi. He was a teacher, like other teachers of his day, who traveled the countryside with disciples. There was no such role for women."[52] One of Jesus' main forums for public preaching and teaching was the synagogue; this too would have been an impossible role for a woman. For historical and cultural reasons, it was necessary that God be incarnated as a male human. But because God is neither male nor female and is imaged in woman and man equally, it was not theologically necessary for God Incarnate to be male.[53]

This line of reasoning is applicable to another argument that many traditionalists invoke, namely, that only men should be church leaders and teachers because Christ chose only men as the twelve apostles. Again, if precedent is the determining factor, then all male Gentiles should be disqualified from leadership ministry. Yet no one would think of limiting the pastorate to Jewish men! Jesus ministered in a society where the people were highly prejudiced against women, as well as any person not of pure Jewish lineage. Jewish law prohibited men from speaking to a woman in public or discussing theology with her under any circumstance.[54] The people of ancient Palestine could not have been less inclined to listen to a theological message delivered by either women or Gentiles. Yet Jesus' apostles needed to be heard, for they were to be the founders of the brand new Christian church.

Jesus often broke with tradition, but he did nothing to undermine the success of the church that would need to be built up from his small band of disciples after he returned to the Father. Jesus did have female disciples, some of whom traveled on occasion with his entourage, and this in itself constituted a disregard for the cultural restrictions on women's activities. He also ignored convention by speaking publicly with women, even offering women theological instruction, which was a necessary first step toward women themselves becoming teachers. But it would have been completely counterproductive for Jesus to have sent women out on teaching missions as he did the Twelve.[55] As Millard Erickson explains:

> It is unlikely that we would find [Jesus], given his historical setting, to be a full practicing feminist, since the radical overturning of cultural mores that would have been involved, for example, in appointing women as some of the apostles, might have prevented his movement from ever obtaining a proper hearing. Nevertheless, there are enough serious breaks with the culture of the time to prove he had great sympathy with women.[56]

During Jesus' earthly ministry, prior to his death and resurrection, the old covenant was not yet fully superseded by the new covenant. (Galatians 4:4 states that Jesus was born under the Law—i.e., the old covenant—to redeem those who were under the Law.) According to the terms of the old covenant, Jewish males had religious privileges that females and Gentiles were denied.[57] Perhaps this is another reason Jesus chose Jewish men for his inner circle of disciples. The Jewishness and maleness of the twelve apostles also affirmed the continuity between the Israel of the old covenant (with its twelve patri-archs) and the church of the new covenant. But once the church was established, neither maleness nor Jewishness were relevant criteria for spiritual leadership.[58]

After Christ had risen from the dead, and his ministry on earth had laid the groundwork for a church in which there is neither male nor female, Jew nor Gentile (Gal. 3:28), God lost no time in calling women to the ministry of the gospel. It was to women that God gave the stag-gering privilege of informing the male disciples that Jesus Christ had risen from the dead and was alive in their midst (Matt. 28:5–10), a central doctrine of the Christian faith, to be sure.

There is no biblical warrant to impute theologically weighty impli-cations to Jesus' maleness. Neither in his instructions concerning women's ministry, nor in any of his Christological discussions, does Paul ever derive any theological significance from the maleness of either Jesus or his twelve disciples. As Erickson points out, "Jesus' maleness is accidental to his meaning as Christ. Much in the act by which he saves us can be best described in human terms by the metaphor of childbirth. He suffered in order to give us birth. Nor did his mothering of us end on the cross, for he continues to nurture us."[59] Jesus even spoke of himself as being like a mother hen (Matt. 23:37).

Biblical references to the incarnation point to the humanity of Jesus Christ, not to his maleness (John 1:14; Phil. 2:7). Scripture has much to say about Jesus, but of his maleness there is no commentary. It sim-ply is not significant. Alistar McGrath states, "The fact that Jesus was male, the fact that he was a Jew . . . all these are secondary to the fact that God took upon himself human nature, thereby lending it new dig-nity and meaning."[60] The theological significance of the incarnation of God the Son in human flesh was that it was *human* flesh, not that it was male flesh.

The Godlike Gender?

What does the imputation of theological significance to Christ's maleness necessarily assume about the nature of God? Or about the creation of woman in the image of God and her re-creation in the image of Christ?

The "Christ as male" argument for a male-only pastorate is grounded in the assumption that knowledge of Christ entails knowing him not only as Savior, Lord, and God Incarnate, but also as a male. Males make better ordained ministers because they better represent Christ, and they better represent Christ because Christ is male, and maleness is "basic" to who Christ is as Christ.

Who is Christ and what did he come to earth to do? The Bible tells us that Jesus Christ is the exact representation of God's being (Heb. 1:3). "He is the image of the invisible God," in whom "God was pleased to have all his fullness dwell" (Col. 1:15, 19). Jesus said, "Anyone who has seen me has seen the Father" (John 14:9). If maleness is basic to who Christ is, then it is basic to his representation of God. If Christ had to be male in order to represent the Father, then God the Father must also be male or male-like. The "Christ as male" argument necessarily assumes that God's nature is more like that of a male than a female.

If Christ's maleness is theologically necessary to his role as our Savior, by which he represented God to humanity, then it must also be necessary to his salvific function of representing humanity before God. But if this is so, then how can female believers be as fully represented as male believers? As Hayter observes, "to make the maleness of Christ a christological principle is to qualify or deny the universality of his redemption. It is the humanity, not the masculinity, of the Second Adam into which we are incorporated."[61] Similarly, Stanley Grenz notes that "the patristic writers and church councils followed the lead of the New Testament in emphasizing Jesus' humanity rather than his maleness. . . . For the church fathers, the focus on the inclusiveness of Jesus' humanity was a theological principle: what the Son did not assume in the incarnation he could not redeem."[62]

The theological necessity lies not in Christ's maleness, but in a view of humanness that does not spiritually differentiate masculinity and femininity. Only as Christ is perceived as sharing with both women and men a common human nature that transcends sexual distinctions does his incarnation and redemption make any theological sense. Jesus himself did not depict either gender as being any more or less like God than the other gender. Rather, as Erickson notes, Jesus demonstrates in his parables "that a woman can represent the activity of God or a righteous individual equally well as can a man."[63] On several occasions, Jesus would tell two parables, each making a similar point, but one featuring a woman and the other a man (e.g., Matt. 25, and Luke 15 and 18). In this, Jesus indicates his desire for people to understand that spiritual reality is no different for women than it is for men. The parables of the woman with the lost coin and the man with the lost sheep in Luke 15 are particularly pertinent; for the man and the woman are each a picture of God seeking out the lost and then rejoicing when the lost is found.[64]

The humanity of Christ, regardless of its maleness, Jewishness, or other physical distinctives, necessarily encompasses all aspects of humanity; otherwise, Christ could not be the Redeemer of Gentiles or of women. To impute a theological significance and necessity to Christ's maleness is to put into reasonable question the efficacy of Christ's redemptive work on behalf of women.

If we are to regard maleness as essential to who Christ is as Christ, not only must we question whether Jesus Christ can represent women as fully as he can men, and not only must we consider men better representatives of Christ, thus barring women from roles of spiritual authority, we must also view women as essentially inferior to men. Women lack the Christlike attribute of maleness that renders men best qualified to represent Christ; and if women are less like Christ than men are, they are simply less than men. They are inferior in their essence or being, not merely in their function or position. It is impossible for Christ's maleness to argue against women in the pastorate without it also arguing against women's essential, spiritual equality with men.[65]

Womanly Ministry

The relationship of an inferior being to a superior being entails the dependence of the inferior upon the superior—even as our deficient human condition necessitates our dependence on God. It is also appropriate that an inferior being should serve the superior being—even as humans find their life purpose in faithful service to their Lord. These are the key elements of a woman's purpose and place in the traditionalist agenda: service of, and dependence upon, a man.

Packer claims that the "nonreversible" roles of men and women are set forth in Scripture and grounded in the nature of the two sexes.

It is in the nature of womanhood to serve a man, and a woman ought not be denied this "womanly satisfaction."[66] "Pastoral oversight," he says, "is not a task for which women are naturally fitted."[67] Some women *do* have "gifts for ministry and a sense of pastoral vocation"; but the pastorate is nonetheless a "man's job," and women who meet the qualifications for this position should be denied it. Qualified women may preach the Word, but they must do so under male supervision and they must not have official presbyterial status.[68]

But wait. Aren't the restrictions on women's ministry grounded in the creational fact that women are not "naturally fitted" to do the "man's job" of pastoral leadership? In making the disclaimer that women may use their preaching and teaching gifts as long as they are not ordained, Packer throws us into confusion over just what he believes women are "naturally fitted" to do. If women are not naturally fitted for teaching and preaching, why should there be a need to offer a provision for them to do so?

This is a tension at the heart of every traditionalist argument for the subordination of women. Are women as able as men to serve in the ministerial roles that are being denied them? To say "no" strengthens the logic of the argument by linking "being" with "function" and making the restriction of women's ministry appear to be just and fitting. But to dwell on this viewpoint for too long reveals women to be inferior to men. Quickly, a disjunct between being and function must be asserted, and assurances offered that women *are* able to do these tasks; their subordination is merely a formality, a matter of function that has no bearing whatsoever on the essentially equal nature of womanhood.[69]

Packer begins his article by referring to women presbyters as "substitute men," and ends it lamenting the preoccupation of such women with "fulfilling a man's role." This is necessarily the perspective of those who believe that a woman forsakes her female nature when she steps out of a role of subordination to male spiritual authority. However, women who believe they are called to the ordained ministry do not aspire to be "substitute men." They do not regard manliness as something to be attained, as though it were superior to womanliness. Rather, they see the pastorate as a calling by which they, as women, may exercise their ministerial gifts out of obedience to God and for the good of the church.

In Conclusion

The question of whether women should be subordinate to the spiritual authority of men is ultimately a theological issue, not simply a women's issue. Far more important than giving women the equal rights that are due them is our obligation to give God the glory that is due him. When men undertake to "stand in Christ's place" and assume a priestly authority by virtue of their maleness, it not only detracts from the honor and glory of Christ's unique place as the "one mediator" between God and humanity (1 Tim. 2:5), but also causes us to view the divine nature through lenses of human sexuality. As a result, God is regarded as essentially masculine or male-like, which, in turn, reduces woman's share in the divine image. By denying woman her full glory (which is the image of God in her), we further deny glory to God, whose glory both women and men were designed to reflect.

At theological center stage in the debate over gender and spiritual authority stands the issue of priesthood, or, mediatorial, representational ministry. Traditionally construed, the man who serves in a priestly capacity, whether in the pulpit or in the home, has the responsibility to interpret God's Word and discern God's will on behalf of those under his spiritual authority. Conversely, the man in such a role is accountable to God for those under his spiritual authority.

But how does this understanding of male ministry line up with the place of priesthood in the new covenant? In the Old Testament, the covenantal relationship between God and his people was mediated by a select number of priests and one high priest, all of whom had to meet strict requirements of gender, tribal heritage, and other physical characteristics. In the new covenant, there are as many priests as there are members of the covenant community; physical characteristics are now irrelevant to qualification for priestly ministry. Moreover, there is now one high priest forever, only one mediator between God and humanity, the Lord Jesus Christ (1 Tim. 2:5). With Christ as high priest, every believer alike can come directly before the throne of God (Heb. 4:14–16). Every believer ministers to God and to others in a priestly role, bringing offerings of praise to God (Heb. 13:15–16), and serving as a representative of God's truth and love to the church and the world (2 Cor. 5:20).[70]

Although its consequences are doubtless unintended by those who advocate it, the introduction of a third category of priests—situated between the high priesthood of Christ and the priesthood of all believers—can serve as a hindrance to the priestly ministries of all believers. Based solely upon physical criteria, members of Christ's body are divided into two spiritual roles: one group is removed a step away from direct access to God through Christ, while the other group is moved up into a role of imitating, or supplementing, the mediatorial ministry of Christ. Those in the first group can become spiritually stunted in a role that predisposes them to spiritual dependency and vulnerability to deception and manipulation. The other group can become spiritually stunted by having their focus shifted from obeying God to playing God; they can become vulnerable to pride, power-mongering, and, finally, burn-out—the result of trying to fill a role that too closely resembles the mediatorial ministry that is rightly Christ's alone.

The God-ordained, new covenant priesthoods—of Christ and of all believers—are both violated in some sense by the addition of a third priesthood, a priesthood of masculinity. The notion of such a priesthood has not come from the New Testament, but from the church's failure to fully apprehend the efficacy of the new covenant, for which Christ is both the one mediator and the final sacrifice (Heb. 9:11–15).

What place can there be in the church of the new covenant for an old covenant type of priesthood, whereby certain human beings are chosen on the basis of their physical characteristics to serve, in some contexts, as mediators between God and other human beings? What sort of arrangement could more effectively curtail the spiritual growth of the body of Christ, or detract from the glory the church should bring to God?

Of course, the male role is not always spoken of as priesthood. In fact, it is frequently described in terms such as "a man's responsibility to provide spiritual leadership." Nonetheless, the spiritual ministry that traditionalists reserve for men is, in essence, a priestly, mediatorial role. In the home, a man represents God to his wife, in the sense that it is his responsibility to make the final determination concerning God's will for her and the family; he also represents his wife to God in the sense that he is spiritually responsible for her and must give account to God for her spiritual condition.[71] The male hierarchy in the church, whereby only men are allowed access to roles that involve high-level decision-making based on discernment of God's will, is the logical extension of the priesthood of masculinity that is prescribed and expressed in traditionalist marriage.

In the debate over gender hierarchy, we are not dealing merely with matters of social order or conflicting psychological definitions of gender. We are debating the theological legitimacy of defining manhood as priesthood, of imputing to the Christian man a divine representational authority that, in one way or another (and however unintentionally), undermines the priestly ministries of Christ and the members of his body.

PART 2

Assessing the Traditionalist Proof Texts

5

In the Beginning

he first three chapters of Genesis can be approached in two different ways. One way is to take the text as it is and to make only the conclusions warranted by the text. The other way (employed by traditionalists) is to read into the text what one expects to find, based on one's interpretations of certain New Testament passages about the roles of women and men.[1]

Biblical feminists regard the New Testament texts on gender roles as culturally specific applications of general biblical principles, such as the priority of the gospel message and the need for Christians to live irreproachable lives in a hostile culture. But traditionalists understand these texts to be direct, unequivocal, transcultural statements of a God-ordained principle of the man's authority and the woman's subordinate domesticity. This is generally defended as the "plain meaning" of the texts, while interpretations that consider these New Testament passages in light of their cultural contexts are scoffed at as "hermeneutical oddities devised to reinterpret apparently plain meanings of Biblical texts."[2]

The "plain meaning" approach, however, is abandoned with alacrity when traditionalists take to interpreting Genesis 1–3. Having already derived a universal principle of male authority and female subordination from culturally relative New Testament texts, they shuttle this principle back to Genesis and attempt to read it between the lines of the creation account. Hierarchical gender roles are then defended on the basis of their having been created by God from the very beginning. For example, John Piper claims that:

> When the Bible teaches that men and women fulfil different roles in relation to each other, charging man with a unique leadership role, it bases this differentiation not on temporary cultural norms but on permanent facts of creation. . . . Just as man was created with a native sense of responsibility to lead . . . so woman was created as a suitable complement to honor this responsibility.[3]

The Genesis account, however, says nothing about man being created with a "native sense" of his authority over woman. Such assumptions must be imported into the creation account from elsewhere.

The meaning of the New Testament instructions concerning gender roles *was* plain to the original recipients of the apostles' letters. But because of the disparities between our cultural situation and the cultures to which these commands were originally directed, these texts must now be looked at with the same hermeneutical common sense that generally is applied to other culturally relative biblical texts, such as those pertaining to the obedience of slaves, the greeting of other believers with a holy kiss, the wearing of head coverings by women in church, and so forth.[4]

Such cross-cultural translation, however, is not necessary in order to determine the purpose or principle that led the biblical author to write what he wrote in the Genesis creation account. The Genesis text does not consist of specific instructions that were written to address an immediate situation; rather, it is a historical record of something that happened long before it was even written down. There is no reason to assume that this text should mean anything other than what it plainly says, or that it should mean what it plainly does not say.

When God Created Humanity

In the Genesis creation account, it is immediately apparent that man and woman are both made by God in the image of God (1:27), and that both are given the charge to rule over the rest of creation (1:28). These primary statements lay the foundation and establish the categories for understanding the expanded account in chapter 2 of the creation of man and woman.[5]

Traditionalists maintain that because the woman was created after the man and was designated as his "helper," she was from the beginning ordained by God to be under the man's authority. But there is no evidence in the text that the man saw any such inequality in their relationship. He simply was delighted that he finally had a partner equal to him, who was like him, and who was very much a part of him (2:23).

After the creation of the woman, marriage was formally instituted by God, with the very nonpatriarchal statement about the man leaving his father and mother and cleaving to his wife (2:24). It is quite clear from this account that the God-ordained ideal for marriage is a lifelong union of one man and one woman, thus definitively ruling out "marriage" between two persons of the same sex. What is *not* clear from the text is any indication that the God-ordained ideal for marriage also includes a lifelong hierarchy of authority, whereby the husband leads and the wife obeys. In fact, there is no mention of either spouse ruling over the other—until after their fall into sin, when God declares to the woman that "he will rule over you" (3:16). This is stated by God not as a command, but as a consequence of their sin.

In order to support their belief that male authority was established by God before the fall, traditionalists point to "hints" in the Genesis account that have to do with the way the man and the woman are referred to in the text, the way they are dealt with by God, and the way they interact with one another. But, as it happens, these "hints" of male rule can more easily be understood as consequences or implications of the simple fact that the man was created first, and this fact in itself tells us nothing of a God-ordained gender hierarchy. It is best to understand the "hints" of male authority that traditionalists find in Genesis 2 and 3 in terms of a fact that the text specifically *does* mention (i.e., man's temporal priority in creation), rather than in terms of a concept of which the text makes no mention whatsoever (i.e., the man's creationally ordained authority over the woman).

"Man" as Meaning Both "Male" and "Human"

What are some of these supposed "hints"? Raymond Ortlund Jr. and other traditionalists see one in the fact that the author of Genesis refers to the human race by the term "man" rather than by the term "woman" or even by a gender-neutral term such as "persons."[6] As Ortlund sees it, what makes "man" the more "appropriate and illuminating designation" for humanity is "male headship," which he understands as the man's spiritual responsibility to exercise authority over the woman. Ortlund also regards the generic use of the term "man" in this passage as a divine legitimation of the use of noninclusive language today.[7]

Before looking specifically at the Genesis account, we should note that the ancient Hebrew language was an expression of patriarchal culture. We cannot conclude, simply because the Bible was written under divine inspiration, that the languages in which the Bible was written were themselves created under divine inspiration. These languages were as male centered as the cultures they reflected and by which they were created. The fact that certain words in a language can be used to refer either to a male human or to humans in general reflects cultural concepts of gender; it says nothing about God's view of gender. We ought not infer that because God made use of androcentric language, God concurs with the premise of such language—namely, that the male fully represents humanity (and thus the same word can serve for either meaning), but that the female is a sexual subset of humanity and does not represent humanity in its fullness.

Actually, Ortlund may well be correct in saying that the use of the word "man" in the creation account hints at male headship; but there is no reason to believe that it hints at a *ruling* headship. Rather, it points to the man being the "head" in the sense that he is the origin or source of the woman and, therefore, existed before the woman.[8] The man existed in relationship to God and to creation for a period of time before woman came into being. During this time, the man is referred to by the Hebrew term "adam," which is translated as "man," "Adam," or "humankind." This is a gender-neutral term that does not refer specifically to a male human, but means simply "human" (or, more literally, "earthling"). The man is called "the human" because he was, at first, the only human in existence, and because the primary significance of his existence was that of his humanness, not of his maleness.

Some have suggested that before the woman was created, Adam was not a specifically male human, but was a sexually undifferentiated human. This idea seems to have some plausibility, given that the biblical text does not refer to Adam as male until after the woman is taken out of him. In Genesis 1:26–27 and 5:1–2, we are told that God created Adam, that Adam was created in God's image, and that Adam was created male and female. These summary statements telescope humanity's two-stage creation, so that—whether existing in the form of a single being or as male and female separate beings—humanity is referred to simply as "Adam." This suggests that before the woman was taken out of the man, Adam had in himself, somehow, a capacity for both maleness and femaleness. Donald Joy sees a parallel here with fetal development, in which every fetus has the form of a female until the ninth week, after which time sexual differentiation begins to occur.[9]

Perhaps, in a sense, ontogeny does recapitulate phylogeny; that is, perhaps the development of each individual human from undifferentiated sexuality to differentiated sexuality echoes the events of the original creation of humanity. As Donald Joy puts it, "We all start out the same in Adam, but we also all start out the same in embryo. Creation revisits every conception."[10] Although, of course, we cannot know these things with certainty, it does appear that the Genesis creation account has in it some mysterious possibilities that should militate against the traditional assumption that "Genesis tells of a male God who created a male human, and afterward, largely as a favor to the male, created a female."[11]

God named male and female humanity "Adam," which means "human" (Gen. 5:1–2). She is human; he is human. In Genesis 2, the man is called "the human" before the woman is taken out of him, and he continues to be designated in this way after she is taken out of him. The man has temporal priority, and the language reflects this. But it does not also reflect a priority of power or authority. Most likely, it is simply for the sake of clarity and continuity that the man is referred to by the same term that had designated him before the woman's creation. There is no reason to regard this use of language as a profound portent of the man's spiritual authority over the woman.

If we were to read a narrative with no record of the man being created before the woman, but which refers to the male human by the same term that designates humanity in general, we probably would get the sense that the male, and not the female, fully represents humanity; and we would conclude that the fully human one ought to have a rank superior to the less-than-fully-human one. Male authority would follow logically from male superiority. But there is no reason to read the Genesis text in this way, because the story tells of an event, namely, the man's temporally prior creation, that accounts for this use of language without any recourse to implications of male superiority.

This points to another problem with Ortlund's argument. He wants to demonstrate male authority but not male superiority from God's "naming of the race 'man.'"[12] But if this were to imply anything of the sort (which it could do only if the man's temporal priority in creation were disregarded), it would imply male superiority, in that the male would be considered more fully human and the female, therefore, less than human. Male rule, then, would be derived from male superiority. In other words, if Ortlund's argument were to prove anything, it would prove too much.

The current traditionalist effort to assert male and female equality concurrently with male authority is a historical anomaly, as well as a logical impossibility.[13] Male authority traditionally has been rationalized by the belief in male superiority. Until fairly recently, it was held that woman did not bear the divine image equally with man, but rather imaged God indirectly through imaging man.[14] From this premise, woman's inferiority and subordination clearly followed. Augustine sets the tone for such thinking in his statement

> that the woman together with her husband is the image of God, so that the whole substance is one image. But when she is assigned as a helpmate, a function that pertains to her alone, then she is not the image of God; but as far as the man is concerned, he is by himself alone the image of God, just as fully and completely as when he and the woman are joined together into one.[15]

In other words, the man is, in and of himself, a complete human who fully images God. The woman does not image God without the man. Abraham Kuyper echoes this traditional, androcentric line of thought in his commentary on Eve: "She is the woman who embodied potentially all that is female. . . . Adam represented more. He embodied not only all that is male, but also all that is human."[16] The idea that the man is primarily a human being, while the woman is primarily a sexual being (in that she is defined in terms of her sexual relationship to a man), continues to undergird the traditionalist system of gender roles today. This leads many people to conclude that a woman is, indeed, quite deficient apart from her association with a man through marriage.

Derived from the Man and Named by the Man

Traditionalists often say that the woman's derivation from the man indicates her subordination to him. Yet the man is derived from the dust of the earth, and he (along with the woman) is supposed to rule over the earth. For that matter, as Paul notes in 1 Corinthians 11:12, ever since the first man, every man has come from a woman. (Based on what we know today of fetal development, this is also true in a sense Paul could not have known about!) Derivation has nothing to do with the determination of authority and subordination. Nor can prior existence be said to entail authority, for then we should have to say that God ordained the animals to rule over Adam.[17]

Traditionalists also have endeavored to demonstrate that male rule existed from the beginning by insisting that the man named the woman before the fall. This argument is based on two assumptions: that the act of naming constitutes an assertion of authority over the one who is named, and that when the man called the woman "woman" (2:23) he was naming her. The first assumption is true only in the rather circular sense that the one who names normally has a higher status than the one who is named (for example, parents name their child).[18] But in this case, the man called the new human "woman" simply in recognition of her identity, not as an act by which he established or exercised his authority over her.

The reason why the man identified the woman, rather than vice versa, is obvious. He had been working in the Garden, processing and categorizing the various items in his world for some time. Then, when the woman appeared before him, he identified her as a woman, *ishshah*, as one who was taken out of man, *ish* (meaning "male"); here, for the first time, the man is referred to as a male. "Woman" is not given as the woman's proper name, but is merely the man's description of her identity as a human who is basically like him, yet with a difference. To identify something is hardly tantamount to ruling it. If, for example, an astronomer looks at a heavenly body and identifies it as a star rather than as a planet, that does not give him authority over it.[19] Nor is identifying or describing something equivalent to naming it.

The man did eventually name the one whom he had initially identified as a woman. After the fall, after the man had begun to rule the woman, he gave her the name "Eve" (3:20). This symbolized not only the imposition of the man's will over the woman's, but also the relational separation of the man from the woman. Before sin entered their relationship, they shared the name "Adam," which God had given to both of them at creation (5:2).

Ortlund acknowledges (in an endnote) the distinction between the man identifying the woman in 2:23 and naming her in 3:20. But, as he sees it, the man was doing to the woman in 2:23 what he had just finished doing to the animals. He was exercising his "royal prerogative" to name and to rule; it was "the climax of his naming of other creatures."[20] However, the man's naming of the animals was a separate event with a very different purpose than the creation of the woman by God and the recognition and identification of her by the man.

Old Testament scholar Joy Elasky Fleming points out that God did not instruct the man to name the woman, as God had instructed him to name the animals. Moreover, the Hebrew language indicates a dissimilarity between the man's identification of the woman as *ishshah* and the true "naming" incidents that occur in the passage.

> When an official act of "naming" takes place in Genesis, there is a distinctive formula that is followed. It includes the specific verb, *qarah* ("call"), followed by the noun, *shem* ("name"). This formula is followed in 2:19–20 where the man names the animals; it appears in 3:20 where the man names (or more correctly renames) Eve; it is employed in 5:2 when God named the two of them "Adam"; and the formula

appears in Genesis 4:17, 25, 26; 5:3, 29; 11:9, and so on. But in 2:23, the formula is absent: the noun *shem* does not appear.[21]

Woman: Man's Helper

Traditionalists maintain that another "hint" of male authority is that the woman was created to help the man, and not the man to help the woman. Paul mentions woman's helping function (along with her origination from man) in 1 Corinthians 11:8–9, and his mention of this is invoked as evidence that God ordained male authority from the beginning. But the significance of Paul's reference to the creation order must be determined in light of his intent in writing the entire passage, not in terms of one's preconceived ideas about the significance of the creation order.[22] The mere mention of a fact proves nothing that the fact itself does not prove. What, then, could be proven by the fact that the woman is referred to as the man's helper?

There are various possibilities for a helper relationship: A helper can be superior, inferior, or equal to the one who is helped. When someone must do a task for which he lacks the requisite knowledge or skills, he will need to get the help of an expert in order to get the job done. The helper/expert, by virtue of her superior expertise, will tell the "helpee" what to do. Usually, in such a helping relationship, roles are determined by expertise (who is knowledgeable), rather than authority (who is in command). But if one person were to have authority over the other in such a relationship, it seems more likely that the helper would have authority over the helpee, as, for example, a school teacher who helps a student with his assignment and who also has authority over the student. Another example with which we should all be familiar is God's role as our helper. Here the helper is superior in both rank and expertise, and the helpee subordinate to the helper's authority.

While this sort of helper/helpee relationship is at least as probable as any other, given the limited information available in Genesis 2, it is clearly not the one traditionalists prefer. The traditionalist view of the Garden of Eden has the man busily ordering things about with all of his masculine authority, but eventually becoming aware that he would be better off with an assistant to help him with his tasks. So the woman comes along to be his obedient helper; she is, therefore, accountable to the man and under his authority.

In general, this describes an employer/employee relationship. Someone who starts a business, for example, designs the product, acquires machinery to manufacture the product, purchases the raw materials, and then hires a worker to put the right nuts on the right bolts. The employer's job is complex and demanding so he needs someone to help him get the job done. The employee's job is simple and fairly straightforward, so the employee needs no helper. The employer has authority over the employee because the employer is the one who knows what needs to be done.

Additionally, the employee's success, status, and identity are directly dependent on the employer's success, status, and identity. If the employer's business prospers, his employee also prospers. Similarly, the employee, whose actual work with nuts and bolts could be performed at many different factories, identifies himself with the product manufactured at "his" factory. So it is with the traditional wife. Her social status depends upon her husband's, she is identified with her husband, and her duties are similar to those of every other "full-time wife and mother."

This seems to be the basic picture traditionalists see in Genesis 2, but with some modifications. In the traditionalist agenda, the area in which a man is to exert his authority (and in which his wife is to serve as his subordinate) does not primarily concern his vocational responsibilities; rather, it seems, his authority is to be exercised primarily over his wife's personal and spiritual life, their marriage, and their children.

However, if the woman is subordinate to the man simply because she was created to meet Adam's need for a helpful assistant, then his authority over her should pertain only to those tasks with which he would have needed help *before* she was created. Her helping tasks should concern only the sort of work for which the man would have had responsibility when he was working in the Garden alone. (Of course, the idea that the man has primary responsibility for the work that God gave humanity ignores the fact that Genesis 1:28 gives responsibility and authority to both male and female at once, with no indication of differing levels of responsibility or authority between them.) At any rate, even if we grant the premise that the woman was created because the man needed a subordinate to help him with his work, this still does not lead to the *personal* authority that husbands are said to have over their wives and families.

In the traditionalist agenda, not only does the husband's authority extend over his wife's entire person, rather than being confined to whatever help she may render as his job assistant, but, as a corollary, the help a woman is expected to offer her husband primarily concerns his personal and emotional life, rather than his vocational responsibilities. This includes not only providing him with meals, clean clothing, a clean house, and well-managed children, but also offering him a "safe haven" of warmth, respect, encouragement, affirmation, acceptance, and love. In other words, her job is to nurture him—regardless of what his job is. Emotional hospitality of this sort is considered to be woman's uniquely feminine calling.

This raises the question of why a man should need a full-time nurturer any more than a woman should need one—or, perhaps more to the point, why only men and not women should be granted the privilege of enjoying this special service. Could it be presumed that a woman needs no nurturing, or less nurturing, than a man? Or that she does not deserve to receive all that nurturing? Since the idea that a woman needs less nurturing than a man implies that she is stronger than the man and emotionally superior to him, it is not likely that traditionalists would choose this rationale. Perhaps it is simply expected of a woman that she will help, serve, and give of herself until there is nothing left to give because this is what womanhood is all about. How many times, after all, have we heard cries of condemnation for the woman who is so "selfish" as to complain of feeling empty or unfulfilled as a person?

A third possibility for a helper relationship is that the helper be equal in status to the one she helps, and that help be mutually given and received between the two persons. In the case of the first woman and man, she could have come to help him in the sense of coming alongside him to join him in his work—not as his assistant or his superior, but as one of equal rank. Instead of assuming that the woman was created secondarily because she was to have a secondary role as the man's subordinate helper, we should consider the possibility that she was called a helper simply because she was created secondarily—after the man had already been at work in the Garden for some time.

Naturally, the text does not say that the man was created to help the woman, for the woman did not yet exist when the man was first created. But when the woman was created, the man was alive and alone and needing help. The woman's appearance changed the situation dramatically for the man, and her purpose is described in terms of this change. The man is no longer alone; he has a partner and a helper.

When the man's temporal priority in the creation order is taken into consideration, the observation that the woman was created to help the man in no way leads to the conclusion that she was created *only* to help the man, or to help him only as a subordinate assistant. There is no reason to assume that once she was created, help was not given and received mutually between the man and the woman. It is unnatural, if not absurd, to overlay a chain of command on a marital relationship of sinless, unfallen love. Man and woman are, after all, equally human, and they equally bear God's image. Why should the purpose of one be simply to serve as a subordinate assistant to the other?

The woman's equality with the man is borne out by God's words, "I will make him an help meet for him" (Gen. 2:18, KJV). Aida Spencer notes that "to 'help' here means 'to share the same tasks' and 'meet' means to do so as 'equal and similar.'"[23] Millard Erickson notes that the Hebrew word translated "meet," *neged,* means "corresponding to" or "equal to" him. The word rendered "help," *ezer,* is used of God in several places in the Old Testament, so any inference of the woman's inferiority to the man is clearly inappropriate.[24] The Key Bible (KJV) has a text note indicating that "meet" means "as before him"—which belies the idea that God intended the woman's help to be of a subordinate nature. The notion that "helper" means "subordinate" must be brought to the Genesis text; it cannot be derived from it. As Spencer puts it, "Woman was created not to serve Adam, but to serve with Adam."[25]

Someone intent on finding positions of superior and inferior rank in the creation order could as easily construe the creation of woman to be man's helper as an indication of the man's inferiority and dependence on the woman. The man could not make it on his own, and he needed help—just as we all rely on the help of God, who is indisputably our superior even when he is helping us. Although the word "helper" is used most frequently in the Bible to describe God's role with respect to his people,[26] the help God offers us does not make him subordinate to us, nor does it put us in authority over, or make us responsible for, the assistance he graciously gives us.

John Piper and Wayne Grudem, however, have a response to the observation that "helper" in itself does not necessarily entail a rank of either inferiority or superiority. Like the more familiar traditionalist argument that the man exercised his authority over both the animals and the woman by naming them, Piper and Grudem seek to find in the man's relationship to the animals an analogy to his relationship to the woman, and thereby to arrive at the conclusion that "helper" in Genesis 2 refers specifically to "one who assists a loving leader."[27] They claim that God had the man look first at all the other creatures to see if one of them could be his helper, and that from this we know that the sort of helper God had in mind for the man was a creature that would be subordinate to him.

How does this follow? Do Piper and Grudem actually think God paraded the animals before the man in order to give him an idea of the sort of helper that would suit him? There is no indication in the biblical text that God had any such notion. Neither is there any support for such an idea from the rest of Scripture. Throughout Old Testament Law, God emphasizes the wrongness of mixing unlike things. How, then, could God have intended that Adam find in his survey of the non-human species any resemblance to what a suitable partner for him should be like? Rather, the fundamental reason God had Adam survey the animals was to impress upon him his need for someone *like* him (not unlike him as the animals were), someone *equal* to him (not unequal to him as the animals were).

The animal survey served as an object lesson for the man, the purpose of which was to demonstrate the unlikeness of the animals to humanity, not the similarity of the animals in any sense to the helper the man would have. The man gets the point of this lesson immediately upon first laying eyes on the woman, and he breaks out in poetry, exulting in her likeness and close relationship to him (2:23).

It almost seems as if Piper and Grudem are thinking in terms of a "great chain of being," as in ancient Greek philosophy, where woman ranks below man but above the animals on a cosmic hierarchy.[28] Piper and Grudem would doubtless deny it, assuring us that the woman is "infinitely different from an animal," and that "no animal can fill her role."[29] But if Adam's inspection and naming of the animals show that God intended Adam's helper to be a subordinate assistant, it also shows that the woman's creational rank is closer to that of the animals than is the man's rank.

The biblical fact is that in no way is the woman any more like the animals than is the man. An unbiased, straightforward reading of this passage reveals that God had Adam see that none of the animals were suitable for him in order to demonstrate that the only creature who could possibly be suitable would be someone like him, equal to him, human like him. The emphasis in the story is on the discontinuity and dissimilarity between the animals and the woman. The story does not demonstrate that the woman is somehow similar to the animals in that she too is under Adam's authority.

If the term "helper" most frequently refers to God, whose status is clearly superior to ours, and if we cannot legitimately regard the relationship of the woman to the man as analogous in any sense to the relationship of the animals to the man, then there is no justification for inferring a subordinate status from the woman's designation as "helper." Traditionalists, however, do not give up that easily. Determined to demonstrate that the woman was created to occupy a rank inferior to the man, some attempt to argue that the act of helping necessarily entails subordination; even God, therefore, is subordinate to us when he helps us. "Subordination is entailed in the very nature of a helping role," declares Ray Ortlund. It is "fallacious" to believe "that God cannot be subordinate to human beings. It is entirely possible for God to subordinate himself, in a certain sense, to human beings. He does so whenever he undertakes to help us."[30] Similarly, Wayne Grudem (evidently thinking better of his and Piper's animal argument) states in his *Systematic Theology* that "whenever someone 'helps' someone else, whether in the Hebrew Old Testament or in our modern-day use of the word *help,* in the specific task in view the person who is helping is occupying a subordinate or inferior position with regard to the person being helped."[31]

This forced construal of God as somehow subordinate to human beings is profoundly unpersuasive. It is, in fact, an example of the fallacy of equivocation. To say that God, who is always helping us, is thereby subordinate to us, is to use "subordinate" in a sense that is radically different from what traditionalists have in mind when they advocate the subordination of women to male authority. It thereby fails to serve as a vindication of female subordination. Humans, after all, have no authority over God, as men purportedly have over their female "helpers." Quite the contrary, in fact.

If we wish to receive God's help in a particular situation, the last thing we should do is to assume some sort of authority over either the situation or (worse yet) our divine helper. Rather, we must acknowledge God's sovereign authority over and responsibility for our own lives, as well as the situation in which we require his help. We then can rest in the knowledge that one who is both loving and omnicompetent is in charge of things, and that we are under his guidance and governance. Any effort to obtain God's assistance while retaining control and responsibility ourselves is doomed to failure. These are not the terms by which God offers us his help. God is our helper when he is also our Lord.

Edenic Equality

The Genesis creation account cannot justifiably be used to demonstrate the existence of male authority and female subordination before the fall. Gender hierarchy cannot be extracted from the Genesis text unless it is first smuggled into the text.

Gilbert Bilezikian comments that the tree of the knowledge of good and evil in Genesis 2, with God's prohibitions concerning it, is a symbolic, visible indication of the fact that there is "one authority structure that permeates all reality and gives it meaning: there is only one God, and to be truly human is to recognize His sovereignty and submit to Him."[32] God's authority over his creation, particularly his human creatures, is a central message of Genesis 2. Genesis 1 establishes another authority structure—twice for emphasis (vv. 26, 28)—whereby God gives the man and the woman joint authority over all the earth and all the creatures God has made to dwell upon it.

These two fundamental authority structures are not presented in the form of hints or clues that can only be seen by reading between the lines. They are unmistakably and undeniably clear; they could not be missed. If any other authority structure had been established at creation, it too would have been presented unequivocally, and not in secret code invisible to the unprejudiced eye.

Conspicuously absent in Genesis 1–2 is any reference to divine pre-scriptions for man to exercise authority over woman. Due to the impor-tance of its implications, had such an authority structure been part of the creation design, it would have received clear definition along with the two other authority mandates. The total absence of such a com-mission indicates that it was not a part of God's intent. Only God was in authority over Adam and Eve. Neither of them had the right to usurp divine prerogatives by assuming authority over each other.[33]

The Genesis account does not hesitate to make authority relation-ships clear where and when they do exist. The absence of any indi-cation of male rule in the original creation order, along with the very clear indication of its presence as a consequence of sin after the fall, militates strongly against the traditionalist effort to discern "hints" of male rule in the creation order, and then to base upon those hints an argument for a permanent, comprehensive, and God-ordained female subordination.

Likewise, the succinct divine commentary on the purpose of mar-riage (Gen. 2:24)—which Jesus refers to as normative (Matt. 19:4–6)—not only is devoid of male leadership overtones, but turns the patriarchal ideal upside down: "For this reason a man will leave his father and mother and be united to his wife, and they will become one flesh." As Bilezikian points out, the woman

> seems to be a free agent, in command of her own life. In this verse, the woman represents the stable point of reference. It is the man who moves toward her after leaving his parents. He attaches himself to the woman. She is not appended to his life. He is the one who adds his life to hers as he "cleaves" to her. The procedure of a man's separating from his father and cleaving to his wife reflects anything but a patriarch-domi-nated society.[34]

In traditional, male-centered society, a woman who marries leaves behind her name, home, family, and identity as an individual and takes to herself her husband's name, home, family, and identity. Despite the obvious reversal of this patriarchal procedure in God's rendering of the first marriage, Ortlund manages to see the man's "initiation" in leaving his own family as a demonstration of "the responsibility of the head."[35]

Even if the man had been created after the woman, those who are bent on justifying male authority would, with a few adjustments, interpret the creation order so as to support this view. Anne Atkins gives a rousing description of how easily this could be done.

> Suppose God had made the woman first, and the man out of her. . . . Now who comes over as the helpless, dependent one, the weaker, inferior partner? Why, the woman again of course! She could not cope alone; man had to be made to bail her out. Part of her body was taken away to make him; she can never again be complete on her own. The man was made last, after the plants, after the animals, and certainly after the woman; he is the crown of God's creation. He was made out of human flesh; she is nothing but dust. Even her name ("man" now of course) is a diminutive version of his ("woman"). She is to "cleave" to him (and, as it happens, this word is "used almost universally for a weaker cleaving to a stronger"; no doubt a great deal would be made of this if the woman were to cleave to the man!). Most significant of all she is to leave her parents and her way of life to join him and adapt to him; she was clearly found to be inadequate on her own.[36]

The fact of the matter is that the temporal order of God's creation of man and woman proves absolutely nothing about which one is the "boss"! If, however, God's creation of the man prior to the woman does not point somehow to man's God-ordained rule over woman, then what does it indicate? Why did God choose to create man and woman at different points in time? Why did he not create both simultaneously? The two-stage creation of humanity highlights the lesson God was trying to teach, namely, that "it is not good for the man [i.e., the human] to be alone" (2:18). God illustrated the point by having the man be alone for a time, and by showing the man that it was "not good."

We would not have had such a clear picture of how fundamentally man and woman fit together, and of how unfit humans are for solitude, if God had created the man and the woman at the same time and in the same way. God's method of creating man and woman demonstrates their interdependence, their oneness, their need for one another, and the basis for their capacity to love one another as partners for a lifetime. It is poetic, picturesque, and to the point. Let us not impose upon this creation story an alien structure of rule and subordination.

138   Assessing the Traditionalist Proof Texts

Adam's "Primary Responsibility" for Sin

Traditionalists find it highly significant that God questioned the man about his sin before he questioned the woman (3:9, 13).[37] But this, along with anything else that may "hint" that God held the man primarily responsible for their sin, need not be attributed to male authority, but (again!) is more appropriately attributed to the simple fact of the man's temporal priority in the creation order.

God made the man first and instructed him in the rules of life in the Garden before the woman was even created. Presumably, she received her instruction concerning the tree of the knowledge of good and evil from the man, who had heard it first from God. Since God had dealt directly and initially with the man about the forbidden fruit (again, because the man was created first), it seems that for this reason God could have chosen to call the man to account before he questioned the woman. Or, perhaps God simply intended to question them each individually, and the order in which he did so did not portend anything in particular.

It is probably true that, if God *had* given the man spiritual leadership over and responsibility for the woman, God would have come to the man first. But in order for the traditionalist argument to be sound, this would have to be the *only* plausible reason for God to have spoken first to the man. Since this is not the case, and there are other reasonable explanations, it is fallacious to say that the sequence of God's questions shows that God had put the man spiritually in charge of the woman. (The fallacy, by the way, is called "affirming the consequent.")

Moreover, the notion that man is spiritually responsible for woman contradicts the biblical teaching that every believer in Christ is directly accountable to God, and that Christ is the only mediator between God and humans. The traditionalist case from this passage is also weakened by the fact that this event took place *after* the fall (when male rule had already begun as a consequence of sin), and so cannot be used to exemplify any sort of creationally ordained order of command.

Even though God speaks first with the man, he also speaks directly to the woman. Clearly, they were each held directly responsible to God for their disobedience. There is no reason to conclude that the sequence of God's interaction with Adam and Eve establishes for all time a pattern whereby the wife receives her spiritual instruction from her husband and her husband is held responsible to God for her sin as well as his own.

"He Will Rule Over You"

After questioning the man and the woman, God says to the woman, "With pain you will give birth to children. Your desire will be for your husband, and he will rule over you" (Gen. 3:16). Male rule and pain in childbearing are clearly presented in this verse as two of the consequences of sin that would be experienced uniquely by the woman. Traditionally, these two items have been viewed as God's declared will for women and, therefore, as normative (which led in earlier centuries to denying women medical relief from pain during childbirth). But these statements are descriptive, not prescriptive. They are not edicts, but explanations of the results that sin, henceforth, will have in the woman's life and in her relationship with her husband. Walter Kaiser notes that there is no grammatical basis to read "he will rule over you" as a command of God.

> The verb contains a simple statement of futurity; there is not one hint of obligation nor normativity in this verb. To argue differently would be as logical as demanding that a verb in verse 18 be rendered, "It shall produce thorns and thistles." Thereafter, all Christian farmers who used weed killer would be condemned as disobedient.[38]

Today, however, the supposed normativeness of gender hierarchy is grounded in the order of creation rather than the fall, and traditionalists generally recognize that Genesis 3:16 refers to the evil effects of sin—effects that should be remediated if possible and not sanctioned or enforced. But advocates of gender hierarchy do not take the reference to male rule straightforwardly, as they do the reference to pain in childbirth. In order to accommodate their claim that benevolent male rule existed by God's decree before the fall, traditionalists must modify the apparent meaning of this verse, insisting that it refers specifically to abusive or domineering male rule. But, of course, the text says simply that as a result of their sin, the man would rule over the woman;

it does not say that the man would *continue* to rule but would now do so in a cruel and domineering fashion. The news to the woman was simply that the man would rule, not that he would rule differently.

The other dire predictions that God pronounces on the man and woman indicate that a negative element is to be added to an otherwise good thing. Pain will accompany childbirth; toil and difficulty will accompany work. But male rule is stated as a negative element in and of itself. God did not say simply, "You will bear children" and expect to be understood as saying, "Now you will bear children with pain." Nor did God announce merely that "You will work," and expect to be understood as saying, "Now you will work with toil and difficulty." Why, then, should we assume that when God said, "He will rule over you," God really meant to say, "He will continue to rule over you, but now with abusive domination"?

The prediction of the man's rule follows the statement about the woman's desire for her husband, and there has been a variety of theories about the relationship between these two statements. Spencer suggests that this verse means the woman will actually desire her husband to dominate her, and he will rule her as a result of her desire for him to do so.[39] This does not seem to be too far off the mark, given that many women do seem almost instinctively to cooperate with and even to encourage male dominance.

Walter Kaiser notes that the word translated "desire" (which appears also in Gen. 4:7 and Song 7:10) was always translated as "turning" until the sixteenth century, when people first took to translating it "desire." According to Kaiser, "turning" is still the more accurate translation, and "it is time the church returned to the real meaning of this word. The sense of Genesis 3:16 is simply this: As a result of her sin, Eve would turn away from her sole dependence on God and turn now to her husband."[40] In sinful response, the man then would take advantage of the woman's emotional dependence upon him by assuming control over her life.

Mary Stewart Van Leeuwen points out that in the beginning, "the man and the woman were equally created for sociability and dominion."[41] This creational intent was skewed when, in the first sin, God's design for human dominion and sociability was misused—in different ways—by the man and the woman. The woman abused her dominion over creation by seeking the knowledge and power reserved for

God, so she lost her place of dominion. Out of balance, the woman's sociability became social enmeshment. The man was thrown off balance in the opposite direction. He abused his sociability by cooperating with his partner instead of obeying God. As a result, he lost much of his propensity for sociability, thus pushing his dominion toward an unsociable, antisocial domination. The man's and woman's sinful proclivities (abusive control and irresponsible passivity, respectively) reinforce each other to create a chronic, "natural" condition of male rule and female subordination.

One interpretation of Genesis 3:16, adopted primarily by traditionalists, casts female desire as the woman's urge to control her husband, and male rule as the man's response to his wife's attempt to dominate him. Whether the man's response is regarded as mandatory or merely inevitable varies among those who hold this position. It is, at any rate, deemed descriptive of the power struggle that typically has characterized the relationship between woman and man since the fall. The exegetical validity of this reading of Genesis 3:16, however, is disputed by biblical scholars on both sides of the feminist divide. By relying entirely on an apparently parallel construction of this verse in Genesis 4:7, this interpretation defines the concepts of female desire and male rule in terms that could not possibly be discerned from the Genesis 3:16 text itself.[42]

Adapting this viewpoint for his purposes, Ortlund states that after the fall, "God gives the woman up to a desire to have her way with her husband. Because she usurped his headship in the temptation, God hands her over to the misery of competition with her rightful head. This is justice, a measure-for-measure response to her sin."[43] Apparently, the woman's desire to reverse male rule by trying to dominate her husband is her special sin, for which God is continually punishing her by means of her husband's domination of her.[44] Indeed, as Bilezikian points out, if the meaning of the woman's desire is to be drawn from the meaning of "desire" in Genesis 4:7, so also must the meaning of the man's rule be drawn from this verse. "In 4:7, the word *rule* has a negative meaning, since God orders Cain to oppose the sin whose desire is for him. This theory would require that Adam treat the woman with the same enmity that Cain was to exhibit toward sin. . . . God would be found allowing men to crush women as if they were sin incarnate."[45]

Nonetheless, this theory seems to hold a lot of appeal for many people, perhaps because it can be employed either as a rationale for male rule, or as an explanation for the intractable, on-going "battle of the sexes" with which we all have to deal.

The Man's Sin of Obedience

All current traditionalist views of the fall begin with the assumption that male authority is instituted in Genesis 2, then violated in Genesis 3 when the woman usurps her husband's authority by eating the fruit without his permission. This, rather than her disobedience to God's command, is deemed her primary sin. However, such an interpretation does not acknowledge that the man, who was there "with her" (Gen. 3:6), offered tacit agreement by his silence.[46] Moreover, the fact that Adam was so willing to follow Eve in eating the fruit suggests that they had *not* been accustomed to functioning along lines of male authority and female subordination.[47]

Traditionalists read a pre-existing chain of command into the statement with which God prefaced his description of the man's share of sufferings: "Because you listened to your wife and ate of the tree about which I commanded you, 'You must not eat of it'" (3:17). In other words, God supposedly blamed the man not only for eating the forbidden fruit, but also for listening to and obeying his wife. But even if God had ordained male authority prior to the fall, God could have delivered the same rebuke to the woman if *she* had listened to and obeyed her husband against God's prior command. Even most traditionalists maintain that if a woman's husband commands her to sin, she must obey God rather than her husband. Moreover, as Ortlund himself admits in an endnote, it is not wrong for a man to listen to his wife and even to follow her advice when it seems to him to be good and godly.[48] A biblical illustration of this truth is found in God's counsel to Abraham to listen to his wife and to do what she said (Gen. 21:12). God's rebuke to Adam in 3:17 is not gender specific and does not presuppose a divine order of male command and female obedience.

The wrong the man did consisted not in obeying his wife, but in disobeying God in order to please his spouse; and this, even according to the traditionalist agenda, would also have been wrong for the woman to do. Both man and woman do wrong if they listen to their spouse when their spouse tells them to do what God has already said they ought not do. Both man and woman do well when they listen to their spouse's suggestions that are in accordance with God's commands.

Marriage, Equality, and the Fall

Because the man was created first and the woman was created later out of the man, they were dealt with somewhat differently—by God, by the text, and by each other. But these differences do not indicate or justify a universal, God-ordained mandate for husbands to rule their wives and wives to obey and submit to that rule. Rather, the Edenic picture is one of mutuality and equality between husband and wife.

Such a marriage seems to be viewed as impossible by traditionalists, who persist in depicting the alternative to male leadership as "female rivalry or autonomy."[49] Apparently, if the man is not in charge, the woman will take charge, thus producing strife and competition. This false dilemma shows up in the antifeminist Danvers Statement, which describes the distortions introduced by the fall into marriage: "In the home, the husband's loving, humble headship tends to be replaced by domination or passivity; the wife's intelligent, willing submission tends to be replaced by usurpation or servility."[50]

Since the purpose of the Danvers Statement is to guard specifically against the perceived evils of evangelical feminism, the question arises as to which of these distortions are believed by the Danvers signatories to be consequences of an equalitarian marriage. Perhaps male domination and female servility are meant to describe the bad male rule introduced by the fall (as opposed to the "good" male rule that existed before the fall), while male passivity and female usurpation describe a feminist marriage. In actuality, however, both of these distorted situations are more likely to arise from hierarchy than from equality in marriage. Male domination occurs when a man's belief in his supposedly God-ordained male authority is not tempered by empathy, and female domination can easily occur when a woman feels threatened by her husband's rule over her. Neither of these distortions, however, are likely to occur in a marriage of mutual love, respect, and submission, wherein authority is shared and husband and wife each have an equal voice in making family decisions.

In the next two chapters, we will look carefully at the biblical picture of marriage in light of the New Testament proof texts that traditionalists use to make their case for the husband's authority over the wife.

6

"The Husband
Is the Head
of the Wife"

any people, at the first whiff of egalitarianism, commence to cite biblical proof texts that they believe clearly establish for all time that a woman should be subordinate to her husband's spiritual authority, that the husband's place is to lead and the wife's is to obey. It does not seem to occur to these people that there is room for debate on this issue within the bounds of biblical authority and orthodoxy.

Dogmatism concerning debatable issues is often due to an ignorance of what is involved in understanding the Bible. For one thing, the distinction between the infallibility of Scripture and the fallibility of our understanding of Scripture is frequently missed. Many Christians have their understanding of the Bible spoon-fed to them by their pastor, and they swallow it whole with no questions asked. Someone who does read the Bible on his own may read a passage that presents to his mind only one message; he then will assume that his understanding of the text is equivalent to the meaning of the text. Many Bible readers are not even aware of the cultural preunderstandings and other elements of the interpretive process that are involved in the reading of any biblical text. In any case, people who have this sort of naive, literalistic approach to the Bible are likely to regard any disagreement with their understanding of a particular text as a disagreement with the Bible itself, which, they assume, can only result from a low view of biblical authority.

An equal and opposite error, frequently made by nonevangelicals laboring under the influence of postmodernist epistemology, is the belief that each person's understanding of what the Bible means is not merely influenced but determined by that person's culturally induced preconceptions and expectations. In this view, the concept of biblical authority is not simply misunderstood; it is rendered meaningless. Because every biblical interpretation is believed to be brought entirely *to* the text, it becomes impossible to derive any authentic message *from* the text. The error in this case does not lie in answering the question of gender roles by a literalistic and legalistic application to our present circumstances of every gender-related instruction in the Bible. Rather, the error lies in looking entirely to the contemporary culture's values and standards (such as they are), and then selecting and manipulating biblical texts to support the contemporary cultural perspective.

The place of truth and sanity is located in the middle ground between these two hermeneutical extremes. Neither absolute certainty nor absolute uncertainty will do. Our understanding of the Bible is always fallible; but good sense, sound knowledge, and the Spirit's leading render possible a humble and reasonable certainty concerning what the Bible truly and infallibly says.

Another reason people tend to become excited before they become educated about interpretational disputes is the common failure to make a distinction between essential doctrine and peripheral doctrine. A debate over a debatable issue (such as evangelical feminism versus traditionalism) should not elicit the level of righteous indignation warranted by a disagreement with a doctrine at the credal heart of Christian orthodoxy. Someone who accepts the core doctrines of the faith but disagrees with your particular view of gender roles should not be labeled a heretic!

How to Do Biblical Interpretation

In order to obtain a clear picture of what the Bible expects of women and men, biblical commands regarding gender roles must be interpreted in light of the cultures for which they were originally intended.[1]

It would seem to be only commonsensical that one cannot directly apply to one's own life the instructions that were written specifically to someone else in quite a different situation. But a false view of spirituality—more akin to superstition—keeps common sense uncommon in much populist-style evangelical biblical interpretation. Many Christians seem to approach the Bible as a magic book: They open it and expect any and all specific commands therein to be directly applicable to their own lives.

This, in large part, is the evangelical heritage of fundamentalist theology. Mark Noll explains that early twentieth-century fundamentalism "emphasized the supernatural character of the Bible to such an extent that the historical contexts of Scripture receded into the background. . . . Under this impetus, the Bible was all too readily taken out of history and read as an artificially unified text."[2] The fundamentalist method (or nonmethod) of biblical interpretation was equated with adherence to biblical authority and inerrancy. "This belief had the practical effect of rendering the experience of the biblical writers nearly meaningless. It was the Word of God pure and simple, not the Word of God as mediated through the life experiences and cultural settings of the biblical authors, that was important."[3] So it is that much of the popular argumentation for traditionalist gender roles takes the form of three or four proof texts strung together into a jigsaw puzzle theology.[4]

In order to understand the meaning of any biblical passage, we must first try to understand the situation of its original audience, so that we can begin to understand why the biblical writer wrote what he did to his intended audience at that time. We then can discern the spiritual principle behind the specific biblical command and apply that principle appropriately to our own lives and cultures. Gordon Fee and Douglas Stuart explain:

> It is possible for a New Testament writer to support a relative application by an absolute principle and in so doing not make the application absolute. Thus in 1 Corinthians 11:2–16, for example, Paul appeals to the divine order of creation (v. 3) and establishes the principle that one should do nothing to distract from the glory of God (especially by breaking convention) when the community is at worship (vv. 7, 10). The specific application, however, seems to be relative.[5]

Hence, the Bible does not demand that women today wear head coverings in church, nor are we required to greet one another with a holy kiss, to wash each other's feet, to abstain from eating meat with blood, or to take wine for the stomach—even though all these things are commanded in the New Testament. But we do need to understand and apply the spiritual truths that initially impelled these commands—which include such universal principles as the need to dress in a way that shows respect for one's family and for social propriety, to love one another, to be humble and willing to serve one another, and to live in a way that is above reproach in the eyes of other believers and those outside the church. As Craig Keener explains, "Although the Bible provides some direct statements of principle, most of its examples are instead descriptions of ideal roles in given cultures, and we cannot glibly impose them on our own culture without thinking carefully how they should really be applied."[6]

In distinguishing between the direct statements of principle and the culturally relative instructions in the Bible, it helps to differentiate those matters that the Bible treats as moral issues from those things that are not inherently moral and, therefore, may change from culture to culture. The apostle Paul's lists of various sins, for example, address moral rather than cultural concerns.[7] The sinful behaviors that Paul prohibits in these lists are always wrong, regardless of their cultural setting. For example, homosexual behavior shows up on these lists (e.g., 1 Cor. 6:9–10), but women preachers and equalitarian marriages never do. Homosexual behavior is also identified as a moral issue in Old Testament Law, where it is clearly condemned and punishable by death (Lev. 20:13). On the other hand, many of the women in the Old Testament who exercised civil and spiritual authority over men were clearly depicted as called and empowered by God for their ministries.[8]

Homosexual behavior and gender equality fall into different categories also when it comes to distinguishing between those matters on which the Bible speaks with a clear, consistent, and uniform voice, and those matters on which there seem to be some contradictions or inconsistencies. Since the Bible never mentions homosexuality except to condemn it, while the Bible sometimes commends and other times restricts women's leadership, this too indicates that the one issue is a universal principle and the other is a culturally relative concern.[9]

Evangelicals today are generally in agreement that, when Paul exhorts both slaves and children to obedience in Ephesians 6:1–9 and Colossians 3:20–22, the obedience of slaves to masters is culturally relative and the obedience of children to parents is a direct statement of principle. Unlike the cultural practices of both slavery and male rule in marriage, children's obedience to parents is a basic moral principle. It is commanded in the Decalogue (Deut. 5:16), and a child's consistent and incorrigible violation of this command was punishable by death under Old Testament Law (Deut. 21:18–21). Moreover, it simply makes moral sense; children are immature and require the governance of an adult. This moral rationale, however, is not applicable to the subordination of slaves and women. Evidence of the distinction between slaves' obedience and children's obedience can also be discerned in Galatians 3:28, where Paul indicates that there has been a change in the male/female and slave/free relationships, but makes no mention of any change between parents and their children.

It is also crucial that individual Bible verses be interpreted in light of both their immediate literary context and the larger context of the teaching of the Bible as a whole. As I hope I have demonstrated in the preceding chapters, the overall testimony of Scripture speaks clearly of the equality of all human beings regardless of their gender, race, or class. The implications of this essential equality are incompatible with the assertion of any universal, spiritual principle of male supremacy.

The basic principle of interpreting biblical texts in light of both their cultural context and the rest of biblical teaching was practiced by those Christians in the nineteenth century who argued for the abolition of slavery—against the traditionalists of the time who believed their proof texts proved that the Bible supports slavery as a universal practice.[10] This principle of biblical interpretation also needs to be understood and applied by those who seek to discern from Scripture the proper "place" of women in the home and the church today.

While the case for biblical equality is based on the general biblical message of equality, the traditionalist case is based primarily on specific proof texts. But when we look carefully at these proof texts, it is apparent that they have enough translational and interpretational ambiguity that they can as readily be understood either way. The equalitarian interpretation of these texts, however, has the best "fit" in light of the rest of biblical teaching.

Does "Head" Mean "Boss"?

Because the doctrine of women's God-ordained subordination runs counter to the overall message of the Bible, the traditionalist system that is built upon selected proof texts has some missing pieces and weak links. In order to construct a complete and consistent doctrine of the universal and God-ordained subordination of women to male rule, it is necessary to add concepts and principles not mentioned in the Bible. Traditionalist doctrine is frequently explained with phrases such as the "chain of command," the husband as his wife's "spiritual covering," and "the man as priest of the home"; but these common expressions are nowhere to be found in the Bible. These concepts appear to rest almost entirely on an interpretation of 1 Corinthians 11 that takes "head" to be a metaphor for authority and then assumes that this makes a man the representative of God to his wife and family. But this meaning is not clear from either the text or the context. In fact, the idea that God has given the husband spiritual authority over his wife, and made him accountable to God for his wife, is directly contradicted by the New Testament account of Ananias and Sapphira (Acts 5:1–11). Husband and wife were each questioned directly and separately about each one's own part in the sin they had committed; they were individually culpable and individually condemned.[11]

Unless the two New Testament references to the husband being the head of the wife (1 Cor. 11:3; Eph. 5:23) can be shown indisputably to speak of a man's authority over his wife, traditionalists are left with the need to make a huge inference, namely, that the exhortations to women to submit to their husbands necessarily entail an exhortation to men to command or exercise authority over their wives. The fact that women are told to submit to their husbands, as all believers are to one another and to the Lord (Eph. 5:21), is in itself inconclusive. It must be inferred that this wifely submission is meant to be both unilateral and universal, and neither mutual nor culturally relative. The Bible never actually tells men to take authority over their wives. That is inferred from the chain of command idea, which is inferred from the idea that husbandly headship means husbandly authority, which, in turn, is inferred from cultural preconceptions about the meaning of head and the role of the husband.

As a result, we have numerous books, radio messages, sermons, seminars, conferences, and magazine articles directly and repeatedly exhorting men to do something the Bible not once directly exhorts them to do, namely, to assume leadership of their wives and families as God's representative to them. Assailed with such teaching on so many fronts, people come to believe that the Bible really does tell men to rule their wives. In fact, one scholarly treatment of evangelical attitudes toward gender roles states that evangelical feminists have a hard time with biblical passages "describing husbands as 'ruling over wives.'"[12] Actually, there are no such passages in the Bible. But there are, as we shall see, passages in Bible paraphrases that say as much (thanks to the authors' efforts to "clear up" obscure texts).

The first place to start in understanding the biblical meaning of the husband's headship is with the fact that in the Greek language of New Testament times, "head" *(kephale)* did not necessarily serve as a metaphor for "chief executive" (as it normally does today). Nor was the head widely regarded as the seat of a person's reasoning and decision-making powers. Rather, the heart was typically seen as the governing center of the body, while the head was regarded as the source of life for the body. An understanding of the head as the supplier of life to the body is clearly the sense in which "head" is used in Ephesians 4:15 and Colossians 2:19, which describes Christ as the source of life, health, and strength for his body, the church.

Another metaphorical meaning for "head" was "source" or "origin," as in the head of a river. The term is used in this sense in Colossians 1:18, which states that Christ is "the head of the body, the church; he is the beginning." "Head" could also be used to refer to that which was in some way prominent or honorable.[13] In their *Greek-English Lexicon,* Liddell and Scott do not include in the definitions of *kephale* any meaning that expresses authority or superior rank.[14] The translators of the Septuagint (the Greek translation of the Old Testament) generally avoided using *kephale* when the Hebrew word for "head" was used to indicate a ruler.[15]

In view of these considerations, we should not assume that New Testament references to the husband as head of the wife mean that he has a God-ordained authority over his wife. Perhaps Paul was referring to the man as the life source for the woman because the first man was the source out of which God created the first woman and this serves somehow as an analogy for the husband–wife relationship. These texts must be interpreted according to their biblical context rather than our own preconceptions.

In 1 Corinthians 11:3–16, Paul does not expand on what it means for a man to be the head of his wife, but employs "head" primarily as a word play or pun in the course of his argument that women should wear a head covering during worship services.[16] But Ephesians 5:21–33 does offer a description of the husband's role as head of his wife; so we will begin by looking at this text, and then turn to 1 Corinthians 11:3–16.

Headship in Ephesians 5:21–33

In this passage we read that the husband is the head of the wife as Christ is the head of the church, "his body, of which he is the Savior" (v. 23). Then we read of how the husband's headship is to mimic the headship of Christ (vv. 25–30). The husband's role is described here as life-giving, self-giving love, which is analogous to the role of Christ as Savior of his body, the church.

The analogy between the husband and Christ obviously is not applicable at every point. We know that, unlike Christ, a husband does not offer a sinless sacrifice of his own life for the sake of his wife's eternal salvation; for he is as much in need as his wife of salvation from sin. So we must note carefully how the passage draws the parallel between the husband and Christ, as well as how it does *not* draw the parallel. It is particularly significant that there is no mention here of either the authority of a husband over his wife (which he had through civil law at the time of Paul's writing) or the authority of Christ over the church (which he has always had in full measure). In order to conclude that Christ serves as a model for the husband's leadership of the wife, it is necessary to presume that "head" has no possible meaning other than authority, or that the reference to the wife's submission necessarily entails her unilateral obedience to her husband's God-ordained authority over her. But neither of these assumptions are warranted by the text itself; they must be brought to the text from previously established assumptions.

The passage does present a parallel between the physical head of a physical body, and Christ as the head of his body the church (vv. 23, 30), and the husband as the head of his wife, whom he is to treat as his own body (vv. 28–30). It is unfortunate that the head–body metaphor, as applied to Christ and his church, and to a husband and his wife, has provoked an inordinate preoccupation with a "chain of command" concept of headship, when the emphasis would more constructively and biblically be placed on an understanding of "body-ship"—that is, our unity and interdependence as one body, whether in marriage or in the larger family of God. In Ephesians 5:21–33, Paul uses the integral unity and interdependence of head and body to illustrate the mystery of the one-flesh union of husband and wife and the one-spirit union between Christ and the members of his body (vv. 28–32; see also 1 Cor. 6:17).[17] This passage depicts marriage not as a hierarchical organization, but as a living, unified (head + body) organism.

The one-flesh unity of husband and wife is highlighted in verse 31, where Paul quotes Genesis 2:24, the divine description of marital union: A man leaves his parents to be united to his wife, and the two become one flesh. To love one's spouse is to love one who has become a part of oneself. As a result, self-interest gives way to self-sacrifice, and the power struggle between two competitors dissolves into mutual submission within a unit that has one goal: their common good. When marriage partners realize that what is good for the other is good for the self (the two having become one), then rules concerning authority and obedience become inappropriate and inapplicable.

It runs contrary to the context and intent of Ephesians 5:21–33 to see the analogy between the husband and Christ in terms of authority. The description of the husband's role speaks of his part in the mutual submission to which Paul exhorts all believers in verse 21; it does not entitle the husband to make decisions that the wife is morally obligated to obey. It should also be noted that the reference to the husband being the head is directed toward the wife, not the husband. Regardless of what Paul meant to convey by the term "head," it seems

clear that this metaphor was pertinent primarily to the wife's understanding of her role. It was not intended to be used by the husband as
his "authorization" from God to be the spiritual ruler of his wife, as
traditionalists today would have it.[18]

Viewing Christ as a model of the husband's authority is inconsistent not only with the general sense of this passage, but also with Jesus'
repudiation—in both action and instruction—of the authoritarian rule
of one person over another.[19] His thoughts on this subject are recorded
in each of the Synoptic Gospels (Matt. 20:25–28; Mark 10:42–45;
Luke 22:25–27). Jesus made it quite clear that the Christlike way is
the way of submission. It was this which he modeled, and this to which
he urged his followers, whether male or female. It would be hard to
imagine anything more antithetical to the spirit of Christ than a doctrine that universalizes and spiritualizes the absolute civil authority
that husbands exercised over their wives in the cultures of New Testament times.

Ephesians 5:21–33 describes the husband as similar to Christ, the
Savior, in that he is a life-giver. In laying down his life—his own
needs, rights, and desires—out of love for his wife (whom he regards
as his own body), a man becomes a source of life for his wife. The
wife is similar to the church in that she must submit to the ministry
of her "savior" if she is to benefit from his life-giving, nurturing love.[20]
The wife's submission, however, is not unilateral; for the husband
also practices submission as he gives himself up for her sake.[21]

The biblical ideal is that as a woman submits to her husband she
receives from him the love that leads to life, growth, and health, even
as Christ's self-giving love serves to nurture the life, health, and growth
of the church, which is his body. Christ's life-giving "head" relationship to his body, the church, is described in Ephesians 4:7–16 and
Colossians 2:19. In imitation of Christ's role as Savior and head of
the church (Eph. 5:25–27), the husband is to love his wife, helping to
make her pure, radiant, and fully alive for service to God.

Aida Besancon Spencer observes that in Paul's description of how
Christ loved and gave himself up for the church, he uses imagery rem-
iniscent of the service of priests to God in the Old Testament. Priests
were to be physically perfect ("without stain or wrinkle or any other
blemish," Paul puts it), and were "washed with water" as part of the
ceremony of consecration. "Even as Christ gave himself so that all

people might become priests (1 Peter 2:9), in the same way husbands are to give themselves to their wives so that the wives might become priests. . . . Paul wants women, as well as men, to function as priests of the most high God and he wants men to help empower them."[22] A woman grows and matures in the ministry to which God has called her when her husband loves her as Christ loved the church.

Biblically, a man is to use his greater social power and male status for the good of his wife, thereby serving as a "head" who provides life rather than commands obedience. The husband is to give up the full exercise of his social privileges and cultural authority in order to love, serve, and honor his wife, even as Christ gave up (temporarily) some of the prerogatives of divinity (Phil. 2:6–8) in order to save and serve the church.

Christ gave his life so that we who were oppressed and enslaved by sin might be set free to rule and reign with him forever (Rev. 3:21; 5:10). Romans 8:17 describes our destiny as "joint heirs with Christ" (KJV); by law, joint heirs have equal power, and neither one has the right to make a decision on behalf of the other.[23] Even so, a husband ought to lay down his life for his wife so that through his self-giving love she may rule as co-regent with him over those aspects of creation with which God entrusted both male and female as stewards (Gen. 1:26–28).

If the analogy between Christ's relationship to the church and a husband's relationship to his wife is so clearly presented here in terms of giving life, why do people persist in seeing it in terms of giving orders? There seems to be a strong tendency to impute to the "head" metaphor the meaning we expect it to have, rather than the meaning Paul gives it. When people see the words "head" and "submit," they think, "submit to authority," when they should be thinking, "submit to life!"[24]

Life-Giving Headship and Ruling Headship

The biblical difference between the roles of husband and wife is not described in terms of levels of authority, but there is a subtle difference nonetheless. Though they are equal in authority and mutual in submission, it seems the husband is in some sense a life-giver or "savior" to the wife in a way that the wife is not to him. There are two reasons for this: creation and the fall.

In the creation of the first man and woman, the woman's origin (or source of life) was in the man. This has a significance beyond that of indicating their complete equality and unity in having been made of exactly the same "stuff." It evidently serves somehow as a parable of the life-giving love that the Lord has for his people, and that God from the beginning intended a husband to have for his wife. As with the first man and woman, though, God is the ultimate Giver and Creator of life, and on him both man and woman depend for their life (as Paul reminds us in 1 Cor. 11:12). However, there is in this picture of Christ and the church, and husband and wife, a "profound mystery" (Eph. 5:32). It seems that, if even Paul was obliged to invoke mystery when trying to explain these concepts and relationships, we shouldn't feel the need to nail down the "head" metaphor with charts and diagrams. Let it retain an element of mystery; let our only rule be love.

After creation came the fall and, as a consequence, the beginning of man's rule over woman (Gen. 3:16). Male rulership and female subjection to that rule is a warp in God's world due to sin.[25] Where does this fallen state of gender relations put the wife? It puts her in a position of helpless subservience to her husband's power and ambition—*unless* her husband lays down his life for her, sacrifices many of his desires for success and domination, and draws from her by God's grace her unique personhood, her gifts, callings, and distinctive character.

Unless the husband counteracts the effects of the fall through his life-giving love for his wife, she will have two choices. She can either become a subordinate assistant whose life consists entirely of serving the needs of her husband, home, and children, or she can break free in an act of autonomous rebellion, such as divorce or separation. The first choice is the traditional one; the second is the modern, secular feminist one. Neither is God's desire for a woman's life.

In a sense, there are two kinds of husbandly headship: life-giving (or biblical) headship, which was instituted at creation, and ruling (or cultural) headship, which began with the fall. Life-giving headship saves women from ruling headship; it is modeled on Christ's life-giving, sacrificial love for the church. The biblical headship of the husband described in Ephesians 5 is redemptive (analogous to Christ's redemption of the church), in that it mitigates that effect of the fall which places the woman under male rule, and it helps to reinstate woman in her creational place of cultural responsibility alongside man.

In life-giving headship, the social privilege and power of maleness is shared by the husband with the wife, and utilized by him according to the terms of love rather than of male conquest and command. By recognizing her personal and spiritual equality with him, and by putting all that he has and is at her disposal, a husband undoes the male rulership of the fall and, by God's grace, saves his wife from its effects.

Ironically, understanding the head of the wife to mean the leader of the wife defeats the biblical purpose of the head as nurturer of the life, health, and growth of the wife. A person cannot grow into full spiritual, emotional, and intellectual maturity if she is denied the opportunity to take responsibility for her own life, if she is treated as a child who needs to have her decisions made for her by someone else.

Yet, the reduction of the wife's role to that of a child's is the ultimate result of insisting that headship means leadership. Because Ephesians 5:25–31 clearly speaks of the husband selflessly serving the wife, as Christ serves and gives life to the church, traditionalists must integrate the element of servanthood into their concept of the husband's hierarchical rule—in order that the husband's leadership be regarded as equivalent to the husband's selfless service. The submissive, self-giving love of the husband set forth in this passage is therefore reshaped and redefined so as to become a permanent, paternal governing of the wife.

Eugene Peterson's paraphrase of Ephesians 5:23 in *The Message* demonstrates how traditionalists are obliged to read this verse: "The husband provides leadership to his wife the way Christ does to his church, not by domineering but by cherishing."[26] In other words, the husband's love for his wife is expressed in his leadership of his wife. This *is* true with respect to Christ and the church. Because the church is so profoundly inferior to Christ in spiritual wisdom and righteousness, it needs Christ's leadership and is served by receiving it. But this is not the case with a husband and wife. The analogy does not extend this far. A husband is not necessarily more righteous or wise than his wife, nor is a wife any more in need of her husband's spiritual leadership than he is in need of hers.

Biblically, the exercise of authority *should* be an act of service. When a person (such as a child) or a group of persons (such as a church congregation) is in need of being guided and governed, then it is hoped that those in authority will govern and guide with the heart of a servant rather than a dictator. But a husband's leadership of his wife is a service to her only if she is childishly in need of supervision by an "adult." The doctrine of male authority denies a wife the status of full adulthood—even if the husband rules with a very light and generous hand.

The only exception to this is what normally happens in truly loving marriages that nonetheless (in theory) endorse the hierarchical model: out of respect for his wife the husband simply refuses to "pull rank." Instead, he permits his wife to participate equally in the decision-making process and to develop fully as an adult person. (When there is mutual love and respect in a marriage, this equalizing of "authority" tends to happen naturally.) However, the husband who regards his wife as more childish and less competent than himself probably will believe he does her a service by governing her.[27]

Hierarchical marriages also stunt the husband's growth in character and sanctification. It is impossible to have a teachable spirit without having a submissive spirit. A person learns by submitting, not by being required to have all the right answers and to come up with all the "final decisions." The man who rejects mutual submission in favor of unilateral leadership is closing the door on the most effective route to spiritual and emotional growth—the learning and loving of two equal partners in the service of Christ's kingdom. Who, after all, is better equipped to encourage a man in the direction of stronger character and more Christlike behavior than the one who loves him more and knows him better than any other? A wife who is not overbearing or demanding, but gentle, loving, prayerful, and patient, can be used greatly by God to facilitate her husband's progress toward spiritual maturity—if he is willing to submit to her as she submits to him.

Headship in 1 Corinthians 11:3–16

What can we gather from the metaphorical use of the term "head" in 1 Corinthians 11:3–16? At the outset we should note that, as Gordon Fee puts it, "this passage is full of notorious exegetical difficulties," and "the books written on this subject express far more certainty than the data allow."[28] These exegetical difficulties create something of a problem for hierarchalists. Unless 1 Corinthians 11:3 can be seen as unequivocally establishing a cosmic hierarchy of authority involving not simply man and woman but God and Christ as well, then the "head" relationships among Christ, man, woman, and God that are set forth in this verse must be seen as merely one element in Paul's argument that female believers in Corinth should cover their heads during public worship. But if the passage is thus shorn of its implications of gender hierarchy, then the "chain of command" doctrine loses its biblical support.

To what metaphorical meaning for "head" does the context point in this passage? For one thing, the order in which the "head" relationships are stated in 11:3 ("The head of every man is Christ, and the head of the woman is man, and the head of Christ is God") suggests that "head" serves here as a metaphor for "source" or "origin" rather than "authority." If this verse were speaking of a chain of command, it should rather say first that God is the head of Christ, then that Christ is the head of man, and finally that man is the head of woman—as do all the diagrams that we have seen illustrating the concept. But instead, the "head" relationships are listed in chronological order of origin.[29] First, man originated from Christ, by whom all things were created (John 1:3; Col. 1:16). Then, woman came from man, according to Genesis 2:21–22. And, in the incarnation, Christ came from God the Father (John 1:1, 14; 8:14, 42).

In verses 8 and 12, Paul speaks of the man as being the source or point of origin for the woman. This reinforces an understanding of "head" as "source" in verse 3; clearly, this concept is not alien to the passage, but serves as an important line of Paul's argument. The idea that Paul is using "head" in verse 3 as a metaphor for "source" was not invented by modern egalitarians. It was held by a number of ancient and medieval theologians, including Athanasius, Chrysostom, Basil, Theodore of Mopsuestia, Eusebius, Cyril of Alexandria, and Photius.[30]

Another way that this text resists an interpretation of "head" as "authority" has to do with the implications of the chain of command for the relationship of Christ to God. The idea that the Son is eternally (but only "functionally") subordinate to the Father is by no means an indisputable doctrine.[31] But it is the position necessarily held by those who also see in this text a permanent (but only "functional") subordination of the woman (or wife) to the man (or husband).[32] The analogy between God's authority over Christ and the husband's authority over the wife breaks down—and with it the chain of command—unless the theologically debatable doctrine of the Son's eternal subordination to the Father can be adequately defended.

Eugene Peterson's paraphrase of this text reflects the traditionalist difficulty here also: "In a marriage relationship, there is authority from Christ to husband, and from husband to wife. The authority of Christ is the authority of God."[33] Peterson adjusts the text so as to have the chain of command begin with Christ rather than with God, thus leaving intact the coequality of God and Christ.

The passage itself offers no reason to understand the metaphorical meaning of "head" as authority, especially considering that the only reference to authority in the entire passage speaks of the woman's own authority (v. 10) and not of any authority that her husband has over her.[34] Unfortunately, Bible translations and paraphrases tend to obscure and even sometimes to reverse this fact. For example, The Living Bible tells us, "So a woman should wear a covering on her head as a sign that she is under man's authority" (v. 10a); but it does admit in a footnote that the literal rendering is, "For this cause ought the woman to have power on (her) head."

In verse 11 Paul qualifies the woman's authority by saying, "However, woman is not independent of man," which would make no sense if he had just referred in the preceding verse to the man's authority over the woman. Paul's idea here seems to be that although a woman has authority over her own head, she should remember that she is not independent of her husband and so should choose to cover her head for the sake of social propriety. A woman should want to honor and not to shame her husband.[35] Paul concludes his qualifying remarks by saying, "For as woman came from man, so also man is born of woman. But everything comes from God" (v. 12). He seems concerned that his readers not make too much of the head relationship of man to woman, but that they balance it with the truth of the interdependence of man and woman and the dependence of both man and woman upon God. Any inference concerning man's superiority over or independence from woman is unwarranted.[36]

Paul speaks of the interdependence and mutuality of husband and wife also in 1 Corinthians 7:4–5, where he refers to them making a decision "by agreement," and says that just as the husband has authority over the wife's body, so the wife has authority over the husband's body (NRSV). It is possible that this statement does not refer only to the physical aspect of marriage, because "by the first century A.D. the word *soma,* translated 'body' (v. 4), included our idea of 'personhood' and was not limited to the physical body as such."[37]

So What Does It Mean?

If the purpose of 1 Corinthians 11:3–16 is not to establish a chain of command by which women are to submit to the spiritual authority of men (as traditionalist interpreters of this passage would have it), then what is the main point? Why did Paul write these words to the church in Corinth at this time? His immediate reason was that he wanted to persuade Christian women in Corinth to wear a head covering during public worship. What is the biblical principle behind the need for a head covering in this situation? Believers ought not distract other believers from their worship of God, and should show respect and consideration for others, especially a woman for her husband by heeding social custom for appropriate public dress. It was shameful, in some cultural sense, for a woman to appear in public unveiled, and this shame reflected on her husband. Therefore, women should wear the culturally proper headgear during the public worship service.

Possibly the head covering was necessary in order to keep from distracting the men, who in that culture were sexually attracted to a woman's hair.[38] This rationale is influential even today in fundamentalist Muslim countries, where women are required to be veiled in public.[39] Another possibility is that the veil was a social symbol of womanhood, which Christian women ought not discard as they might have been tempted to do by their newfound freedom in Christ or by neighboring Greek or proto-Gnostic religions that urged women to deny their femaleness and become spiritually male. (Unlike some of the pagan religions that allowed women public ministry, the early Christian church allowed women to pray and prophesy in public as women, not as imitators of men.) Paul was concerned that Christian men and women not deny the distinction between the sexes, as culturally expressed.[40]

At any rate, because woman came from man (which makes man her head), she is, in a sense, a reflection of him. She is man's glory (v. 7), and she should dress and act in a way that honors and reflects well on her husband.[41] Many take Paul's explanation for why woman is man's glory—that she was created from man and for man (vv. 8–9)—to be an exposition of woman's subordination to man. But, as already noted, Paul indicates in verses 11 and 12 that this is not the meaning he intends to convey. Rather, as Gordon Fee explains,

> Paul really is reflecting the sense of the Old Testament text to which he is alluding. Man by himself is not complete. . . . The animals will not do; he needs one who is bone of his bone, one who is like him but different from him, one who is uniquely his own "glory." In fact, when the man in the Old Testament narrative sees the woman he "glories" in her by bursting into song. She is thus man's glory because she "came from man" and was created "for him." She is not thereby subordinate to him, but necessary for him. She exists to his honor as the one who having come from man is the one companion suitable to him, so that he might be complete and that together they might form humanity.[42]

7

Marriage and Mutual Submission

omen are told to submit to their husbands in Ephesians 5:22–24, Colossians 3:18, Titus 2:5, and 1 Peter 3:1–6. This chapter will focus primarily on the more extended passages, where the meaning and context of submission is given the most explanation and clarification.

The Greek word translated "submit" refers to being put or ordered, or to putting or ordering oneself, under another. Whenever it is exhorted of wives—or of Christians in general—it is in the sense of submitting oneself voluntarily, rather than being put forcibly under submission.[1] The general meaning is of self-surrender, of a "readiness to renounce one's own will for the sake of others . . . and to give precedence over others."[2] Christian submission is presented in the New Testament as transforming one's "place" in the social order from a situation of onerous obligation and slavish obedience to an expression of one's devotion and ultimate submission to Christ, within a context of reciprocal submission among all believers. In this "redeemed" submission, obedience is rendered where it is legally required, insofar as it does not conflict with obedience to God.[3]

It is important to understand that submission (having a disposition of deference, humility, and respect toward another person) is not the same as obedience (acting under command from a higher authority). Obedience can follow from submission, but obedience is not necessarily entailed by submission. In biblical usage, "to 'submit oneself' could mean to 'give in' or 'cooperate,' and need not mean 'obey.'" In fact, "the closest thing Paul gives to a definition of the term" in the context of Ephesians 5:21–33 (the longest New Testament passage on marital roles) "is the word 'respect' in 5:33, where he plainly summarizes his whole exhortation to wives."[4]

The New Testament states clearly that submission is an attitude all believers are to adopt (Eph. 5:21); in humility each person should regard others as better than himself (Rom. 12:10; Phil. 2:3; 1 Peter 5:5). In a relationship of mutual submission no one puts oneself above or over another, but rather defers to the other and does not insist on one's own priority or preeminence. Submission is presented in the epistles and exemplified in the life of Christ as the normal Christian position; it is contrasted with the too-human tendency toward self-promotion and self-defensiveness (see 1 Peter 2:21–23).

To submit is essentially to count the other person greater than oneself, to give up one's own rights, and to defer to the wishes or needs of the other. A complete and wholehearted submission amounts to giving oneself so completely that one lays down his or her life for the other. This, in fact, is precisely what husbands are told to do in Ephesians 5:21–33. Ironically, this is the passage most frequently used to mandate the wife's universal and unilateral submission to the husband's authority over her.

Mutual Submission in Ephesians 5:21–33

The call to mutual, reciprocal submission in Ephesians 5:21 establishes the framework for the instructions to wives and husbands that follow. Verses 21 and 22 should be considered part of the same thought, for the verb "submit" in verse 22 is not in the Greek text but is borrowed from verse 21. Wives, therefore, are to submit to their husbands in the same way that all believers are to submit to one another. This text is not advocating a unilateral female submission to male authority. Rather, it is presenting the submission of wives as one application of the basic principle of mutual submission that is to be applied by all believers within the context of the body of Christ. The admonitions to wives to submit and husbands to love are balanced in this passage by commands to all believers to love and submit to one another (Eph. 5:1–2, 21). "Husbandly love and wifely submission in this context thus become examples of those more general virtues, rather than statements that love is only the husband's role, and submission only the wife's."[5]

Because it is clear that this passage is teaching mutual submission in some sense, traditionalists often try to affirm the coexistence of hierarchy and mutual submission within marriage. The wife's submission is defined as obedience, while the husband's submission is defined as a paternalistic concern to determine what is best for the person in his charge. This is how one commentator explains "the way in which husbands submit to their wives" according to Ephesians 5:21–33: It is "not a burdening of the wife with the decision-making responsibility . . . but rather it means making decisions according to her needs and her welfare, even when it means a decision she may not like."[6] In other words, the wife benefits from being governed by her husband, because he knows—better than she knows herself—what is best for her. When husband and wife "submit" in such different ways, for such different reasons, and to such different degrees, the claim that submission is "mutual" is far from convincing.

Some traditionalists maintain that verse 21 does not speak of all believers submitting to all other believers, but only of believers in some groups submitting to believers in other groups. The groups of submitters and submittees to which this verse refers are then delineated in the verses that follow (Eph. 5:22–6:9), namely, wives to husbands, slaves to masters, and children to parents.[7] This reading of the text assumes that submission is equivalent to obedience, and ignores the element of reciprocity that is present in the "one another" in verse 21; it also disregards the immediately preceding exhortations, which are clearly directed toward all believers.

According to the commentator for Ephesians in The NIV Study Bible, "The grammar indicates that this mutual submission is associated with the filling of the Spirit in verse 18. The command 'be filled' (v. 18) is followed by a series of participles in the Greek: speaking (v. 19), singing (v. 19), making music (v. 19), giving thanks (v. 20), and submitting (v. 21)."[8] Craig Keener explains that "the Greek phrase 'submitting to one another' retains here its usual force in the context of the parallel phrases that precede it: a subordinate participial clause dependent on the preceding imperative. In other words, the submission of 5:21, like the worship of 5:19–20, flows from being filled with God's Spirit (v. 18)."[9]

Verse 21 must remain conceptually connected not only to the verses that follow it, but also to the verses that precede it. Just as all believers are to speak and sing to one another (v. 19), so all believers are to submit to one another (v. 21). No believer is immune from the imperative to be filled with the Spirit (v. 18); nor is any believer immune from the imperative to submit to other believers. To read Ephesians 5:21 in any way other than as exhorting mutual and reciprocal submission without respect to any believer's social status is to read it in light of one's own preconceptions. C. E. B. Cranfield comments that the question of the meaning of submitting to one another in this verse "is to be solved not by attempting to explain away the idea of reciprocity, but by recognizing that [the word 'submit'] here does not mean 'obey.'" He then points to Romans 12:10 and Philippians 2:3 as texts that "mean essentially the same thing" as Ephesians 5:21.[10]

Another traditionalist objection to the idea of mutual submission within marriage is that the New Testament never uses the word "submission" to describe the husband's behavior. Wayne Grudem finds it "very significant that the New Testament authors never explicitly tell husbands to submit to their wives."[11] Laying down one's life for someone (as Ephesians 5:25–30 instructs husbands to do for their wives in imitation of Christ) evidently does not qualify as a description of submissiveness, in Grudem's estimation. Although the New Testament authors may not use the actual word "submit" when speaking to husbands, the idea is certainly present both in the general directives to all believers and in specific exhortations to husbands.

The fact that the Bible never tells husbands to rule, take authority over, command, or otherwise provide direction and decisions for their wives seems far more significant than that husbands are not specifically told to "submit." Nonetheless, men are routinely informed by traditionalists that the Bible tells them to assume spiritual leadership of their wives and families. Such a role, however, is not commanded of husbands in Scripture, but is inferred from an understanding of "head" as necessarily indicating authority, and from the assumption that wives' submission consists of a universal and unilateral obedience to their husbands' God-ordained authority over them.

Certainly, we ought not negate the biblical injunction for wifely submission. But neither should we assume that it precludes mutual submission or that it demands the wife's unilateral submission to the husband's spiritual authority over her; to go this far is to go beyond the words of Scripture. In biblical times, men had a great deal of socially sanctioned authority over their wives; but the New Testament counters this cultural reality with instructions to husbands to treat their wives with respect and love. The biblical counterpoint to the wife's submission is not the husband's rule of his wife, but the husband's love for his wife—a love that he is told to express with the same devotion and concern that he exercises in caring for his own body (Eph. 5:28).

By ancient standards, Paul's exhortations to husbands to love their wives self-sacrificially were quite radical, while his instructions to wives to respect and submit to their husbands were rather watered down. Craig Keener explains that

> The household codes [of Greco-Roman society] normally instructed the head of the household how to "rule" or "govern" his wife, rather than how to love her. Paul is certainly among the minority of ancient writers in that he devotes more space to the exhortations of husbands to love in Ephesians 5 than to that of wives to submit. In our culture, his exhortation to wives to submit stands out more strongly; in his culture, the exhortation to husbands to love, rather than the normal advice to rule the home, would have stood out more strongly. Further . . . he does not urge the husband to inculcate submission in his wife. Paul's only instructions to the husband are to serve her as Christ served the

church, and, since husband and wife are "one flesh" (Gen. 2:24), to love her as he would his own body.[12]

Paul does not tell wives to *obey* their husbands as he tells slaves to obey their masters, and children their parents (Eph. 6:1–9; also Col. 3:20–22); he only tells wives to submit, as believers are to submit to one another and the church to Christ (Eph. 5:21, 24). In Paul's instructions to husbands and wives, he "avoids the nuances of 'obedience' and 'ruling,' but he does not mind calling on wives to submit or husbands to love, because this was behavior that should indeed characterize all Christians."[13]

Unlike the husband's love and the wife's submission, the husband's rule of the wife is not commanded in Scripture—probably because, unlike love and submission, it is not particularly an outworking of Christlike character. It is, rather, what society at that time expected a husband to do. The Bible does not require us to conclude that the husband's rule of the wife in that culture is also what God demands of a man as a matter of spiritual principle.

The description of the husband's role in Ephesians 5:25–31 indicates that the wife's submission "is not a one-sided submission, but a reciprocal relationship. . . . To give oneself up to death for the beloved is a more extreme expression of devotion than the wife is called on to make."[14] Culturally, the husband ruled the wife. But spiritually, he was to respect her as an equal, care for her as he cares for his own body, and nurture her as Christ does the church—all in the context of a loving relationship of mutual submission.

Paul summarizes his exhortations in the final verse of the passage: A husband should love his wife and a wife should respect her husband (Eph. 5:33). Any hint of the husband ruling his wife and the wife obeying her husband is conspicuously absent in this summarizing statement. It is far from apparent that Paul's intent in this passage is to establish a spiritual principle of husbandly rule and wifely obedience. Such a conclusion would require much more than what is provided in the text alone.

What Paul describes in Ephesians 5:21–33 is not a role relationship of two functionaries performing their respective job descriptions within a hierarchical authority structure. Rather, it is a relationship that flexes and flows with the mutual, submissive love that follows always and only from husband and wife being filled with the Holy Spirit (Eph. 5:18–21).

Why the Emphasis on Wives' Submission?

In New Testament times, women were well aware of their legal obligation to be submissive to their husbands' civil authority. Why, then, did the apostles Paul and Peter emphasize the need for wives to be submissive? It seems there was both a spiritual reason and a cultural reason for this. In Ephesians 5:22–24, wives are told that they should submit to their husbands because the husband is to the wife as Christ is to the church; that is, he loves her, looks out for her, and gives up his own life for the sake of her welfare. This gives wives' submission a spiritual context, redeeming it from being merely a legal obligation. Women with believing husbands have a new, spiritual reason to be submissive. Their husbands are supposed to have the same loving, self-giving concern for them that Christ has for the church. A wife has nothing to fear, nothing to resent, if her husband loves her as Christ loves the church.

This reason for a wife's submission is still applicable to us today. Even in our modern society of equal rights, men possess a cultural clout, a social if not legal authority, that is greater than that of women. A wife needs to guard against resentment of her husband's greater freedom and social power, and to remain selflessly disposed toward her husband, with her heart open to receive the ministry of his love for her. Biblically, a wife's submission is not an end in itself, not a unilateral and permanent subordination of one partner to the other. It is a means to the end of a marriage characterized by equality, mutuality, oneness, and fellowship. The exhortation to the husband to lay down his life for his wife, to give up his male power and prerogative for the wife's benefit rather than to use it for his benefit, is likewise pertinent even today. And in doing this, the husband completes the circle of mutual submission and love that characterizes a godly marriage.

It was also for a cultural reason that the New Testament writers stressed the need for women to submit themselves willingly to their husbands, whether or not their husbands were believers. A wife's obedience to her husband was required by both Jewish and Roman law, and was the generally accepted cultural norm of ancient societies.[15] Christian wives were to submit to their husbands for the same reason that all believers were to submit to the civil governing authorities and slaves to their masters (see 1 Peter 2:12–3:7). Christians needed to conduct themselves as respectable and responsible members of society, so that non-Christians would see in their good behavior the goodness and glory of God. "For the sake of their witness and their survival, Paul portrayed Christian ethics in terms that would best communicate to their culture the moral superiority of Christianity."[16] Because submission is a Christlike virtue that all believers should practice, the New Testament writers readily admonished Christian wives to be submissive; but they stopped short of admonishing husbands to rule.

The concern for social propriety and Christian witness is not irrelevant for wives today. For example, it is still the cultural convention for a wife to take the last name of her husband. A married couple who have different last names are likely to be regarded askance by the conservative element; to some people, such a practice hints darkly at radical feminist ideology or of living together without benefit of matrimony. Although it is not wrong or sinful in itself for a Christian married woman to keep her maiden name, it is possible that, in some circumstances, it could mar the credibility of the couple's Christian witness. Therefore, it may be advisable for a wife to follow the cultural convention on this, even when she and her husband do not agree with the underlying premise of the convention (that in marrying, a woman's identity is subsumed under that of her husband's). In the New Testament church, it was not merely advisable but necessary for wives to submit to their husbands' civil authority, even though the law's underlying premise (of women's spiritual and intellectual inferiority) was clearly unbiblical. Submission in itself is certainly not unbiblical, and when it becomes mutual between husband and wife, then so much the better.

Submission and Domesticity in Titus 2 and 1 Timothy 5

Understanding the New Testament concern for purity and propriety helps clarify the meaning of Paul's words in Titus 2:3–5, where he encourages women to be submissive to their husbands and to busy themselves in domestic pursuits "so that no one will malign the word of God" (v. 5). In the context, he also instructs old men, young men, and slaves to behave with integrity and propriety, "so that those who oppose you may be ashamed because they have nothing bad to say about us" (v. 8), and "so that in every way they [i.e., Christian slaves] will make the teaching about God our Savior attractive" (v. 10).

Those who advocate rigid gender roles point to Titus 2:3–5 as evidence that a woman's place should always and only be in the home, serving the needs of her family. Therefore, she ought not occupy herself with vocational activities unrelated to homemaking. But this is not the governing principle of the text; the main point, rather, is that women should learn to be "self-controlled and pure," as opposed to being busybodies who spend their time slandering others and getting drunk on wine. The issue here is the need to live a life that is above reproach. For women in Greco-Roman culture, that meant being managers of their homes, loving their children, and loving and submitting to their husbands. Paul contrasts this with being a busybody, gossiping, and getting drunk (see also 1 Tim. 5:13–14), because this was a probable alternative for the woman in ancient Greco-Roman society who did not occupy herself responsibly with household management as a wife and mother.

There *are,* however, a variety of responsible and respectable vocational options for women in our society today—options that did not exist for women during New Testament times. The modern-day application of Paul's principle in this passage is not that women ought not pursue work outside the home, but that, for example, homemakers who are addicted to talk shows and soap operas should begin to use their time and talents responsibly—whether in the home or outside it. The management of a household today does not normally require the amount of effort and industry that it did in earlier times, and so for this reason also it is not irresponsible, unbiblical, or a "bad witness" for Christian wives to make something other than homemaking their primary vocation—provided, of course, that children's needs are not neglected. We do not need to re-create the culture of ancient societies in order to lead lives consistent with biblical teaching. We need, instead, to understand the governing principle behind specific biblical instructions, and then to apply that principle appropriately to our own lives.

Despite Paul's insistence on social propriety for Christians, and despite the cultural authority of the man in ancient society, he avoids instructing men to rule their wives. Quite the contrary, in fact. In 1 Timothy 5:13–14, a passage similar to Titus 2:3–5, Paul tells women to manage, or to rule, their households. The term used here clearly denotes authority. Even in the patriarchal Greco-Roman world, a woman's place in her home was to be a place of authority. In 1 Timothy 3:4 and 12, Paul also tells the deacons and elders (who probably were men at that time) to manage, or rule, their households, and to govern their children well.[17] And children are told to obey *both* parents in Ephesians 6:1 and Colossians 3:20. The equal authority of husband and wife over their children was also affirmed in Old Testament Law (Lev. 19:3, Deut, 5:16, 21:18–21). Biblically, husband and wife are both to have authority over their household and their children.

Submission and Sarah's Obedience in 1 Peter 3:1–7

Peter expresses his desire for Christians to behave in a socially irreproachable manner when he says, "Live such good lives among the pagans that, though they accuse you of doing wrong, they may see your good deeds and glorify God on the day he visits us" (1 Peter 2:12). He then proceeds to exhort believers to be submissive to the civil government, and slaves to their masters; for Christ is our example (2:22–24). And, "in the same way"—that is, in the same Christlike spirit of submission—wives are to be submissive to their husbands, so that by their blameless behavior their unbelieving husbands may be encouraged to accept Christ. This wifely submission is described in 1 Peter 3:4 as a "gentle and quiet spirit." Peter is speaking here not only of the fulfillment of a legal obligation, but also of an inner attitude of Christlike servanthood.

The women with unbelieving husbands to whom Peter directs his exhortation had already been unsubmissive to their husbands' authority when they rejected their husbands' pagan gods in favor of Jesus Christ.[18] Because submission to God always takes precedence over submission to civil authorities, Peter approved this sort of unsubmissive behavior. However, the refusal of these wives to submit to their husbands' religious beliefs made it that much more important for them to be submissive in other areas of life, in the hope that their "gentle and quiet spirit" would win their husbands to Christ. William Barclay explains that

> Peter's advice to wives is six times as long as his advice to husbands . . . because the wife's problem was far more difficult than that of the husband. If a husband became a Christian, he would automatically bring his wife with him into the Church, and there would be no problem. . . . For a wife to change her religion, while her husband did not, was unthinkable. In Greek civilization the duty of the woman was "to remain indoors and to be obedient to her husband." . . . Under Roman law a woman had no rights. . . . When she was under her father she was under the patria potestas, the father's power, which gave the father even the right of life and death over her; and when she married she passed equally into the power of her husband. She was entirely subject to her husband, and completely at his mercy. . . . The whole attitude of ancient civilization was that no woman could dare to make any decision for herself. What, then, must have been the problems of the wife who became a Christian while her husband remained faithful to the ancestral gods?[19]

First Peter 3:1–6 cannot be understood to be advocating a wife's submission to her husband's spiritual authority, for the lack of these women's submission to their husbands' authority in the spiritual dimension is deemed a good thing in this context. Peter is urging wives to submit to their husbands' *civil* authority, not to their authority in spiritual matters. Because this text is directed to wives of unbelieving husbands, it cannot be used as a proof text for a spiritualized "chain of command," whereby the husband decides what God's will is and the wife is obliged to obey his decisions.

To illustrate the wifely submission to which he urges Christian women, Peter refers to Sarah, who "obeyed Abraham and called him her master" (v. 6). Like all illustrations, this one is not precise at every point. As Keener observes, "Although Peter explicitly advocates only 'submission' (v. 1), he cites Sarah as an example even of 'obedience,' which was what Roman male society demanded of their wives."[20] Also, Peter is speaking primarily to wives of unbelieving husbands, yet Sarah's husband was a believer.

It is not entirely clear how much of Sarah's stated behavior Peter is urging specifically upon the wives to whom he is speaking. He does not say, "You are Sarah's daughters if you also obey your husband and call him your master." Rather, Peter says, "You are her daughters if you do what is right and do not give way to fear" (v. 6b). It would be going beyond the evidence in this passage to conclude that wifely obedience to husbandly authority is the universal, spiritual principle governing Peter's words. Rather, it seems that the fundamental principle here is that believing women (and men, for that matter) should imitate Christ in their submissive spirit and resolute righteousness in the face of persecution and hostility from those outside the faith. (This was particularly pertinent for women who were in the difficult circumstance of being married to unbelievers.)

A Christlike attitude of submissiveness may or may not lead to acts of obedience, depending on the requirements of the situation. But since in Roman society obedience was required of slaves to masters, wives to husbands, and everyone to the civil governors, obedience probably was entailed by the submission that Peter urged upon the recipients of this letter. Nonetheless, the emphasis here is on having a submissive attitude and demeanor, rather than on simply fulfilling the obligation of civil obedience.[21]

In any case, the sort of submission Sarah exemplifies is not as extreme as it may sound. The reference to Sarah calling Abraham her "lord" or "master" (depending on the translation) does not mean that their marriage was akin to a master–slave relationship. "When Peter refers to the master of a slave . . . he uses another term, *despotēs* (2:18), which shows that that is not what he is thinking about in this verse."[22] Keener notes that "one should not read too much into Sarah's calling her husband 'lord' here . . . it was a polite way to address someone of higher authority or one to whose status one wished to defer."[23] The term is probably intended here as a title of honor and respect, similar to the term "sir." Millard Erickson points out that the feminine of the Hebrew term meaning "lord" or "master" is used to describe Sarah's relationship to Abraham in Genesis 20:3.[24] Interestingly, the only time the Old Testament records Sarah referring to her husband as "master" (Gen. 18:12) is when she is talking to herself and Abraham is not even around to hear her!

The word translated "obeyed" in 1 Peter 3:6 can also be rendered "to listen." In Acts 12:13 this term is translated "hearken" (KJV), "listen" (Berkeley), and "answer" (NIV, NASB, NRSV); in Romans 10:16, it is translated "heed" (NASB), "listen" (Jerusalem, Berkeley), and "obey" (KJV, NRSV). The Hebrew equivalent to this word is used in Genesis 16:2 and 21:12, where Abraham is said to have "listened" or "agreed" to what Sarah said—meaning that he did the thing she asked him to do. The second time he "listened to" and obeyed Sarah, it was because God told him to do so.[25] Sarah was not a servile spouse who did nothing but what her husband asked; rather, she had her own ideas about things, and on at least two occasions it was Abraham who obeyed Sarah. The idea that Peter's words should be understood in light of the fact that Abraham also obeyed Sarah is not a feminist observation of recent origin. In his commentary on this passage, church father John Chrysostom writes, "This is what I want to point out, that both he obeyed her in all things and she him."[26]

Sarah is commended for her submission and obedience, but even in the highly patriarchal culture of their time, Abraham was not averse to obeying Sarah's wishes. Whatever the exact nature of Sarah and Abraham's relationship, it evidently was not one of unilateral rule and submission. Peter emphasizes the wife's submission (exemplified by Sarah's obedience) for cultural reasons; but this does not preclude "reciprocal obedience in the sense of listening to one another and supporting one another's wishes where they do not conflict with obedience to God."[27] Submission, deference, obedience, and self-sacrifice should flow back and forth in a marriage from one partner to the other as love takes its God-given, God-blessed course.

Peter also has a word for believing husbands. They too, "in the same way," are to exemplify the submissive spirit of Christ by exercising consideration and respect for their wives (1 Peter 3:7). Peter gives two reasons why husbands should behave in this way. First, women were in a weaker position socially than men and their welfare depended upon their husbands' considerate treatment of them. Second, women and men are spiritual heirs together, equal inheritors of God's gracious gift of life. In acknowledging women's full religious equality with men, Peter deviates radically from the traditional Jewish thought of his time.[28] Concerning this text, Barclay points out that "women did not share in the worship of the Greeks and the Romans."

Similarly, "there was no part for women in Jewish worship. Here in Christianity there emerged a revolutionary principle. Women have equal spiritual rights; granted that, the whole relationship between the sexes was changed."[29]

In terms of social status, women were inferior to men; but spiritually they are men's equals, and it is the spiritual reality that should guide the behavior of Christian husbands. The exhortation to husbands in 1 Peter 3:7 echoes the understanding of headship outlined in Ephesians 5:21–33. The husband is to use the resources and benefits that are at his disposal in order to serve and build up his wife, thus enhancing her life in ways that would not otherwise be possible.

Slavery and Wife Abuse in Light of 1 Peter 2 and 3

The exhortations in 1 Peter 2 and 3 should not be taken as timeless commands for Christian behavior. Few would care to argue today that anyone enslaved in any sense to an abusive master should always simply endure it, as Peter advises slaves in 2:18–20. Rather, in keeping with the theme of the entire epistle, these words should be understood as the apostle's specific advice to Christians caught in circumstances of oppression and persecution. Different times call for different applications of Christlike submission. Lee Anna Starr observes that if

> 1 Peter 3:1–6 is binding on subsequent generations; if it is an entailment, then we must face the fact that 1 Peter 2:13 [obedience to the king and other authorities], and 2:18 [slaves' obedience to masters], are entailments also. We cannot generalize the one and restrict the others as to time and place. We cannot abjure the "divine right of kings" and hold to the "divine right" of husbands; we cannot manumit the slave and drive an awl through the ear of the wife.[30]

In other words, Peter's instructions must be understood in light of the cultural conditions of the Christians to whom they were addressed. The principle behind his words remains true: Christians ought to submit to those in authority over them—as long as it does not entail disobedience to God (see Acts 4:19–20). But this general principle needs to be applied differently in different cultures and by no means demands that we reinstitute today the authority structures of ancient societies.

Traditionalists, however, believe that the basic principle behind Peter's command to wives to be submissive is not simply that believers should submit to those in authority, but that husbands ought to be in authority over their wives. If this be so, then the basic principle of the preceding verses (1 Peter 2:18–19), where slaves are commanded to obey their masters, must be that some humans ought to claim ownership of other humans, or, at least, that such an arrangement is morally legitimate. In other words, if 1 Peter 2:13–3:7 is to be interpreted as teaching the principle that a man has the divine right to rule his wife, this passage must also be interpreted as teaching the principle that some humans have the right to own other humans.[31] It would be more consistent with overall biblical teaching to regard the instructions to both slaves *and* wives, not as divine approbation of the authority structures that demanded their submission, but as the godly response to the existence of those authority structures at that time.

Traditionalists typically object to the slavery/marital hierarchy analogy by pointing out that God did not ordain slavery from the beginning as he did the institution of marriage (see Gen. 2:24 and Matt. 19:4–6).[32] But this observation, while true enough, misses the point. The question is whether male rule in marriage was ordained from the beginning, not whether marriage itself was ordained by God. No one is disputing the institution of marriage per se; the interpretational dispute concerns whether the dynamic of rule and obedience is an essential, God-ordained element of marriage.

Perhaps some traditionalists miss this distinction because they see hierarchy as fundamental to the meaning and essence of the sexual difference and, hence, to the marriage relationship. But while the law of rule and obedience is the very essence of slavery, without which there can be no institution of slavery, the law of rule and obedience is not a necessary element of the marriage relationship. Marriage not only can exist without hierarchy, it thrives without it! To regard the master-slave hierarchy as culturally relative is also to regard slavery as a culturally relative institution. But to regard the husband–wife hierarchy as culturally relative is *not* to regard the institution of marriage as culturally relative.

In rendering transcultural the authority structure of marital hierarchy (and, by implication, slavery), the traditionalist interpretation of 1 Peter 2 and 3 also renders transcultural the nature of the submission that Peter considered appropriate for Christian wives and slaves living in the cultures of that time. Just as slaves are to follow the example of Christ by submitting to the authority of their masters even when they are treated harshly and unjustly (2:18–23), so also "wives, in the same way" (3:1), are to be submissive even when their husbands are harsh and abusive. If, as the traditionalist interpretation would have it, this text is a direct, transcultural statement of wifely virtue defined as obedient submission to the husband's authority, then this "suffering in silence" sort of submission must also be required of wives today. Although Peter clearly tells husbands not to act harshly (3:7), his only command to wives is to submit. Even if the husband does act harshly, the wife is still to submit.

The implications of this hermeneutical perspective are borne out in much traditionalist teaching on the subject. James and Phyllis Alsdurf report that Bill Gothard (one of the most rigid "chain of command" teachers) believes that this passage requires abused wives today to "suffer for righteousness' sake," and not to rebel against their circumstances.[33] James Hurley says that Peter's instructions are not culturally relative but are as applicable to the present as they were to their original audience. And he recognizes that Peter is speaking of submission even under oppressive conditions, and of a wife living "a godly life even with an abusive pagan husband," which demonstrates "the willing suffering and love of Christ for his church." Hurley admits that "it is not an easy calling which Peter lays before the Christian wife of an unbeliever!"[34] Presumably, if a wife is required always to submit (as a universal principle of righteousness) to a cruel and unloving non-Christian husband, she must also submit to a cruel and unloving "Christian" husband.

Similarly, Wayne Grudem—who also sees these commands as "absolute" rather than culturally relative—notes that wives are instructed in this passage to be submissive to husbands who are harsh and unkind as well as to those who are good.[35] He qualifies his remarks with an endnote, stating that the Bible does not condone and even forbids the harsh and abusive treatment of wives by husbands, and that churches should try to protect wives in these situations.[36] However, this qualification does not specifically sanction abused wives' resistance to hostile husbands; women whose churches do not intervene in their defense are apparently without any biblically sanctioned recourse. [37]

In view of the potentially harmful teaching that can easily follow from the traditionalist interpretation of Peter's words to wives, it is crucial that this passage be understood in its cultural context. This text is a historically specific application of the universal principle that believers should live blamelessly according to the standards of their society, which includes being in submission to those who are in authority over them (insofar as it does not entail disobedience to God). Such submission was especially important for the recipients of Peter's epistle because of the need for Christians to be good witnesses in a culture that was hostile to Christianity. They needed to live in a way that was above reproach, so as to counter the cultural suspicions that Christianity was socially subversive. Moreover, in an authoritarian society such as theirs, resistance to unjust authority was not a viable option. In the case of the believers to whom Peter was writing, an attempt at resistance would have done more harm than good. The fact that wives were under the civil authority of their husbands, just as slaves were ruled by their masters and all members of society by the governing authorities, is the context of Peter's instructions to wives and is crucial to discerning the intent of the entire passage (2:13–3:7).

The reasons that wives in Peter's day needed to submit to their husbands' rule—even when it was unkind and oppressive—are no longer applicable. Christianity is not considered socially subversive today, and husbands have no civil authority over their wives. A woman living with an abusive husband has many choices in a modern, democratic society that wives in Peter's time did not. Whereas at that time it probably would have been unwise or impossible for a woman to resist harsh treatment from her husband, today the wisest choice normally would be for a woman to find a way out of such a situation.

However, we should not go so far as to assume that Peter believed the cultural situation at that time required Christian wives to submit to treatment that was physically harmful or dangerous. Peter was admonishing wives and slaves to bear up in a Christlike manner in situations from which they had no escape. He was not commanding wives and slaves to choose abuse when they had the option of seeking freedom from abuse. Moreover, physical violence against wives was quite rare in New Testament times, so it is unlikely Peter even had this in mind.[38] Because Roman law did not allow a man to beat his wife,[39] physical abuse would not have been included in the husband's legal rights to which a wife was obliged to submit. Peter also states that he does not want women to live in fear (3:6). The submission to which he exhorts women, therefore, would not entail submission to circumstances that are downright frightening. Nonetheless, biblical counsel to women who are living with abuse in modern times can differ greatly, depending on whether the instructions in this passage are interpreted as culturally relative or timeless and absolute.

Summarizing Biblical Submission

The New Testament texts instructing women to submit to their husbands were saying nothing new in the cultures of that time; women knew that they were socially and legally obligated to be submissive. However, the instructions to husbands to be considerate, respectful, loving, and self-sacrificial toward their wives were revolutionary and countercultural. Because these exhortations to husbands were not a reflection of cultural values, we may take them to be transcultural and universal. But we cannot justifiably assume that the cultural setting of the New Testament wherein wives were required to submit to their husbands' authority necessarily reflects a universal, God-ordained order for marriage.[40] Gordon Fee and Douglas Stuart explain that

> The degree to which a New Testament writer agrees with a cultural situation in which there is only one option increases the possibility of the cultural relativity of such a position. Thus, for example, homosexuality was both affirmed and condemned by writers in antiquity, yet the New Testament takes a singular position against it. On the other hand, attitudes toward slavery as a system or toward the status and role of women were basically singular; no one denounced slavery as an evil and women were held to be basically inferior to men. . . . [T]o the degree to which [the New Testament writers] reflect the prevalent cultural attitudes in these matters they are thereby reflecting the only cultural option in the world around them.[41]

If the New Testament exhortations for wives' submission were intended as a universal pronouncement legislating husbandly authority and wifely obedience for all believers for all time, then we would expect to find, along with the commands for the submission of wives, corollary commands for husbands to take charge and lead. But this element in the equation is conspicuously missing.

If, on the other hand, the New Testament emphasis on the submission of wives to husbands was occasioned primarily out of concern for culturally appropriate Christian behavior, and not as an expression of a universal, spiritual principle of God-ordained male authority, we would expect to see counterbalancing instructions to men to treat their wives as their spiritual equals. This we do see. In the most extended passage on this subject (Eph. 5:21–33), the admonition to husbands to love, respect, and honor their wives is lengthier and more detailed than the admonition to wives to submit.

While we see in Scripture a concern that husbands who have legal authority over their wives not abuse that authority, we do not see any scriptural license for husbands who have *no* legal authority to assume *spiritual* authority over their wives and to wield it in the name of God. The New Testament speaks of the spiritual equality of women and men (Gal. 3:28; 1 Peter 3:7), and it recognizes the husband's cultural authority over the wife. But it does not authorize the husband to assume spiritual authority over his wife, nor does it sanction or validate the husband's cultural authority by specifically telling him to rule his wife. All of this strongly suggests that whatever husbandly authority may have been assumed by the New Testament emphasis on wifely submission, it was a civil function, not a spiritual function. Those who claim the New Testament mandates the husband's spiritual authority over the wife are reading these texts as though they were written directly to people in the late twentieth century rather than the first century.

The general intent of the apostles Paul and Peter in writing these passages, it seems, was to advocate conformity to cultural custom insofar as it was consistent with biblical principles, so that believers would be seen by the outside world as being above reproach. Blatant rebellion against social codes would have hindered rather than helped their Christian witness. It is a biblical principle that people should be subject to the authorities; hence, believers are exhorted to do so. But a wife's submission to the civil authority of the unbelieving husband should not extend to the acceptance of his religious ideas, for this would be to disobey the Lord. It is also a biblical principle that people should be loving, submissive, and respectful in their attitudes toward one another, and to this all believers are admonished. Out of concern for cultural propriety, special emphasis is put on the submission of wives, but this does not entail a universal command to husbands to rule their wives. Rather, the wife's submission is one aspect of the mutual submission that should exist between a husband and wife.

By contrast, the idea that one believer should have authoritarian (absolute and final) rule over another believer is antithetical to the biblical teaching of Christlike submission and the equality of all persons under God; therefore, husbands are *not* told to rule their wives. If anything, they are told not to, but rather to treat their wives as they treat themselves (Eph. 5:28), and to respect them as "joint heirs" of their spiritual inheritance in Christ (1 Peter 3:7). Rather than endorsing male rule, the exhortations to husbands to love their wives with a self-sacrificial love serve to mitigate the culturally sanctioned authority of men over their wives. The instructions to husbands reflect the biblical truth of woman's essential, spiritual equality with man, the oneness and unity of husband and wife, and the mutual submissiveness that should characterize the marriage relationship.

Even within the context of a culture in which men legally had full authority over their wives, the biblical picture of marriage stresses mutual submission, love, and respect, rather than a structure of authority and obedience. Not only is the wife to yield her rights and life to her husband, the husband is to yield his life and rights to his wife.

A Marriage of Equality

Many people seem to have a hard time imagining how a marriage could exist without a chain of command. We hear comments such as, "A ship can only have one captain," and "Someone has to make the final decision." Very frequently equalitarian marriage is perceived as role reversal, wherein the wife is dominant and the husband passive—which is precisely what a marriage of equals is not! In view of such confusion and consternation, a practical word of clarification on the subject seems to be in order.

How is a marriage of mutual submission different from a traditionalist marriage? The answer to this question can be found in a conversation I had with an associate pastor who holds to male leadership in the home but not in the church (not an uncommon position, by the way).

When I asked her how her "chain of command" marriage would be different from my "mutual submission" marriage, she told me that she would not accept a request for public ministry without her husband's approval. I responded that this is not the difference, for I also would do no ministry without my husband's approval. But, I added, neither does he accept offers of ministry without my approval. "Ah," she said, "there is the difference. My husband pretty much has free rein."

This woman's initial understanding of equalitarian marriage illustrates the paucity of categories many people have in assessing the options. It is commonly believed that either women submit unilaterally to their husbands, or women do not submit at all. However, the difference an equalitarian marriage makes is not primarily in the wife's behavior, but in the husband's—as he learns to adopt a habitual attitude of respect, deference, and humility toward his wife. Over the years my husband and I have learned the spiritual importance of our submission to one another. One time Doug went ahead on a ministry project even though I told him I did not think it was wise for him to do it at that time. It turned out to be quite an ordeal, from which we both suffered considerably, and which did not seem to have God's full measure of blessing and protection. This experience taught us a valuable lesson: Spiritual power and protection for ministry are available in full measure only when husband and wife are in full agreement.

In a marriage where each partner maintains an attitude of submission toward the other, each will take turns "obeying" the other, yet without either taking authority over the other. Neither submission nor obedience will be unilateral; both will flow in both directions. On more than one occasion I have done something simply because my husband wished me to do it, or I have not done something simply because he wished me not to do it. In fact, I do not believe I ever have or ever would blatantly contradict his earnest and loving desire for what he believes is best for me to do. So far, this sounds a lot like a traditionalist marriage—except that we do not stop at this point. He, too, submits to my convictions and concerns about what is best for him and for us. In a marriage of mutual submission, husband and wife defer to each other's desires and yield to each other's judgments. There is a natural give and take, an ebb and flow that is unprogrammed and undiagrammed.

This should not be regarded as a particularly difficult or unusual arrangement; it often occurs naturally. The better the relationship and the deeper the friendship of a married couple, the less likely it is that they will be concerned about their respective roles and statuses. When each partner regards the other as equally deserving of respect, and each loves the other wholeheartedly, role equalization and mutual submission tend to follow as a matter of course.[42] There probably are many more Christian marriages that are equalitarian in practice (if not in theory) than many traditionalists would like to acknowledge!

But—everyone always wants to know—who will make the final decision in a marriage if no one person is in charge? The simple answer is that husband and wife together will make all decisions that affect them both. Why does it often seem so difficult to imagine such a thing? Perhaps it is because we forget that marriage is first and foremost a relationship, not a business enterprise that requires officers and managers (although even in business two people can be co-managers with equal rank). We fear that if we remove structured hierarchy from a marriage, angry anarchy will be the result. Such fears are unfounded. If each partner in a marriage is lovingly committed to the welfare of the other, and is devoted to making decisions that will be for the good of the other, then shared decision making will be in no danger of becoming a power struggle between competing selfish demands for the fulfillment of one's own rights, needs, and desires.

How does this work out in practical reality? Again, the answer is surprisingly simple. Until both partners believe a certain course of action is God's will for their lives, that course of action will not be taken. But what about those rare instances in which one thing or another must be done immediately, and it is impossible to wait for agreement and clarity of understanding? Then, whoever will be most affected by the decision or is best qualified to make an informed decision should probably carry the most weight in the decision-making process. This would not occur because the "informed" partner tells the other partner what to do, but because the less informed partner defers to the other out of respect for the other's judgment and concern for the other's best interests. Marilyn Quayle offers a slightly altered version of this rule for a successful marriage of equals. She says that whenever she and Dan disagree (which doesn't happen often), "whoever feels more strongly about an issue wins."[43]

Usually, however, decisions do not need to be made immediately, and a husband and wife can wait until they reach agreement before making their decision. This is the surest way to hear clearly from God so that his will can be obeyed. When decisions are made according to what only one partner (the husband) believes is God's will, then the family is more likely to get off track. For example, once when Doug and I were in the throes of indecision as to whether we should remain in our present church or begin to attend elsewhere, we reached a point of definite disagreement. He decided he wanted to go to another church, but I did not feel at all comfortable with the church he had chosen. I wondered, was my discomfort my own problem, or was it an indication that this church was not God's will for us? In my distress, I even wondered if I should simply submit to my husband as the spiritual authority in this matter, as the traditionalist view would have it. Failing to arrive at either answers or agreement, we waited and we prayed. Finally, and suddenly, God made it clear to both of us that we should remain in our present church. After we made this decision, time testified to the rightness of it. We were very grateful that we persevered in our distress and indecision until God confirmed his will to both of us.

Traditionalists often fail to see that there is another possibility besides the roles and rules of traditional marriage and the secular feminist marriage of two self-centered individuals. A marriage of mutual submission holds to an equalitarian relationship between husband and wife, not because each demands equal rights, but because each loves the other so completely and selflessly that neither would have the other be deprived of any opportunity that would help that person grow into maturity and fullness of life. Each partner's personal rights and liberties are protected by the other, and both are set free to be who they are in Christ. And the rule book is irrelevant.

As Gretchen Gaebelein Hull observes, a unilateral husbandly rule and wifely submission "undermines the biblical ideal of the 'one flesh' union in marriage. A system built on a dominant/subordinate concept of male-female roles will by its very nature discourage any deep relationship between man and wife. Truly meaningful relationships only occur where both parties participate equally in all aspects of their relationship." This is well illustrated by comparing David's friendship with Jonathan to his relationship with his assorted and numerous wives and concubines. David's lament upon Jonathan's death is quite telling: "I grieve for you, Jonathan my brother. . . . Your love for me was wonderful, more wonderful than that of women" (2 Sam. 1:26). Hull points out that "such a close friendship was possible because David and Jonathan were equals, whereas David's use of his wives and concubines indicates his inability to accept their equal personhood."[44]

On a "20/20" television program about marriage and housework, it was stated that experts have identified one problem that is almost universal in troubled marriages, namely, the assumption that the man's life—his career, his plans, his desires—comes first.[45] Unfortunately, the secular solution to this problem is couched not in terms of mutual submission, but of equal rights. Marriage is seen not as an opportunity to learn loving sacrifice for one another, but as an opportunity—indeed, a right—to have one's own needs met by one's spouse.

Equality in marriage *can* mean that women become as selfish and demanding toward their mates as men often have been. The inevitable result of two self-centered partners is a breakdown of the relationship. But equality can also mean that men begin to act as selflessly and sacrificially toward their mates as women have been expected to do. The inevitable result of two self-giving partners is a long and happy union. The former sort of marital equality typifies secular feminism; the latter describes biblical equality (as well as marriages that are hierarchical in theory but not in practice).

Love not only recognizes the other person's rights, it acknowledges and obeys the call to sacrifice. Love transforms a sterile arrangement of roles and rules into a warm, give-and-take personal relationship in which both partners not only are given opportunity to exercise their own rights of personhood, but frequently will lay down some of those rights in order to facilitate the fulfillment of the other person's rights. In marriage, self-fulfillment is not possible apart from self-sacrifice. As each partner sacrifices for the other, each is fulfilled. Women who are wives and mothers are no strangers to the self-fulfillment that comes through self-sacrifice. But they often are deprived of the self-fulfillment that comes through their husbands' self-sacrificial love for them. When the one-way submission street is opened up to two-way traffic, then the relationship—and the persons in it—will be opened up to grow in a way that would not otherwise be possible.

In an essay written by a man who had decided to forego his seminary presidency in favor of caring for his wife, who was stricken with Alzheimer's disease, an oncologist was quoted as commenting, "Almost all women stand by their men; very few men stand by their women."[46] Mutual submission has men acting with the same sacrificial devotion to their spouses that traditionally has been expected from women.

Self-sacrifice ought not be an alien concept for people who have already given their lives to Christ in response to the sacrifice of his own life for us. Only as a husband and wife are filled with the self-giving love of Christ is a marriage of mutual submission possible. James Houston observes that apart from Christ, "Eros remains fixed as acquisitive love, whose aim is simply self-satisfaction." Such love "is wholly incompatible with Christian love, which is identified as self-giving—an inconceivable reality outside the Christian faith."[47]

In the end, there is but one rule for a husband and wife: the rule of Christlike love. From this, all that is good and godly for a marriage will follow.[48]

8

The Bible and Women in Leadership

he New Testament states that women are not to speak in the church, nor may they teach or have authority over men (1 Cor. 14:34–35; 1 Tim. 2:11–15). That should about take care of the matter, if it were not for the fact that the New Testament also teaches that both male and female are one in Christ as equal heirs of God (Gal. 3:26–28; 1 Peter 3:7). Why is it, then, that in the church—where spiritual status should be most apparent—the positions of men and women should be the most unequal? Why should the male be given the voice of authority in spiritual matters and the female be silenced and subordinated before the male's spiritual authority?

Compounding the apparent biblical contradiction is the fact that a number of women in the Bible did teach and speak authoritatively on spiritual matters. As Aida Besancon Spencer points out, "If even one woman could be found who was affirmed [in the Bible] as an apostle, a prophet, an evangelist, a pastor, or a teacher, then one could—one must—conclude that women have been given gifts from God for positions to which we now ordain people and for positions considered authoritative in the first-century church."[1]

Old Testament Women in Spiritual Leadership

There were female leaders and prophets even in the era of the old covenant: Miriam (Exod. 15:20; Micah 6:4), Deborah (Judg. 4–5), Huldah (2 Kings 22:14–20; 2 Chron. 34:11–33), Noadiah (Neh. 6:14), the wife of Isaiah (Isa. 8:3), and Anna (Luke 2:36). Traditionalists often try to explain that a ministry of such power and prominence as Deborah's was an exception to the rule of male authority in the Bible. But exceptions to rules occur in the natural and social realms; they do not occur in the realm of God's moral law. If God called Deborah to her ministry, female leadership cannot be said to violate moral principles ordained by God.

It seems clear, for two reasons, that Deborah was put in her position of civil and spiritual leadership by God. First, her leadership was clearly a spiritual blessing and a force for righteousness at a time of national crisis. Second, because she ruled in a highly patriarchal society and was not the wife or daughter of a ruler, we may safely surmise that she could not have been propelled into her position merely by cultural forces. God had a definite and purposeful hand in Deborah's rise to power, which shows that there is nothing inherently unfitting or immoral about a woman occupying a position of civil or spiritual authority.

Because there is no account in the New Testament of any woman wielding the high level of authority with which God entrusted Deborah in the Old Testament, the example of Deborah tends to be pushed aside when traditionalists propound the principle of God-ordained male authority that they believe is taught in the New Testament. (Apparently, women of the new covenant are under an even more restrictive law of male authority than were the women of the old covenant.) Deborah is regarded as a bizarre blip on the historical screen of universal male rule. Her leadership, in one way or another, is put into a different category than that of the male prophets and rulers of Israel. John Piper and Wayne Grudem believe that Deborah's leadership actually affirmed "the usual leadership of men" by serving as a rebuke to the men of Israel who should have had the courage to take on leadership of the nation themselves. They also insist that Deborah's gifting and calling by God does not necessarily make her an "ideal model for us to follow in every respect."[2]

Another traditionalist tactic is to construe Deborah's prophetic leadership of Israel as being less authoritative than that of the men who occupied the position of prophet. Thomas Schreiner, for example, finds significance in the fact that the Bible does not say Deborah prophesied in public but only in private, and that she did not actually lead men into battle as did the male judges of Israel. Schreiner also finds it significant that the Bible does not come right out and say that God raised up Deborah, as it does when speaking of the important male judges of Israel. He concludes that Deborah's rule "was different from that of the other judges in that she did not exercise leadership over men."[3]

Although male prophets of the Old Testament did utter public pronouncements, they were often reviled and ignored. Deborah, however, was sought out by the people of Israel, and her words of prophetic wisdom were respected and obeyed. There is no reason to believe that only women took her counsel as authoritative, or that her judgments pertained only to private matters and not to the public realm. Moreover, she was not only a prophet, but the judge, or ruler, of all Israel (Judg. 4:4). This puts Deborah's ministry—much more than that of the "public" male prophets—in line with the traditionalist concept of authority as a position that commands obedience.[4]

There is also no reason to believe that the level of Deborah's authority was not equal to that of the male rulers of Israel. Although she did not lead the men into battle herself, she directed the man who did. She would not have marched into battle with the male soldiers in any case. Being a woman, she was unsuited for and untrained in the battlefield skills of the ancient world. But her exclusion from active military duty did not make her spiritual and political leadership any less authoritative. As Stanley Grenz observes, "Schreiner's concern to harmonize the account with his male headship principle is foreign to the concern of the biblical author. Deborah commanded Barak to assemble the army. To suggest that this does not entail the exercise of authority over a man in an official capacity presses the text into a procrustean bed."[5]

Judges 2:16 clearly states that "the Lord raised up judges, who saved them." Surely this applies to all the judges of Israel, whether or not the account of their exploits specifically reiterates this point. As Merrill Unger notes, the judges of Israel acted, for the most part, as agents of the divine will, regents of the invisible King, holding their commission directly from Him or with His sanction. . . . As to the nature of the office, it appears to have resembled that of the Roman dictator, to which it has been compared, with this exception, that the dictator laid down his power as soon as the crisis that had called for its exercise had passed away; but the Hebrew judge remained invested with his high authority throughout his life. . . . The origin of their authority must in all cases be traced ultimately to Jehovah, owing to the very nature of the theocracy.[6]

This is the sort of position to which God called a woman—even before the new covenant in Christ did away with all spiritual distinctions between male and female! Deborah may have been the only female judge of Israel, but she was a judge, nonetheless, called by God to rule with both civil and spiritual authority. Those who wish to derogate the importance and authority of her rulership on account of her gender find no encouragement toward this end from the actual biblical text.

Huldah is another remarkable Old Testament prophet. King Josiah was one of Judah's few righteous kings, and during his reign the high priest "found" the Book of God's Law in the temple, where it apparently had been lost during the many years of apostasy and idolatry. When King Josiah became acquainted with the contents of the Book, he was horrified at how angry God must be at the nation's disobedience. He immediately told the high priest and some other men to go find a prophet who could tell them what to make of it all. So the men went directly to Huldah, not to Jeremiah or to any other male prophet of the period. Huldah spoke the word of the Lord to the men who had sought her out, her message was accepted as authoritative by the king, and, as a result, the nation was purged of idolatry and restored to obedience under the Law of God for the remainder of Josiah's reign.

It seems obvious that if the king specifically consulted and obeyed Huldah, she must have been regarded as an authority of considerable prominence and respect in spiritual matters. Nonetheless, Huldah, like Deborah, is dismissed by traditionalists as less authoritative than those whom the Bible records as prophesying publicly.[7] Perhaps it is not clear to the detractors of such powerful female ministry that because a "public" prophet in Old Testament times was neither appointed nor elected to the position, he had no "official" authority with which to command the obedience of others, so people were free to heed or to disregard his pronouncements. The closest a prophet could come to being "authorized" would be for a public official to seek out and accept as authoritative that person's prophetic word (as King Josiah did with Huldah). Moreover, since the "public" prophets, including Isaiah, were also sought out for private consultation, there is no reason to assume that Huldah's private counsel to King Josiah was the only sort of prophetic function she ever performed. She could well have prophesied publicly also.[8]

New Testament Women Who Ministered with Authority

The new covenant was instituted at the resurrection of Jesus Christ. God's first move after this momentous change in the spiritual order was to commission the women who had come to the empty grave with the ministry of proclaiming the Good News (the gospel) to the other believers (Matt. 28:1–10; Mark 16:1–7; Luke 24:1–10; John 20:11–18). This was God's clear refutation of the Jewish belief that women were liars and, hence, could not be trusted as witnesses.[9] It also was an intimation of the truth of Galatians 3:26–28. The old order, in which religious life was almost exclusively in the hands of free Jewish men, had given way to a new order, in which there should no longer be any distinction in spiritual roles or privileges between Jew or Gentile, slave or free, male or female. Under the old covenant, Jesus chose free Jewish males for his apostles. Under the new covenant, women were the first to be commissioned to preach the gospel message.

With the outpouring of the Holy Spirit at Pentecost, the gift of prophecy (speaking on behalf of God) became available equally to both male and female, according to the Old Testament prophecy of Joel that was applied by Peter to the New Testament age (Acts 2:17–18). The four daughters of Philip all had the gift of prophecy (Acts 21:8–9). It is clear from 1 Corinthians 11:4–5 that both men and women were praying and prophesying publicly in church meetings; the only restriction Paul gives is that women wear a head covering, which, in the context of ancient culture, addressed the issue of sexuality, not authority.[10]

The role of prophet was one of high status and authority, for the prophets spoke the word of God to the people, and, according to 1 Corinthians 14:3 and 31, their words served both to instruct and to encourage. Prophecy, as defined in this text, consists of "giving encouragement and hope as well as speaking to men in order to build them up in the faith," and is the "functional equivalent of authoritative teaching."[11]

Whenever the different gifts and ministries are mentioned in the New Testament there is no hint of any qualifications or limitations as to which groups of people are eligible for the leadership gifts and which are not. All the spiritual resources necessary for all the ministries are distributed by God's grace to various people without respect to race, class, or gender. In speaking of the different gifts and ministries, Paul states that "it is the same God who activates all of them in everyone [which includes both male and female]" (1 Cor. 12:6 NRSV).

A number of women who had leadership ministries are cited with approval in the New Testament. Priscilla and Aquila were a married couple, each of whom were very involved in teaching and pastoral ministry as fellow workers with Paul and as leaders of a church in their home (Rom. 16:3–5; 1 Cor. 16:19). Priscilla and Aquila offered doctrinal instruction to Apollos, a teacher and leader in the church, who received their instruction as authoritative—even though it came in large part from a woman (Acts 18:24–26).

The New Testament references to Priscilla and Aquila make it clear that, despite the male-dominant culture, Aquila was not the leader and Priscilla his assistant. In fact, of the seven times the two names are mentioned together, Priscilla is listed first five of those times (Acts 18:18–19, 26; Rom. 16:3; 2 Tim. 4:19). Because it was the custom to list the husband's name first, this reversal indicates Priscilla's importance in the minds of the New Testament writers Luke and Paul.[12] It also indicates that Priscilla was not teaching as a secondary partner under the "covering" of her husband's spiritual authority. If there were a universal spiritual principle requiring a woman to be subordinate to the teaching authority of the man, Priscilla would not have been referred to in terms indicating either her equality or her prominence in the Priscilla–Aquila teaching team.

Paul praises two apostles in Romans 16:7, a man named Andronicus and a woman named Junia (NRSV). In recent centuries translators and commentators have earnestly endeavored to explain that Junia was either not a woman or, if a woman, not an apostle but merely esteemed by the apostles. Early church fathers, however, acknowledged that the text indicates Junia was both a woman and an apostle. John Chrysostom wrote, "Oh! how great is the devotion of this woman, that she should be even counted worthy of the appellation of apostle!"[13] It wasn't until the thirteenth century or so that a commentator first took to referring to these two as "men." Junia's gender has been hotly contested ever since.[14] Her name, as well, has been tinkered with in the attempt to render it masculine rather than feminine; it appears in some translations as "Junias," which is assumed to be a contraction of a longer masculine name, such as Junianus. However, while Junia was a common Roman name for a woman in ancient times, there is little if any evidence of "Junias" appearing as a man's name during this period.[15]

As for whether Andronicus and Junia were apostles themselves or merely esteemed by the apostles, Craig Keener observes that it is

> unnatural to read the text as merely claiming that they had a high reputation with "the apostles." Since they were imprisoned with him, Paul knows them well enough to recommend them without appealing to the other apostles, whose judgment he never cites on such matters. . . . Paul nowhere limits the apostolic company to the Twelve plus himself, as some have assumed (see especially 1 Cor. 15:5–11). Those who favor the view that Junia was not a female apostle do so because of their prior assumption that women could not be apostles, not because of any evidence in the text.[16]

Piper and Grudem contend that even if Junia were a woman and an apostle, her ministry would not have carried much authority. Since Junia and Andronicus were evidently not in, or closely associated with, the "unique inner ring" of apostles, their apostleship would have consisted of an itinerant teaching ministry, which would have been "significant but not necessarily in the category of an authoritative governor of the churches like Paul."[17]

To say that a person's ministry carries less spiritual authority than that of the apostle Paul is not to say a great deal. None of the ministries that traditionalists want to reserve for men today are as authoritative as the apostleship of Paul. Moreover, Paul describes Junia's apostleship as "outstanding" or "prominent" (NRSV), which would seem to indicate something of more significance than Piper and Grudem allow. It is unwarranted to assume that Junia and Andronicus were not eyewitnesses of Jesus or closely associated with those who were. Many in the early church and among the church fathers believed that these two apostles were in this category.[18]

At any rate, it is both natural and customary to include Andronicus and Junia with those apostles who were not of the Twelve, but who—like the Twelve—were sent by Jesus Christ with the authority to preach the gospel and build up the church. The New Testament does not list the names of all the apostles outside the Twelve, but they include Paul, Barnabas, James the brother of Jesus, Andronicus, and Junia.[19] The New Testament also speaks of apostles in the nontechnical sense of messengers sent by a specific church for a specific mission. Second Corinthians 8:23 and Philippians 2:25 are the only instances in which Paul uses "apostle" in the simple sense of messenger or representative.[20] Yet this is the sort of ministry to which Piper and Grudem wish to consign Andronicus and Junia, for no apparent reason other than that the apostolic ministry of a woman must be construed as less authoritative than the pastor/elder ministries traditionalists seek to reserve for men.

Phoebe was a minister, or deacon *(diakonos)*, of the church at Cenchrea (Rom. 16:1–2). The term used to describe Phoebe's ministry is also used by Paul to describe the ministries of Apollos, Timothy, Tychicus, Epaphras, and, most frequently, Paul himself.[21] With respect to these men, *diakonos* probably refers to ministry in general rather than a specific church office. In the case of Phoebe, however, Paul speaks of her work as a *diakonos* specifically in connection with the church at Cenchrea, which points toward her serving as deacon in a more or less official capacity.[22] The nature of the office of deacon is never described in detail in the New Testament, but evidently included administrative and general ministerial responsibilities.[23] "The lack of any feminine equivalent for *diakonos* makes it likely that there was no distinction seen between the office of male and female deacons. Phoebe was a deacon, not a deaconess having completely distinct duties."[24] Paul also describes Phoebe as a benefactor or patron *(prostatis)* of the church, which implies a position of prominence and authority.[25]

Female teachers are referred to in Titus 2:3 as "older women" *(presbutis)*, which would more accurately be rendered "female elders."[26] These women were teachers specifically of women but not necessarily only of women. Female elders *(presbytera)* are also mentioned in 1 Timothy 5:2, following the reference to male elders *(presbyter)* in 5:1. Of the church fellowships specifically mentioned in the New Testament, more were designated as meeting in the homes of women than of men.[27] It should be remembered that, until the third century, churches normally met in the private homes of the church leaders.[28] The "elect lady" to whom John addresses his second epistle may have been the leader of the church that met in her home.[29] Examples of other women who probably served as church overseers (a position comparable to the present-day position of pastor) include Chloe (1 Cor. 1:11), Lydia (Acts 16:40), and Nympha (Col. 4:15).[30] Paul speaks of Euodia and Syntyche as his co-workers in ministry (Phil. 4:2–3), a term which elsewhere describes the ministries of Paul, Timothy, Titus, Epaphroditus, Mark, Luke, Priscilla, and Aquila.[31] Historical evidence concerning the Christian church in the first and second centuries indicates that women occupied roles of church leadership to a far greater extent than in later church history.[32]

It is apparent that there *were* women in the New Testament church who ministered in a teaching capacity and who exercised authority over both women and men—with Paul's approval and commendation. Clearly, it cannot be said that the New Testament prohibits women from having any authoritative or teaching ministry in the church. Nonetheless, fewer women than men occupied such roles. This need not be interpreted to mean that God prefers men for such ministries. The deficit in female ministers can easily be explained by cultural considerations, not the least of which is the fact that women were less likely than men to have been trained in the Scriptures, a clear prerequisite to serving in a teaching ministry.

The socially acceptable role for a woman in New Testament times was as the manager of her home; as a rule, this would have been the primary focus for women in the New Testament church. On several occasions, the apostles Paul and Peter exhorted Christian women to conduct themselves in a socially suitable manner, so that in the eyes of the world they would be above reproach (1 Tim. 5:11–14; Titus 2:3–5; 1 Peter 3:1–7). The plea for believers to be mindful of social propriety was especially urgent in situations of instability, where the church was threatened by heresies and persecution.

Relatively few women in the Greco-Roman world had opportunity to rise above their socially restricted circumstances and become qualified to serve in church teaching and leadership. Craig Keener observes that the constraints on women in the New Testament church were practical, not theological.

> Scandal would have arisen had Paul included women among his traveling companions, but once this fact is taken into consideration, the percentage of women colleagues Paul acknowledges is amazing by any ancient standards. . . . In other words, it was not women's gender per se, but the place of their gender within their culture, that limited some of their ministry.[33]

The biblical texts forbidding women to speak or teach or have authority over men cannot be taken as universally normative, lest the Bible be regarded as contradicting itself when it commends women for speaking, teaching, and serving in leadership ministries.[34] The apparent meaning of these restrictive texts must be adjusted and limited through the interpretive process, and this is true whether one is a hierarchalist or an egalitarian.

The Traditionalist Hierarchy of Spiritual Authority

Traditionalists account for the presence of female leaders and teachers in the Bible by ranking ministry positions within a hierarchy of male authority. The general principle undergirding this system is that the highest levels of spiritual authority are occupied only by men, while the lower levels may hold both men and women. This, by the way, highlights the fact that traditionalism entails not merely a "difference" in function between men and women, but a restriction of function for only women.

The traditionalist ordering of the hierarchy of ministries seems to go like this: At the top are the senior pastors of local churches; at the next lower level are the associate pastors and elders of local churches; finally, there are all the rest of the ministries (this is generally where the women are allowed to join in). These ministries include prophecy, evangelism, Bible college and seminary teaching, Sunday school teaching, missions, speaking, writing, and so forth. Not all traditionalists permit women to serve in all of these third-level ministries; there is a multiplicity of views as to just which of these ministries should be identified as "male only." Most traditionalists deny women entrance to any ministry above the third level, although some who hold a moderate position allow women any ministry but that of senior pastor.

What has happened here? Apparently, Paul's ranking of the spiritual gifts and ministries (1 Cor. 12:28; Eph. 4:11) has been reorganized according to two criteria. First, the ministries that are said to be the most authoritative do not include any of the ministries that the New Testament unequivocally records women performing. Since, as Susan Foh observes, "there are no examples of women teaching the assembly or even a miscellaneous group of people," this particular activity is marked as the ministry that carries the highest level of spiritual authority, and which, therefore, should be limited to men.[35] This criterion renders private instruction less authoritative than public instruction, and the ministry of prophecy less authoritative than that of teaching. It is, however, unclear why it should be considered a less authoritative ministry to tutor a noted church leader in Christian doctrine (as Priscilla did) than to teach doctrine to an assemblage of ordinary church members.

Traditionalist efforts to construe prophecy as less authoritative than teaching are also unpersuasive. D. A. Carson, for example, points out that the "apostolic deposit" of teaching, such as came from Paul, is nonnegotiable and, therefore, more authoritative than prophecy, which must be judged (1 Cor. 14:29).[36] Thomas Schreiner maintains that because New Testament prophecy does not have the "absolute authority" of Old Testament prophecy, "the church does not accept such 'revelations' uncritically, but weighs them carefully."[37] New Testament prophecy may well be less authoritative than Old Testament prophecy, and prophecy in general less authoritative than the teaching of the founding apostles. Such observations, however, do not prove that teaching per se is more authoritative than prophecy.

The point at issue in the debate over women's ministry is not whether women may be permitted to exercise the authority of the Old Testament prophets or the founding apostles. There are, after all, no more openings in these departments; the canon has been closed, and the days of the old covenant are behind us. Rather, the question under discussion is whether or not to deny women the normal, ongoing teaching authority of ordinary pastors. And this sort of teaching, no less than New Testament prophecy, needs to be judged and evaluated according to biblical standards, and should never be accepted uncritically (as were Old Testament prophecy and apostolic teaching, according to the traditionalist arguments).

The second mark of spiritual authority in the traditionalist system is having a title, a position, and the social or ecclesiastical "clout" to make others do one's bidding. This too puts the local church with its officials at the top of the hierarchy. According to this criterion, spiritual authority parallels the structures of authority in a male-oriented society. The overriding concern in such a system is not so much that the leader must empower and enable the people to do what they *all* have agreed is right to do, but that the leader must possess the authority necessary to cause the people to do what *he* believes is right to do.[38]

True spiritual authority, however, is more free ranging than the traditionalist understanding allows. Divine authority is, essentially, the authority to stand and speak in God's place. Such an authority is exemplified most fully in the life of Christ—who, in his life on earth, had no social or ecclesiastical authority by which he could command obedience. The apostle Paul is another example of this type of authority, which he saw as a greater authority than that which is ecclesiastically conferred. In Galatians 1:11–2:10, Paul makes quite a point of demonstrating that his authority to preach the gospel came directly from God, and not from the church leaders—although he did eventually receive their approval and cooperation. God has a way of speaking to the church through people outside the "official" ecclesiastical loop. The ministries of prophet, evangelist, and apostle do not describe official positions in churches today. But the person truly called to one of these ministries has a powerful deposit of spiritual authority that comes directly from God—which ultimately could influence the church at large more profoundly and powerfully than would the ministry of the average church pastor.

The central rationale behind traditionalist teaching on gender roles seems to be that there is a universally applicable biblical principle whereby spiritual authority in the church and home is to be exercised by the available men. But if this is the case, then *all* spiritual ministries that claim to speak the word and will of God should be restricted to men—not simply those ministries that entail ecclesiastical authority in a local church body.

There is a curious conflation of categories in the traditionalist system. Traditionalist-defined male authority is not simply spiritual authority, because it is understood in terms of the structures of social and political authority, which entail the right to issue commands and enforce obedience. But neither is it merely social or political authority, for its limitation to males is deemed a spiritual principle that is ordained by God and is not strictly applicable to secular society (at least, not according to late twentieth-century traditionalism), but only to the church and home where the making of decisions based on the discernment of God's will is to be ultimately a man's job.

What happens if this traditionalist-constructed hierarchy of spiritual authority is *not* used as a hermeneutical template overlaying the entire Bible? There emerges from Scripture a very different picture of the place of women in ministry. In a *Christianity Today* interview, F. F. Bruce expressed his conviction that there are no biblical grounds on which to restrict the ministry of women. When asked for his interpretation of 1 Timothy 2:9–15, he declared that "it is merely a statement of practice at a particular time." Bruce's succinct assessment of this troublesome text is not merely his personal preference, but a view that is grounded in Paul's overall approach to women in ministry.

> Paul's teaching is that so far as religious status and function are concerned, there is no difference between men and women. . . . Men receive praise, and women receive praise for their collaboration with him in the gospel ministry, without any suggestion that there is a subtle distinction between the one and the other in respect of status or function. Anything in Paul's writings that might seem to run contrary to this must be viewed in the light of the main thrust of his teaching and should be looked at with quite critical scrutiny. . . . If, as evangelical Christians generally believe, Christian priesthood is a privilege in which all believers share, there can be no reason that a Christian woman should not exercise her priesthood on the same terms as a Christian man.[39]

Let us, then, begin to look "with quite critical scrutiny" at the few texts that do "seem to run contrary" to Paul's usual approach, and see whether they are compelling enough to oblige us to judge the rest of Scripture in their light.

"Silent in the Churches"

In 1 Corinthians 14:34–35, Paul declares that women should be "silent" and "in submission." However, he could not mean complete silence, if for no other reason than the fact that just three chapters earlier Paul speaks of both men and women praying and prophesying in the public assembly (1 Cor. 11:4–5). Traditionalists, therefore, are unable to claim that this passage silences women from praying or prophesying publicly; but they do maintain that it sets forth a transcultural mandate for some sort of silence and subordination. The type of mandated silence varies, depending on the traditionalist; in general, the silence extends to preaching, teaching, and other forms of public speaking that fall outside the category of prayer and prophecy.

Sometimes the silence is interpreted, on the basis of the preceding verses, to refer to speaking in tongues or to judging prophecies.[40] But Paul offers nary a clue that his instructions concerning tongues or the judging of prophecies pertain only to men. When he says that "the others" should weigh the prophecies carefully (14:29), it seems clear that "the others" include everyone but the speaker of whatever prophecy needs to be judged. To maintain that "the others" are limited to the elder-teachers in the church (who must be male) is to read into the text a great deal more than is entailed by the text itself.[41]

Usually, traditionalists simply interpret this text to mean what they interpret 1 Timothy 2:12 to be saying, namely, that Paul is stipulating a universal principle whereby women are not to speak in such a way as to exercise authority over men. Hence, Piper and Grudem maintain that 1 Corinthians 14:34–35 prohibits women from speaking in any way that "compromises the calling of the men to be the primary leaders of the church."[42] It seems, though, that the type of silence being demanded of women in this text should be determined, if possible, from the text itself and its context, rather than from a disputed interpretation of another text. When the interpretation of this text must be derived not from the text itself, but by superimposing upon it an interpretation obtained elsewhere, then 1 Corinthians 14:34–35 cannot be said to prove anything in and of itself.

In interpreting this text, it is necessary to delineate the type of silence and the context of the subordination that Paul requires here, in order not to contradict the rest of the New Testament where women are not completely silent and subordinate, but are actively involved in ministry. The directive for women's silence should be understood as applicable only to the type of speaking that was at issue in the specific situation to which Paul directed these words.

The context of this passage concerns the maintenance of order in the worship service. The same word used of women's silence is commanded of those who would speak in tongues without an interpreter (14:28).[43] Paul's intent is evidently to silence only disruptive speaking. The particular type of disruptive speaking that is mentioned with respect to women probably has to do with interrupting the public speaker with questions—a practice that was common at this time.[44] Paul says the women should save their questions to ask their husbands after they get home (v. 35). This "indicates that he is primarily concerned with women interrupting teaching, not women engaged in teaching."[45] Apparently, women had been asking questions out loud and disrupting the order of the church service. This may have been happening because the women in the church were less educated than the men and so would seek clarification from the preacher during the sermon.

The silence to which women are admonished in verse 34 and the speaking that is considered disgraceful for a woman in verse 35, then, refer specifically to interrupting the pastor's message with irrelevant questions. The solution Paul prescribes is for the women's questions to be answered after the church service by their husbands (who, presumably, were better educated in the Scriptures than the women). This not only would remove the disruptive element from the service, but would help solve the root of the problem by having the men instruct their wives in Christian doctrine.[46] The universal principle behind Paul's words is not the permanent silencing and subordinating of women in the church, but the curtailing of practices that disrupt the flow and order of the public assembly of believers.

Some people maintain that because Paul invokes "the law" in admonishing women to be silent and in submission, this command should be seen as universal and transcultural. This is a problematic premise on which to establish the universality of the silence and subordination being advocated here. Nowhere in Old Testament Law are women ever actually told to be silent or subordinate—although Paul could possibly be referring to the generally subordinate status of women in Old Testament times. While Paul "does not require believers to keep all the stipulations of the law, he expects them to respect standard customs that could derive support from the law."[47]

Another possibility is that "the law" refers to the body of Judaic interpretive traditions related to Old Testament Law, which imposed numerous restrictions on women, including their silence in synagogue worship. Perhaps here Paul is referring to Jewish law as representative of culturally appropriate behavior, which he frequently urges Christians not to disregard.[48]

Whatever the referent of the term "the law," it does not require that this command be regarded as transcultural. Rather, it seems to indicate that the issue at stake in this text is propriety, which in this case required that women not be talkative and disruptive in the church service but submit to the private instruction of their husbands. Craig Keener sums it up:

> The fact that Paul addresses his argument in this particular letter to the specific situation in Corinth, and that his injunction to silence cannot contextually mean more than that the women should not ask ill-conceived questions during public lectures, mean that the inspired principle he articulates calls us to order in worship, not to the silence of women.[49]

However, several evangelical biblical scholars see textual evidence that this command to silence women did not come from Paul. Walter Kaiser and others believe that in 1 Corinthians 14:34–35 Paul is quoting from a letter he had previously received from the Corinthians, in which they cited the Jewish law of the Talmud and Mishnah where women are commanded to be silent. Paul, therefore, is not teaching the silencing of women in any sense, but is indicating his disapproval (in verse 36) of the Jewish rule concerning a woman's absolute silence in public.[50]

Gordon Fee and others believe these verses are an interpolation; that is, they were added after the original Pauline manuscript was written. This view is supported by the fact that different ancient manuscripts have these verses in different places. Usually they appear where they are in our Bibles, but in the Western text, which was used in the Latin church for at least three hundred years, the verses silencing women come at the end of the chapter. Fee sees no reason why these verses would have been shifted around had they originally been in one place or the other. It is more likely that "they were not part of the original text, but were a very early marginal gloss that was subsequently placed in the text at two different places."[51]

Another reason to view verses 34 and 35 as an interpolation is that they do not seem to belong in Paul's argument in chapters 12 through 14, "which to this point has only to do with manifestations of the Spirit in the community"; nor do they fit very well in the immediate argument of 14:26–40. In fact, the passage reads more smoothly and sensibly without these verses.[52] Moreover, the statements in 14:34–35 silence women absolutely, without modification or qualification, and, therefore, contradict 1 Corinthians 11:5, as well as the emphasis in chapter 14 on the participation of *all* believers in the worship service. Fee concludes, "On the whole, therefore, the case against these verses is so strong, and finding a viable solution to their meaning so difficult, that it seems best to view them as an interpolation."[53]

Elders and Deacons in the New Testament Church

Other New Testament passages that have been used to restrict women's ministry include Paul's lists of qualifications for elders (1 Tim. 3:1–7; Titus 1:5–9), in which he stipulates, among other things, that an elder be "the husband of but one wife." This is taken by traditionalists to mean that elders must, in principle and for all time, be men.

However, Paul also says that an elder must have obedient children. By the logic of the traditionalist argument, an elder must be not only a man, but a married man with children who obey him. But, of course, the argument is not carried through consistently. A church that allows only men to be elders normally will not ban from the position of elder those men who have no children, who are unmarried, or who have rebellious and disobedient children.

This passage does not specifically require that an elder be male any more than it requires that an elder be married with children. Paul's point here is that an elder who is a married man with children should not be a bigamist or an adulterer, and should be a responsible "family man" who disciplines his children properly.[54] It probably was expected that an elder would be a married man with children because "these were necessary aspects of being respectable in antiquity," and Paul was aware, as always, that "a persecuted minority sect needed to protect itself against public slander."[55] Here again Paul indicates his concern for propriety, "for the reputation of the church within the larger Greco-Roman society" (as also in 1 Tim. 2:2–4; 3:7; 5:14; 6:1; Titus 2:7–10).[56] But there is no reason to conclude that this expectation was based on theological and not merely cultural reasons.

Craig Keener notes that when Paul says an elder should be the husband of but one wife, this should be taken as a

> general statement that might admit certain obvious exceptions . . . most [ancient] writers stated principles this way. Paul's requirement that an overseer be "husband of one wife" . . . could not apply to Paul [who was not married] and probably could not apply to Timothy, either. Does his general prohibition nullify his own teaching and that of Timothy, whom no one was to despise (4:12)?[57]

Paul could not be requiring an elder to be married for the additional reason that such a requirement would contradict what he says in 1 Corinthians 7:32–35, where he extols the advantages of singleness for the person who wants to serve the Lord.[58] Since Paul's lists of qualifications for elders cannot be used to exclude from church leadership unmarried men (such as Paul and Timothy), neither can they be used as a biblical basis for excluding women.

While the expectation at the time was that elders would be men, room is left for women to qualify for the position. First Timothy 3:1 says, "If anyone aspires . . ." which refers not to a male but to a person of either gender. Once women had submitted to theological instruction, they too could meet the qualification of being "able to teach" (3:2).[59]

The church at Ephesus may have had some female deacons. In the section discussing the qualifications of deacons (1 Tim. 3:8–13), verse 11 is directed to the women and verse 12 to the men. Some translations have verse 11 referring to the wives of the deacons. But because the text says, "*the* women" rather than "*their* women" (the same Greek word could mean either "women" or "wives"), it is probably more natural to read this verse as referring to women who are deacons.[60]

Whether or not Paul is referring here to women who are deacons at the church in Ephesus, he does refer approvingly in Romans 16:1–2 to a woman named Phoebe, who was a deacon at the church in Cenchrea. Therefore, when Paul says that a deacon must be the husband of but one wife (1 Tim. 3:12), he clearly could not mean by this that all deacons must always be male. When assessed in light of its cultural context and the rest of Paul's writings, the phrase "husband of but one wife" cannot legitimately be taken as stipulating that all church leaders be men.

It is telling that when a biblical passage listing qualifications for church leaders includes a reference to the prospective leader's wife, this is taken as a requirement of maleness for the position. But when a biblical passage describing the qualifications of a disciple refers to the prospective disciple's wife (Luke 14:26–27), it is quite naturally and appropriately understood as referring to a general principle that is applicable to all believers, regardless of gender.[61] The reference to the disciple's wife is correctly understood to mean that *if* the disciple is a married man, his love for his wife and other family members must take second place to his love for Jesus Christ.[62]

In the next chapter we will look at the pivotal proof text in the traditionalist arsenal. The argument for banning women from positions of ministerial authority stands or falls on the degree of certainty that can legitimately be imputed to the traditionalist interpretation of 1 Timothy 2:11–15.

9

"I Do Not Permit a Woman . . ."

irst Timothy 2:11–15 presents a problem for traditionalists similar to the one presented by 1 Corinthians 14:34–35. Neither of these texts can be taken at face value as a direct statement of universal principle, because, as we have seen, women in the Bible did teach, speak publicly, and exercise authority over both women and men in the course of their various ministries. Those who interpret 1 Timothy 2:11–15 as a permanent, transcultural restriction of women's ministry need to modify and qualify the statement that a woman may not "teach or have authority over a man." The usual traditionalist approach is to allow women to teach and have some authority over some men in some sense, but to restrict their opportunities to do so to some degree.

The particular areas of restriction vary widely among traditionalists. Some say a woman may not preach from behind the pulpit during a Sunday morning worship service, but she may give the same message to the same audience on a different occasion (such as an evening service). Some say a woman who is a missionary may serve as the leader and teacher (i.e., pastor) of a church in a foreign country, but may not fill a pastoral role in an American church. Some allow women to perform leadership and teaching functions in a church context, but not to bear the title (or receive the paycheck) given to the men who perform similar leadership and teaching functions. Some allow women to perform all pastoral duties and to fill any pastoral position except that of senior pastor. Some say that women may not teach authoritatively in a public worship service, but they may offer authoritative instruction to a man in private (as did Priscilla); some even allow women to write books on Christian doctrine and to teach men in seminaries. Some say that although women may teach the tenets of the Christian faith to their sons and grandsons—after all, Paul commended the faith Timothy learned from his mother and grandmother (2 Tim. 1:5)—women may not teach the same truths to other men of comparable age in the church. And so forth.

All those who hold these views—despite their divergent applications of the text—appeal to 1 Timothy 2:11–15 as the biblical basis for their position. In other words, even those who insist that the Bible presents a transcultural restriction of women's ministry cannot find clear direction from this text or any other biblical text as to what, exactly, that restriction is.

Rather than acknowledging that the meaning of 1 Timothy 2:11–15 is more consistent with the rest of Scripture if it is understood as directly applicable only to its specific cultural and historical context, traditionalist interpretation begins with the assumption that this text is universally normative. This then requires an ad hoc modification of the terms of the prohibition, so as to allow for any ministry by women for which there is unequivocal biblical evidence and example.

Drawing Lines and Choosing Alternatives

The question of where to draw the line between what is and what is not permissible for women is a difficult one, simply because there is nothing in the text to indicate any qualification or limitation of the ban on a woman teaching or having authority over a man. Taken as a transcultural command, as a direct statement of a universal principle of the spiritual authority of men, this text proves too much, even for traditionalists. It becomes necessary to draw lines around certain types of teaching and authority ("hermeneutical gerrymandering," David Scholer calls it), thereby making distinctions in levels of authority in ministry that are not delineated in Scripture.[1] It seems, though, that "anyone who argues for the 'timeless,' absolute character of any scriptural injunction should be prepared to take such a text without qualification or equivocation."[2]

Vague though its parameters may be, it is nonetheless this text to which traditionalists must turn for a biblical rationale for barring women from the higher-status positions of ministry. Without 1 Timothy 2:11–15, traditionally interpreted, there would be no case at all for the universal restriction of women in ministry.

The case based on this isolated text is weakened not only by the apparent contradiction of this passage with the broader biblical picture of women in ministry, but also by the numerous translational and exegetical difficulties in these few verses. Because the restriction of women's ministry depends on interpreting this text as universally binding, traditionalists must be able to demonstrate that theirs is the only viable interpretation. Unfortunately for the traditionalist cause, there *are* plausible alternative interpretations that do not demand that all women for all time be barred from teaching and leadership ministries. Therefore, the traditionalist interpretation of this text cannot justifiably be advanced as the final, binding, and authoritative word on the subject.

If 1 Timothy 2:11–15 can legitimately be understood as a prohibition relevant only for women in a historically specific circumstance (which it can), and if there is no other biblical text that explicitly forbids women to teach or have authority over men (which there is not), and if there *are* texts that assert the fundamental spiritual equality of women with men (which there are), then women who are not in the circumstance for which the 1 Timothy 2:12 prohibition was intended may safely follow whatever call they may have to ministry. In other words, it ought at least be acknowledged that the traditionalist interpretation is debatable on biblical grounds. This being the case, we should give the benefit of the doubt to any woman who is called to and qualified for pastoral leadership, and allow her the opportunity to use her gifts in this way. If we do not have sure reason to judge her, then we dare not risk quenching the Spirit's ministry through her.

The interpretational ambiguities in this text, however, do not deter traditionalists from making it the basis of a biblical doctrine of women's ministry. Yet it does not seem that our understanding of an important biblical teaching should begin with, and be based upon, an isolated text in which there are numerous exegetical uncertainties. Rather, such a study should begin with the clear message of the whole of Scripture—which is incompatible with any doctrine that deems spiritual authority a male prerogative.[3] Obscure and isolated texts need to be interpreted in light of and in conformity with the overall message of the Bible.

A Universal or Culturally Relative Prohibition?

The fundamental question that needs to be answered with regard to 1 Timothy 2:11–15 is whether this prohibition was advanced as a temporary corrective to a specific problem situation, or as a universal theological principle whereby upper echelon spiritual authority must be reserved for men and denied to women. Which of these two alternatives is more plausible, when judged in light of the whole Bible and the specific context of the passage?

Traditionalists maintain that Paul's prohibition here is a reminder of what Timothy and the New Testament church generally knew to be the case. But Paul does not state the prohibition in the form of a reminder, and it is not mentioned elsewhere in the New Testament. How can traditionalists be so certain that it was "Paul's position in every church that women should not teach or have authority over men," and that he was giving "explicit teaching on the subject here simply because it has surfaced as a problem in this church"?[4] Craig Keener observes that "what is most significant about the wording of the passage . . . is that Paul does not assume that Timothy already knows this rule. . . . Paul often reminds readers of traditions they should know by saying, 'You know,' or 'Do you not know?' or 'According to the traditions which I delivered to you.'"[5] But in this case, there are no such indications that Paul is merely reminding Timothy of an established rule that Timothy would already have known about. Moreover, there are no parallel texts in the New Testament to support the view that New Testament churches normally denied women teaching authority. "Since this passage is related so closely to the situation Timothy was confronting in Ephesus, we should not use it in the absence of other texts to prove that Paul meant it universally."[6]

In understanding 1 Timothy it is important to remember that Paul wrote this letter to a specific person at a specific church in order to address a specific set of problems confronting the church at that particular time. So, what were the circumstances at that time, and how should Paul's response to them be understood?

The purpose of the epistle is set forth at the outset: Paul is providing Timothy with instructions on how to carry out his assignment of dealing with the false teachers in the church at Ephesus (1 Tim. 1:3).[7] Some form of heresy was evidently being taught in many of the house churches by the presiding elders. As Gordon Fee explains, "It seems certain from 2:9–15, 5:11–15, and 2 Timothy 3:6–7 that these straying elders have had considerable influence among some women, especially some younger widows, who according to 2 Timothy 3:6–7 have opened their homes to these teachings, and according to 1 Timothy 5:13 have themselves become propagators of the new teachings."[8] In 1 Timothy 5:13, these women are described as busybodies going about from house to house (or perhaps house church to house church), "talking foolishness and speaking of things they should not."[9] As a result, some have already "turned away to follow Satan" (5:15). Fee notes that "to talk foolishness" is a better translation than "gossip" (NIV); for this word was "used in contemporary philosophical texts to refer to 'foolishness' that is contrary to 'truth.'"[10]

Paul's solution to this situation is, first, that women in the church comport themselves modestly and decently, in dress, demeanor, and occupation, conforming to the domestic roles that were considered culturally appropriate for respectable women at that time (2:9–10, 15; 5:14). Second, Paul counsels women to "learn in silence with full submission" (2:11, NRSV). This in itself was a radical move; in Paul's day, women generally did not receive theological instruction. But it was necessary for them to do so if they were to guard themselves against deception by teachers of false doctrine. Keener points out that "the word used here for 'silence' normally refers to respectful attention or a quiet demeanor. The *whole* church is exhorted to this kind of quiet lifestyle with the same word in this very context (2:2)."[11] Learning "in silence with full submission" describes the attitude which, at that time, was considered characteristic of and proper for all wise persons and students of Scripture.[12] Studying the Scriptures—one of the many religious privileges that previously had been reserved for men—was now open to and even required of women as well.

The final element of Paul's solution to the problem of Ephesian women being duped by false teachers was that they should not be permitted to teach or to domineer over the men. In general, women were not as well taught in the Scriptures as were the men, and so needed to learn before they could be qualified to teach. Moreover, as Keener notes, "much of the false teaching in Ephesus was being spread through women in the congregation. This is not to say that women are more prone to lead others astray than men—the false teachers themselves seem to have been men. But in that culture the uneducated women seem to have provided the network the false teachers could use to spread their falsehoods through the congregations (1 Tim. 5:13; 2 Tim. 3:6–7)."[13] In short, the women's knowledge of true doctrine was severely limited and their interest in false doctrine had reached dangerous proportions. Therefore, women were to submit themselves to the teaching of the men who were the church leaders at the time (but not, of course, to those men who had been teaching false doctrine; Timothy had been instructed to deal with them).

If, as it seems most reasonable to believe, Paul's proposed measures were designed to remediate a specific and immediate problem, then the proper understanding of their import would be in the context of their applicability to the particular situation in the Ephesian church. It is inconsistent to regard the dress code in 1 Timothy 2:9 as culturally relative and, therefore, temporary, but the restriction on women's ministry in 2:12 as universal and permanent. All these instructions are part of the same paragraph, the same flow of thought, and are elements of an epistle that was written, not as a general "church manual" applicable to all churches everywhere, but specifically for Timothy with respect to his assigned task of dealing with the false teaching in the Ephesian church at that time.[14]

What Was Paul Prohibiting?

The question of the universality of Paul's prohibition is not the only point of debate. It isn't even entirely clear what Paul was prohibiting. The word in verse 12 that is translated "authority" *(authentein)* is not the word used elsewhere in the New Testament to denote the positive or legitimate use of authority *(exousia)*; in fact, this word occurs nowhere else in the New Testament. Moreover, it had a variety of meanings in ancient Greek usage, many of which were much stronger than mere authority, even to the point of denoting violence.[15] Given that there is so much uncertainty concerning the word's intended meaning in this text, any definitive statement that Paul was forbidding women to exercise authority per se seems unwarranted. Yet this is the only biblical text that appears specifically to forbid female leadership; therefore, those who wish to use this prohibition to impose a permanent ban on women in leadership must somehow demonstrate that the meaning of *authentein* in this verse points unequivocally to authority in the ordinary, neutral sense of *exousia*.

Extensive recent research into ancient Greek usage of this term suggests that at the time Paul wrote this letter to Timothy, *authentein* did not refer to exercising authority in the capacity of an authorized official. Rather, it "included a substantially negative element (i.e., 'dominate, take control by forceful aggression, instigate trouble')."[16] Therefore, it seems forced and unreasonable to view 1 Timothy 2:12 as denying women the ordinary and appropriate exercise of authority. It appears far more likely that the prohibition refers to a negative and harmful use of authority—which, in principle, would be prohibited for men as well as for women, but in this case probably referred specifically to the women who were teaching the heresy against which Paul had written 1 and 2 Timothy. Thus Paul would not have intended this prohibition to exclude women from either the ministry of sound teaching or the legitimate exercise of ecclesiastical authority.[17]

Richard and Catherine Clark Kroeger suggest that *authentein* may be used here to mean that a woman was "not to teach or to represent herself as originator of man." According to this use of the term, Paul's statement would be a direct refutation of a proto-Gnostic teaching that may have been the heresy that was circulating in Ephesus at the time, namely, that the man came from the woman and that Eve brought spiritual enlightenment to Adam.[18]

Scholars disagree on whether "to teach" and "to have authority" refer to two different activities or just to one activity of teaching authoritatively.[19] Some traditionalists hold that the central point of the prohibition is not teaching, but authority; teaching men is off limits for women only if it is authoritative teaching. Not surprisingly, different traditionalists have different ideas about what makes teaching authoritative. In general, the prohibition is understood in terms of serving in the church office of elder or pastor, or in any ministry that requires ordination.

All traditionalist interpretations, of course, require that *authentein* be defined in the sense of the normal, neutral exercise of authority. Because this definition of *authentein* is indispensable to viewing this text as the biblical basis for restricting the upper levels of church authority to men, traditionalists are unable to accept alternative definitions of this term. The case for biblical equality, on the other hand, is strengthened by, but is not dependent upon, an alternative definition of *authentein*. For the sake of argument, the rest of this chapter will assume the traditionalist understanding of this term.

"Adam Was Formed First"

Traditionalists maintain that the prohibition of 1 Timothy 2:12 is universal and transcultural because it is followed by the statement, "For Adam was formed first, then Eve; and Adam was not deceived, but the woman was deceived and became a transgressor" (2:13–14). This reference to the creation account is regarded as the causal basis for Paul's prohibition; and if the prohibition is based on the creation order and not merely on a temporary cultural situation, then it must be absolute and not relative.

But is the prohibition grounded in the creation account, or is it simply explained or illustrated by the creation account? The grammar here does not require us to understand Paul's reference to Adam and Eve as the causal basis for the prohibition. The word "for" does not necessarily mean "because"; it can be used simply to express a connection or continuation of thought, as it does in 1 Timothy 2:5.[20] If this is the case here as well, then verses 13 and 14 could simply be supplying an analogy that explains why women must, at this time and in this church, learn from the men who are in leadership. Walter Kaiser puts the question:

> Do we have here the argument from the orders of creation; or do we have an argument from the fact that the men in Timothy's church, like Adam, had teaching which the women did not have [God gave his instructions concerning the tree directly to Adam before the woman was created], and thus the women, like Eve, would be more vulnerable to deception and trickery in situations that called for an adequate grounding in the Word?[21]

If the problem that Paul is seeking to remediate here is the deception of Ephesian women by false teachers, then it is quite possible that verses 13 and 14 serve to illustrate the seriousness of this problem by comparing it with Eve's deception and its consequences. Because the women in the Ephesian church were being deceived by false teaching (see 1 Tim. 5:13–15; 2 Tim. 3:6–7), and because Eve's experience shows deception to have very serious consequences, the women in Ephesus were to guard themselves from false teaching by submitting themselves to the teaching of the men who were qualified to teach.

Understanding the reference to Adam and Eve as an analogy does not do violence to either text or context, and it neutralizes the argument for the universality of the prohibition. This is not the only time that Paul uses Eve as an object lesson for Christians in danger of being deceived. In 2 Corinthians 11:3, Eve serves to illustrate the deception to which both men and women in the church seemed to be inclined. This text, by the way, shows that the reference to Eve in 1 Timothy 2:14 does not mean that Paul regards Eve as prototypical of a female penchant for being deceived.[22] Men, as well as women, can be taken in by false doctrine and need to guard themselves with the true Word of God.

An alternative understanding of verses 13 and 14 is supplied by the Kroegers' proposed definition of *authentein*. If the women in Ephesus were teaching the heretical doctrine that woman was the originator of man, and were retelling the story of woman's deception so as to make Eve the hero who brought knowledge and enlightenment to Adam, then Paul's statement that Adam was created first and Eve was deceived would serve simply as a direct refutation of this heresy—which Paul does not permit women to teach.[23]

According to traditionalists, the reference here to Adam being created first is actually a reference to what they perceive to be the implication of this order of creation, namely, that woman was created from the beginning to be permanently subordinate to man's spiritual authority over her. It is this perceived implication of the creation order that links it with the prohibition and makes the prohibition universal and permanent. Paul does not actually say that the creation order signifies a universal mandate for male authority; nowhere, in fact, is this stated in the Bible. Paul simply says that Adam was created first—which, in itself, is merely a statement of fact, not of theological principle.

As even John Calvin observed, "The reason which Paul assigns, that woman was second in the order of creation, appears not to be a very strong argument in favour of her subjection; for John the Baptist was before Christ in the order of time, and yet was greatly inferior in rank."[24] Calvin acknowledges that this verse must be supplemented by an interpretation of Genesis 2 that sees in the order of creation God's intent that woman "might be a kind of appendage to the man," so that in creating woman, God "added to the man an inferior aid."[25] Determined as Calvin was to subordinate the woman, he nonetheless recognized that verse 13 in itself proves nothing.

Those who interpret this text on the basis of the assumption that Paul prohibits women from teaching men because God ordained women to be permanently subordinate to men are obliged to infer that Paul's reference to woman being created after man is actually a reference to woman's subordination to man. However, inferring the meaning of a text from preconceived ideas is not the same as understanding the meaning of a text based on what the text and its context actually say. The argument for the universality of the prohibition in 1 Timothy 2:12 hinges entirely on the traditionalist supposition concerning the theological significance of Adam's temporal priority in creation. Without this supposition, which cannot be derived conclusively from the text (or, for that matter, from the Genesis account), the argument from verse 13 for the universality of the prohibition is groundless.

Besides its dependence on inference, there are other problems with the traditionalist interpretation of verse 13. If the point of the verse is the universal subordination of women to the spiritual authority of men, then why would this pertain to subordinating women in the teaching ministry, yet leave unrestricted other ministry gifts, such as prophecy, which are equally, if not more, authoritative?[26] And if Paul's creation-order rationale here renders universal and transcultural the prohibition of women teaching authoritatively, then why doesn't Paul's creation-order rationale for women's head coverings (1 Cor. 11:6–9) make the wearing of headgear a universal and transcultural requirement for women in church?

Unless Genesis 2 is interpreted in light of the traditional interpretation of 1 Timothy 2:12–14, a doctrine of male authority cannot be derived from it. Genesis 2 taken on its own terms does not teach that because woman was created after man, she was created subordinate to man.[27] John Piper and Wayne Grudem's comment on 1 Timothy 2:13 illustrates the circular reasoning of traditionalists. "In the context of all the textual pointers" in Genesis 1–3, "we think the most natural implication of God's decision to bring Adam onto the scene ahead of Eve is that he is called to bear the responsibility of headship [i.e., authority]. That *fact* is validated by the New Testament when Paul uses the fact that 'Adam was formed first, then Eve' (1 Tim. 2:13) to draw a conclusion about male leadership in the church."[28] An implication that traditionalists believe is hinted at by "textual pointers" in Genesis becomes a veritable "fact" when it is perceived in light of the traditional interpretation of 1 Timothy 2:12–13. But the traditional interpretation of 1 Timothy 2:12–13 presupposes the traditional interpretation of Genesis 1–3, which in turn relies on the traditional interpretation of 1 Timothy 2:12–13 in order to turn the "textual pointers" in the creation account into actual "fact."

In addition to the usual "hints" and "textual pointers" that traditionalists see in Genesis 2, some see particular significance in the ancient patriarchal custom of primogeniture. For example, Grudem declares that "the creation of Adam first is consistent with the Old Testament pattern of 'primogeniture,' the idea that the firstborn in any generation in a human family has leadership in the family for that generation."[29] Along the same lines, Craig Blomberg argues that "an ancient Middle Eastern mind-set would have had little problem in accepting a rationale like that of verse 13; order of creation implies some kind of hierarchy. Paul is thus arguing here from a timeless creation ordinance, which contemporary interpreters may not simply set aside because they do not like it."[30]

Again, Paul can only be understood to be arguing from a timeless ordinance if his reference to Adam's temporal priority is presumed to be a reference to an ordained creational hierarchy. Paul does not actually make this connection himself. Blomberg believes he didn't need to make it because the ancient Middle Eastern mind would have supplied the inference, given the cultural assumptions about the superior privileges due the firstborn.[31] In other words, Paul is saying here that male authority is a universal law because the man has the rights of the firstborn.

In order to derive this meaning from Paul's reference to the order of creation (i.e., that the man's temporal priority equals his superior status), one must assume that Paul believed this was what the Creator intended to signify in choosing to create the man prior to the woman. If Paul did *not* believe that God intended for the creation order to be understood in terms of the law of primogeniture, then, presumably, Paul would not have invoked this law (however elliptically) in support of male authority as a timeless ordinance. So then, the most important question here is not what the ancient Middle Eastern mind was likely to infer from man being created first (although that is a relevant consideration), but what God intended to signify by creating man first. Did God believe (long before there even was an ancient Middle Eastern mind-set) that the firstborn ought to have special privileges? Did God regard primogeniture as something of a universal law operative even at creation? Is this likely? Is it consistent with Scripture?

It seems more likely that the God who chose Jacob over his older brother Esau (Mal. 1:2–3), Ephraim over his older brother Manasseh (Gen. 48:13–20), the tribe of Judah over that of the eldest, Reuben (Gen. 49:8–10), and David over all his older brothers (1 Sam. 16:4–13), does not put much stock in the patriarchal custom of primogeniture. At these crucial junctures in Israel's history, God's mind differed sharply from the ancient Middle Eastern mind. God's criterion for choosing leaders is described in 1 Samuel 16:7: "The LORD does not look at the things man looks at . . . but the LORD looks at the heart."[32]

It does not even seem probable that the ancient Middle Eastern mind would have regarded the practice of primogeniture as relevant to Adam and Eve; for this custom pertained to male siblings, not to a husband and wife.[33] The analogy does not obtain. Eve was not born *after* Adam, she was "born" *from* Adam. Eve's familial relationship to Adam is more analogous to a person's relationship to his or her mother than to a man's relationship to his oldest brother. Furthermore, as Grudem notes, primogeniture applied only to the generation of the firstborn. If this practice were to be applied to Adam and Eve, then it would apply *only* to them. Men and women of successive generations would be governed by whoever was born first!

Again, it seems, we need to recall Paul's words in 1 Corinthians 11:8, 11–12. Though the first woman came from the first man, ever since then man has come from woman, and, ultimately, everything comes from God. In other words, let us not get involved in drawing cosmic diagrams of who is in first place, but let us recognize our mutual dependence on one another and our ultimate dependence on God.

At any rate, the argument from primogeniture does not escape the necessity of relying on conjecture. It requires that we infer that Paul intended his audience to infer male supremacy from the creation order. This appears to be a bit of a stretch. Such inferences of inferences are brought to the text, not demanded by the text.

In view of the difficulties plaguing the traditionalist effort to wrest a rationale from verse 13 for women's permanent subordination to the spiritual authority of men, it seems that the best way to view this verse is as an introductory and correlative element in Paul's primary illustrative point in verse 14.[34] As Gordon Fee points out, Paul's emphasis in verses 13 and 14 is not the fact that Adam was created before Eve, but the fact that Eve, and not Adam, was deceived. The former is merely stated without any amplification. "Its application can only be inferred. The second point, however, from Genesis 3, seems to be his real concern, since it receives an elaboration and leads directly to the conclusion in verse 15."[35]

Perhaps, as several biblical scholars have suggested, Paul intends in these verses to connect Eve's deception with her being created after Adam. Gilbert Bilezikian explains:

> In the fateful story of the fall, it was Eve, the lesser-informed person, who initiated a mistaken course of action and who led herself into error. Eve was not created first or at the same time as Adam. She was the

late-comer on the scene. Of the two, she was the one bereft of the first-hand experience of God's giving the prohibition relative to the tree [Gen. 2:16–17]. She should have deferred the matter to Adam, who was better prepared to deal with it since he had received the command directly from God. Regarding God's word, Adam had been teacher to Eve, and Eve the learner. Yet, when the crisis arrived, she acted as the teacher and fell into the devil's trap. Her mistake was to exercise an authoritative function for which she was not prepared.[36]

In other words, the point of the illustration is that, in order to avoid deception and serious error, those who lack instruction in God's Word (as did Eve and the Ephesian women) should defer to the expertise of those who are more thoroughly instructed (as were Adam and the male leaders in the Ephesian church). Thus, Paul's intent in referring to Adam and Eve is not to say that women in general should submit to the spiritual authority of men, but that women—and, in principle, men as well—who do not have adequate spiritual understanding should defer to and learn from those who do.

"But the Woman Was Deceived"

Whether or not a dependence on presuppositional inference in verse 13 is seen as problematic, other difficulties arise in the traditionalist treatment of verse 14. If verses 13 and 14 are to be viewed as pre-senting a causal connection between the orders of creation and women's permanent subordination to the teaching authority of men, then the logic for verse 14 must go as follows: Since the first woman was deceived, this failing is somehow characteristic of *all* women. Because of their propensity for deception, women are less fit than men to give spiritual instruction and leadership.

Traditionally, this has been the rationale most readily invoked by writers and commentators for why women should not be spiritual lead-ers and teachers.[37] But this reasoning assumes that it is worse to have a leader or teacher who can be seduced to sin (like Eve) than to have one who sins willfully with his eyes wide open (like Adam). It also assumes that it is acceptable to risk having women teach false doc-trine to women and children, but not to men—who, presumably, would be less likely than the women and children to be deceived by the false teaching. Some traditionalists today seem to be recognizing these difficulties and making various efforts to avoid them.

Craig Blomberg solves the problem by detaching verse 14 from verse 13 and grouping it instead with verse 15, suggesting that this more accurately reflects how these verses relate conceptually to one another.[38] Douglas Moo regards verse 13 as the causal basis for woman's permanent subordination to man's spiritual authority; he then switches to viewing verse 14 as illustrative—but with a strange twist. The issue becomes, in his view, not the woman's deception exactly, but her insubordination. Thus Moo proposes that "Eve was deceived . . . in taking the initiative over the man."[39] This, of course, reflects Moo's premise that Genesis 2 establishes male authority from the beginning—which renders Eve's primary sin not that she ate the fruit against God's command, but that she did so by her own decision, in violation of Adam's authority over her.[40]

Even allowing Moo's premise, it is a bit forced to define an act of usurping authority as tantamount to an act of deception. They are two quite different types of sin; the one does not follow from the other. But because Moo perceives the problem at Ephesus to be the women's insubordination to the universal law of male authority, he sees the reference to Eve's deception as a warning to women not to be insubordinate to the authority of men. Moo concludes with the claim that "this explains Paul's emphasis in the verse better than any other alternative."[41]

James Hurley also tries to avoid an interpretation of verse 14 that says women in general are more prone to deception. Like Moo, he maintains that Adam's God-ordained authority over Eve is the main point of this verse. But Hurley then undertakes an odd maneuver, suggesting that because the man was appointed by God to exercise spiritual discernment and decision making on behalf of the woman, Adam was "prepared by God" for this task and Eve was not. She was deceived because she did not discern the serpent's lie; and she did not discern the lie because she was assigned and equipped by God to receive obediently God's truth imparted to her by the man; and she was assigned and equipped thusly because this is the God-ordained purpose and role of womanhood. Therefore, in order not to fall into deception, the woman must rely on the spiritual authority of the male.[42]

But if Eve's supposedly God-ordained subordination to Adam's authority in spiritual matters was paradigmatic for all women and men who follow after, and if Eve's ineptitude at spiritual discernment was a consequence of this permanent, God-ordained hierarchy, then such spiritual ineptitude must be a constant characteristic of all women for all time.

In the end, Hurley affirms what he strove to deny. If women's spiritual faculties are not as well prepared by God to undertake the serious, responsible, spiritual discernment and decision making for which God has assigned and equipped men, then the conclusion is unavoidable: Women are more easily deceived in spiritual matters than men. It seems an odd theological entailment that a sovereign Holy Spirit should be restricted by a person's gender.[43] It is also interesting to note how readily and reasonably woman's spiritual inferiority follows from woman's universally mandated subordination to the spiritual authority of the man.[44]

"Saved Through Childbearing"

The first part of verse 15 reads literally, "But she will be saved through the childbearing."[45] The "she" in verse 15 refers to "the woman" in verse 14 who was deceived, and who now serves as an object lesson for the women of Ephesus. As Gordon Fee notes, the fact that the woman was deceived and fell into transgression

> is exactly the point of 5:15—such deception of woman by "Satan" has already been repeated in the church in Ephesus. But, Paul says in v. 15, there is still hope. She can be saved (eschatological salvation is ultimately in view, but in the context she shall be saved from her deception with its ultimate transgressions), provided she is first of all a woman of faith, love, and holiness. This, then, is the point of the whole—to rescue these women and the church from the clutches of the false teachers. Their rescue includes proper demeanour in dress, proper demeanour in the assembly (including learning in all quietness), and getting married and bearing children (one of the good works urged in v. 10, seen in light of 5:9–10).[46]

David Scholer also sees verse 15 as the "conclusion to the discussion of the place of women in the church, [which] must mean that women find their place among the saved (assuming, of course, their continuation in faith, love, and holiness) through the material and domestic roles that were clearly understood to constitute propriety *(sophrosyne)* for women in the Greco-Roman culture of Paul's day."[47] Thus the passage begins (vv. 9–10) and ends (v. 15) on the same note: Women are to behave with social propriety, conforming to current cultural standards of respectability.

Paul's instructions and prohibitions concerning women's place in the church should always be interpreted in light of this clearly artic-ulated concern. Counseling women to attend to their maternal duties was particularly pertinent advice for the believers in Ephesus, given that the heresy circulating in the Ephesian church forbade marriage (1 Tim. 4:3) and in general "assaulted and abused what was consid-ered appropriate and honorable behavior for women."[48] The princi-ple behind these exhortations to domestic responsibility is that women are to conduct their lives in whatever way is deemed proper and hon-orable in the society in which they live, not that subordinate domes-ticity is to be the universal role for women regardless of what their culture deems honorable and respectable.

Another interpretation of verse 15 is offered by Craig Keener, who views it as a reference to women being kept safe through childbirth. Because women in ancient cultures offered many prayers to various deities for "salvation" (i.e., safety) in childbirth, "the most natural way for an ancient reader to have understood 'salvation' in the con-text of childbirth would have been a safe delivery."[49] According to ancient Jewish tradition the curse of painful childbirth even included death for women who were particularly sinful. But verse 15 offers hope: "As impiety delivered one over to the effects of the curse, so also piety could deliver one from certain effects of the curse."[50]

Paul, therefore, is trying to mitigate and qualify his reference in verse 14 to the woman's deception and transgression by offering assur-ance that God provides salvation from the effects of original sin, specifically, from the curse of painful childbirth. The curse should not be considered normative for women. "Paul does not appeal to the curse [in verse 14], but to Eve's sin; and here [in verse 15] he merely makes plainer that the curse itself was never part of God's ideal plan for his people and that his appeal to the example of Eve's sin does not sup-port the continuance of the curse."[51] In other words, "Paul may be saying in 1 Timothy 2:15: 'Eve sinned and is a warning about what these women in Ephesus can do; but I must qualify my point: the curse that followed her sin is reversed for true followers of Jesus Christ.'"[52]

Another possibility is that verse 15 refers to the bearing of the Christ child. Although transgression entered the world through Eve's disobedience, salvation has come through the obedience of Mary in giving birth to the Savior. This interpretation is supported by Paul's use of the singular article ("the") to modify "childbearing."[53] Perhaps Paul is offsetting the dire effects of Eve's disobedience by noting the redemptive effects of Mary's obedience, which saves womanhood from the taint of the first woman's sin.

Mark Roberts proposes that verse 15 offers the promise that woman's subordination is not permanent. Salvation (in the sense of restoration or deliverance) "from the very condition which demands her churchly silence" is in view. This occurs in two ways. First, the woman's bearing of the Messiah "avenges woman's deception and transgression."[54] It saves her from her reputation as the first sinner. Second, the childbearing function of womanhood serves to counterbalance the order of creation in which the first man "bore" the first woman from his own body. Thus Paul is qualifying his reference to Adam's temporal priority in creation in much the same way as he qualified it in 1 Corinthians 11:11–12. In other words, whatever significance one may wish to derive from the fact that the first woman came from the first man, it needs to be balanced by the fact that ever since, man has come from woman. The restorative effects of woman's bearing of the Messiah and of women's childbearing capacity in general, however, are insufficient. Individual women must also "continue in faith, love and holiness, with propriety."[55]

A different variation on the theme of verse 15 is offered by the Kroegers, who suggest that Paul may be refuting the Gnostic notion that women must somehow surrender their femaleness and become "male" if they are to secure spiritual salvation. Contrary to the Gnostic doctrine of the spiritual superiority of masculinity, Paul affirms that "woman can be saved while she still possesses that distinctive which most decisively sets her apart from man."[56]

Whatever Paul's intention in relating childbearing to salvation, it does seem that verse 15 "provides, within the structure of Paul's argument, a positive conclusion to the negative statements in 2:11–14."[57]

In this final word, Paul is encouraging the women of Ephesus to take heart in God's promise of salvation, restoration, and deliverance.

Summarizing the Situation

The difficulties with the traditionalist interpretation of 1 Timothy 2:11–15 include the following:

1. Interpreting the prohibition as a statement of a universal principle of women's subordination to the spiritual authority of men contradicts the biblical principle of the spiritual equality of all believers, as well as the biblical examples of women who served in ministries that included teaching and having authority.
2. The traditionalist interpretation necessitates a fair amount of "hermeneutical gerrymandering" between those teaching and leadership ministries deemed permissible and those deemed nonpermissible for women. Traditionalists disagree on where to draw the line because there is no limitation on the prohibition of 1 Timothy 2:12.
3. First Timothy 2:11–15 is isolated in that it is the only biblical text that specifically restricts women's authority to teach. It is also troubled with translational and exegetical ambiguities. These factors make 1 Timothy 2:11–15 a shaky leg on which to construct a transcultural ministry restriction for all women for all time.
4. There is no need to interpret this text as teaching a universal principle whereby women must be excluded from top levels of spiritual authority, when the prohibition can be adequately explained as Paul's specific response to the cultural and ecclesiastical conditions of the Ephesian church at that time.
5. The intended meaning of the word translated "authority" *(authentein)* is not known with certainty, but it probably does not mean authority in the usual, neutral sense of *exousia*. If it refers to authority in any sense, it probably refers to a domineering, abusive authority, which, of course, would be biblically prohibited for both men and women.

6. The way in which verses 13 and 14 ostensibly serve as a time-less, causal basis for a universal subordination of women to the spiritual authority of men is not as obvious or straightforward as traditionalists claim, but is riddled with hidden presuppositions and contradictions.

There are, essentially, two ways to approach 1 Timothy 2:11–15. One way is to begin with the assumption that spiritual leadership is essentially a male function, and, therefore, to regard this text as a direct statement of this fundamental principle. This template of male authority must then be placed over the whole of Scripture, and every other biblical reference to women's ministry must be made to conform to it.

In order to reserve the most authoritative ministries for men, all the ministries of women in the Bible must be construed as either not authoritative, less authoritative, or authoritative in a different way from the ministry prohibited in 1 Timothy 2:12. Straws must be grasped at in order to render Deborah's jurisdiction over Israel less authoritative than that of the male judges, to categorize the ministry of prophecy as less authoritative than teaching, to assure that, even if Junia were a woman and an apostle, her ministry would not have entailed much authority, and to deem spiritual instruction given in private to a male church leader to be less authoritative than spiritual instruction given publicly to the general congregation.

Another approach is to view this text in light of the overall teaching of the Bible, and, therefore, to conclude (with sufficient exegetical support from the text itself) that 1 Timothy 2:11–15 is a temporary, culturally relative restriction. Regardless of one's approach, the applicability of this text must be limited in one way or another. Considering the many difficulties with the traditionalist effort to limit the types of teaching and the levels of authority from which women are to be excluded, it seems to be more consistent with both the context of the passage and the general teaching of the whole of Scripture to limit instead the time, place, and circumstances of the prohibition's relevance.

Thus, texts such as 1 Corinthians 14:34–35 and 1 Timothy 2:11–15 are best regarded as specific instructions that are directly applicable only to the situations for which they were originally intended.

Our knowledge of the cultural contexts of these two texts provides ample justification for interpretations that are historically specific—but still relevant for us today, since the basic biblical principles governing culturally relative instructions can be discerned and applied in any culture.

10

Ending
the Stalemate

e have seen that the broad sweep of biblical thought aligns more readily with gender equality than gender hierarchy, and that the traditionalist proof texts do not present an open-and-shut case in favor of universal male authority. Where, then, should we go from here? What can end the stalemate between those who are convinced the Bible mandates a hierarchical and unequal relationship between women and men, and those who are just as convinced that it does not?

Most of the discussion thus far has been spent in feverish debate over the exegetical intricacies of the traditionalist proof texts. Although faithful exegesis is certainly crucial, a myopic fixation on a handful of biblical texts will not ultimately resolve the gender debate. It is doubtful that either side will ever be able to put to rest all of the hermeneutical questions and objections concerning each "problem passage." In and of themselves, the biblical texts that specifically address male and female roles simply do not spell out this issue with cut-and-dried clarity.

Some reputable evangelical scholars believe the New Testament urges its readers to be respectable and law-abiding members of society, and yet to remember that women and men are essentially equal in rights, gifts, and spiritual ministries. Other reputable scholars believe that the central message of the New Testament is fundamentally in agreement with the cultural custom of reserving social and spiritual leadership for men, but that it modifies this custom such that male leadership is to be exercised wisely and lovingly. Both interpretations of the traditionalist proof texts are exegetically plausible; both respect the authority of Scripture. How can we decide which to choose?

We need to widen the scope of the debate and look beyond the proof texts to the teaching of the whole of Scripture, to a theology of God and sexuality that is derived from Scripture, and even to the sciences. And, perhaps most importantly, we must cooperate with the Holy Spirit in encouraging repentance, forgiveness, and reconciliation between Christian men and women. Galatians 3:26–28 states that in Christ there is oneness and unity between male and female, Jew and Gentile, slave and free. Ephesians 2:14–18 describes this oneness in terms of Jew and Gentile. It is likewise applicable to women and men. "For he is our peace; in his flesh he has made both groups into one and has broken down the dividing wall, that is, the hostility between us . . . for through him both of us have access in one Spirit to the Father" (Eph. 2:14, 18 NRSV). This issue needs to be discussed and debated, but not without the grace of God to forbear and forgive, the courage to take a stand for what one believes is true, and the equanimity to "speak the truth in love" (Eph. 4:15) with civility, courtesy, and consideration for others.

When we look to the message of the Bible as a whole, we find no contradiction between the equalitarian view and the clear biblical proclamation of the ultimate inclusion and equality of all classes of people within the redeemed community. The hierarchical view, on the other hand, does entail a contradiction with this fundamental message of equality; it, therefore, requires the logically problematic "equal in being, unequal in function" concept in order to harmonize gender hierarchy with the biblical teaching of the essential equality of all persons.[1]

A viable and biblically consistent theology of sexuality must be firmly grounded in these biblical principles: the creation of man and woman as equally imaging God, the priesthood of all believers, the unique high priesthood of Jesus Christ, and the equality in spiritual status of women and men in Christ. The implications of these fundamental principles seem clearly to rule out any universal hierarchies or cosmic principles of male supremacy. The theological difficulties that are generated by assigning spiritual authority along lines of gender furnish a strong argument in favor of biblical equality.[2]

The burden of proof, it would seem, should be on the one who seeks a clear and consistent biblical mandate for a universal exception to the biblical ideal of mutuality and equality among the members of the body of Christ. Careful examination of the proof texts that supposedly support such an exception seems to indicate an inability to bear this burden of proof. To assert a universalized and spiritualized gender hierarchy in the home and church is to go beyond what is clearly stated in these texts, and to go against the teaching of the whole of Scripture.

What do we find when we look to the sciences, and how should we approach our investigation in this area? Both God's natural revelation and God's written revelation are legitimate sources of truth, and both require that they be interpreted in order to be understood. David Basinger states that "Since both involve finite humanity's attempts to interpret an infallible revelation, it is, in principle, no more likely that either is more accurate than the other. Both must be given serious consideration."[3] If there seems to be a conflict between the two sources of revelation, we should consider the possibility that our interpretations of either source are incorrect. Of course, there are certain core doctrines of the Christian faith about which the Bible is sufficiently clear that any apparent contradiction with natural revelation should be corrected by adjusting our interpretation of nature rather than of Scripture.

But in areas of inquiry that are not essential to the central core of orthodoxy, and about which the biblical witness is unclear or even appears to be contradictory, natural revelation can help us arrive at the truth. Before science informed people otherwise, it was commonly believed that the Bible taught that the earth was at the center of the universe. Now, in the light of modern scientific interpretation of God's natural revelation, we know that we live in a solar system with the sun at the center, and that this truth is not inconsistent with a proper interpretation of the Bible. Christian philosopher J. P. Moreland believes that this same approach can be applied helpfully to other issues pertaining to the integration of science and the Bible. A biblical interpretation that is strongly favored by natural revelation should be preferred, as long as it is exegetically defensible. So, for example, it would seem to be better to choose the theory of progressive creationism over that of young earth creationism because the former harmonizes with what appears to be true according to natural revelation, and it can also be harmonized with God's written revelation.[4] In other words, when a debatable interpretation of the Bible seems to fly in the face of the natural evidence, it should be reconsidered in light of such evidence.[5]

This principle is also applicable to the question of biblical teaching on roles for women and men. Upon first encountering the traditionalist proof texts, the immediate impression of the average twentieth-century reader is likely to be that the Bible teaches the superiority of men in some sense. But once these biblical texts are studied carefully in light of their cultural contexts, as well as their context within the whole of biblical teaching, it becomes clear that the equalitarian interpretation is both exegetically and theologically sound. Natural revelation helps tip the scales even more toward gender equality, for the evidence here favors the egalitarian view, but lends little support to traditionalist gender roles.

The Significance of Gender Differences

Traditionalists often attempt to support their case by invoking scientific "proof" for the existence of gender differences. But merely demonstrating the existence of gender differences does not justify male authority and traditionalist gender roles. One must also demonstrate certain things to be true about these differences.

First, men and women must be shown to be different innately, as opposed to merely culturally. There must be gender differences that derive from biology rather than social conditioning. Most people on both sides of the feminist divide are willing to acknowledge this much. There appear to be some generalizable biological differences between men and women that influence functions other than reproduction.

Second, these innate gender differences must be shown to be significant and substantive; their effects on human behavior must be more than incidental, minor proclivities. These differences must have a direct bearing on behavior, such that different roles and statuses follow necessarily from them.

Third, these innate and significant differences must somehow be shown to be part of God's original design for men and women, and not a sinful distortion of that design. To demonstrate that men, for example, "naturally" tend more toward violence and aggression is not to demonstrate an aspect of God's creational plan for the male nature.

Finally, having ascertained the existence of innate, significant, and God-ordained gender differences, traditionalists must show that these differences indicate that men are better suited to lead and women are more in need of being led. They must clearly show men to be better equipped intellectually for serious cultural and scholarly endeavors and women to be better suited for domestic duties. Men and women must be shown to be inherently fitted for unequal status.

Traditionalists, however, do not seem overly concerned to establish a link of logical necessity between the gender differences that have been suggested by scientific research and their belief that women should occupy roles of subordinate domesticity while men exercise social and spiritual leadership. Rather, it seems that whatever the evidence for gender differences, it is readily interpreted as supporting traditionalist gender roles. For example, in Gregg Johnson's discussion of the differences in brain structure between men and women, he notes that women's brains "are generally capable of receiving and meaningfully processing more sensory nerve input" at one time. But "males, with their more lateralized brains, tend to have thought processing more regionally isolated and discreet, with fewer interconnecting nerve interactions and perhaps more straightforward, quick reactions to important stimuli."[6]

An unprejudiced assessment of the data Johnson presents might well judge women's brains better equipped for those jobs that require leadership of a number of people and projects, and men better suited to work alone on whatever their assigned task may be. For Johnson, however, the significance of this difference in brain function is that it uniquely equips women for child care—in which "there is great advantage in being able to receive and process multiple stimuli in order to monitor multiple children and other social contacts."[7]

Biologically based gender differences such as Johnson points out are not only frequently misapplied, but also overgeneralized. If someone were to assume that because I am female, I am mentally equipped for child care or multiple-stimuli management responsibilities, that person would be profoundly mistaken. I am all too aware of my brain's abject inability to process stimuli in the way that Johnson claims women are especially equipped to do. It is simply wrong to assume that all women are like all other women, and all men are like all other men, and all women are unlike all men. Many, many factors coalesce in the formation of a person's temperament and mental abilities, and of these, the biological difference of sex is only one.

The crucial question is not, "Are there differences between men and women?" but, "What difference do these gender differences make?" As Lisa Sowle Cahill points out, to say that there exist some differences between women and men

> is not to say, however, that emotional and cognitive traits vary greatly between the sexes or are manifested in comparable degrees by every member of each sex; or that the fact that males and females may fulfill certain roles somewhat differently implies that each sex can fulfill only a certain set of social roles, much less the devaluing of one sort of role or set of roles, and the subordination of it to that of the opposite sex.[8]

Frequently, a "scientifically proven" gender difference will create quite a public stir, even though it makes little or no difference in the behavior of men and women. For example, when a recent study showed that male and female brains work differently when performing the task of decoding words, many people were excited to have "scientific proof" that men and women really are psychologically different. However, this particular difference in brain function makes no difference in actual behavior; men and women perform this high-level cognitive task equally well.[9]

Similarly, an ABC News special, which reported scientific studies showing differences in behavior and brain function between men and women, was hailed by traditionalists as antifeminist and profamily (a label frequently—and unfortunately—used to refer to hierarchical gender roles).[10] But, again, simply to assert the existence of gender differences is not necessarily to oppose gender equality and support gender hierarchy. For one thing, this program explicitly described as "sexist" the gender ideology of the 1950s—an ideology that traditionalists typically revere and attempt to emulate. Moreover, traditionalist gender roles received little, if any, support or justification from the "scientifically proven" gender differences that were reported on this program (assuming that a television show can even begin to depict accurately the highly nuanced field of scientific research). Questions such as which gender is most inclined to attend to details (female), or which is most likely to have a better sense of direction (male), are not relevant to a determination of which gender is best suited for subordinate domesticity and which for public leadership.

This program did not disagree with, but rather supported, the fundamental feminist belief that women should have equal rights and opportunities with men. John Stossel, the host of the program, explicitly stated that gender differences should not mean that anyone should be excluded or their choices limited. Yet, the practice of exclusion and limitation by reason of gender is the central contention of traditionalism with which feminists disagree. Even more to the point, this news program argued that women are probably better suited for leadership than men, and that the reason most leaders are men is not because they are better at *doing* the job, but because their aggressiveness makes them better at *getting* leadership jobs.

Stossel closed with these perceptive observations: "Aren't we all better off when everyone is allowed the freedom to choose what we want to be? Thank God for the women's movement!" "People vary so much that *individual* differences are often much greater than the differences between the sexes." "Why not let people's natural inclinations take them wherever their potential allows?" Would that traditionalists actually agreed with the perspective of this program as much as they seem to think they do.[11]

This program did, however, share in common with traditionalists the tendency to describe modern feminism solely in terms of 1970s-style feminism, which abhors the very idea of studying or acknowledging gender differences. Entirely omitted from the presentation was any mention of the many contemporary feminists who do have an

interest in studying and even basing feminist theory upon generalizable differences between women and men.

The program also neglected to mention the fact that most of the
demonstrable psychological differences between men and women are
relatively small. Even in the largest differences, there is more than a
fifty percent overlap between women and men.[12] This means that there
are always more men and women who are alike than who are different—even in those areas in which men and women are most unalike.
Psychological gender differences, therefore, do not justify treating all
women differently from all men. And, as Stossel *did* point out, the
differences that do tend to exist do not support the thesis that women
are less qualified than men for leadership. If anything, the evidence
points in the opposite direction, indicating that a relational (or "feminine") leadership style is probably more effective than an authoritarian (or "masculine") leadership style.

Common sense tells us that it is counterproductive and unfair to
pass over a qualified female for a leadership position and to install an
incompetent male instead; yet this is what must sometimes be done
when authority is deemed an exclusively male prerogative. Indeed,
experience has proven women to be more than competent for leadership roles, both within and without the church. As Craig Keener
observes:

> Since I have learned from women professors and ministers, studied
> alongside women colleagues in doctoral-level classes, worked along-
> side women colleagues in ministry, taught women students, and so on,
> the intolerance of those who pronounce judgment on women's calls
> strikes me as insensitive and demeaning. Spiritually, intellectually, and
> in leadership ability these women are complete equals of their male
> colleagues; biblical evidence for their subordination would have to
> appear much more compelling than it does for me to grasp how sub-
> ordination could even reasonably be applied in their case.[13]

Not only are many women naturally gifted in leadership abilities,
while many men are not, but families are likely to be better off in a
home where authority and parenting responsibilities are shared equally
between husband and wife.[14] Taken together, the biblical, historical,
sociological, psychological, logical, and theological perspectives form

a strong cumulative argument in favor of a biblically defined equality between women and men.

What Is at Stake?

Probably the biggest hindrance to a productive approach to the gender debate is the perceived threat of the "slippery slope." Many fear that a rapid descent into a secular, liberal, or pagan feminism would be the result if evangelicals were to accept a nonhierarchical, flexible, equalitarian approach to gender relations. In view of this fear, it is crucial that we understand what is and what is not at stake in this debate, as well as what biblical equality is and what it is not, and how its premises, goals, motivation, and historical roots differentiate it from the various forms of modern feminism. What *is* at stake is the opportunity for women to pursue their callings whatever they may be, as well as the opportunity for both men and women to benefit from the full range of women's gifts and to learn from and relate to women as whole persons. What is *not* at stake is biblical authority, biblical morality, the integrity of the church, or the preservation of the family and civilized society.[15]

As far as marriage is concerned, I can see no harm that could possibly result from a marriage relationship characterized by mutuality in love, respect, and submission. If each partner is primarily concerned not for his or her own privilege or betterment, but for the spiritual health and vitality of the other partner and their life together, then it seems that such a relationship could only be Christlike, spiritually fruitful, and mutually fulfilling.[16] Moreover, since the traditionalist proof texts never tell men to rule, but do tell women—as well as believers in general—to submit, then there can be no disobedience to Scripture in a husband and wife submitting to one another. Mutual submission is, after all, a recurrent theme in the teachings of Jesus and the apostles.

So much more stands to be gained than lost in a marriage of equality. Genuine respect, affection, appreciation, commitment, and loving friendship tend to grow naturally out of a relationship in which mutual submission is practiced consistently and both partners share equal status and equal authority. When one partner holds a permanent and comprehensive authority over the other, the mutuality and reciprocity that characterize a good marriage do not come as easily or naturally; often, it seems, the couple must expend considerable effort to achieve a measure of emotional intimacy in their relationship.

Even more serious is the potential for abuse in a hierarchical marriage. We all—male and female alike—are sinful human beings easily corrupted by power. Because of this fact of human nature, a man's traditionally defined "headship" can slip into an abusive exercise of his superior status, especially if his behavior goes unchallenged by a meek, domesticated wife. This need not happen, nor does it normally happen. But it stands to reason that it would be more likely to happen in a marriage in which the wife is more submissive than the husband, the husband is not accountable to his wife as she is to him, and the husband has ultimate control over the family members and the freedom to do whatever he chooses. The statistics, in fact, confirm that the second-best predictor of sexual abuse in a family (after alcohol and drug addiction) is the family's acceptance of conservative, religious teaching on rigid, hierarchical gender roles.[17]

On the other hand, a marriage of equality can have the disadvantage of being less "efficient," with decisions sometimes taking longer to make and the allocation of responsibilities requiring some negotiation. Moreover, the husband may resist having to be accountable to his wife for his actions, and the wife may be initially frightened at the prospect of sharing equal responsibility in decision making. These elements, however, are not reasons to reject a marriage of equality, but are the necessary "growing pains" of both partners as they move toward maturity in mutuality.

What about the question of women's roles in church ministry? If we decide that the Bible does not universally prohibit female pastors and elders, and we recognize the call of those women who are gifted and equipped by God for this ministry, then what do we stand to lose if we are wrong? As long as church leadership is limited to those persons (whether male or female) who are genuinely godly, gifted, and Spirit filled, and as long as they perform their ministries to good effect with the Holy Spirit's clear blessing, then it does not seem that this could lead to apostasy or heresy (as some claim it would). Of course, those who are unworthy or ineffective, whether male or female, should not be allowed to enter or to continue in pastoral ministry.

But what if we decide that pastorally gifted women should be kept in a place of subordination to men who may or may not be as well qualified for such positions? And what if we are wrong? For one thing, women whom God has called to the "male only" ministries will not have full opportunity to grow spiritually, intellectually, and emotionally in the direction God intends for them. Even more importantly, the church as a whole will suffer for lack of opportunity to benefit from *all* those whom the Lord has called to leadership and teaching ministries. Men will be deprived of valuable teaching when spiritually mature and gifted women are allowed to offer their insights and instruction only to other women. The women of the church—who have opportunity to benefit from the ministry of everyone who is called to teach (whether male or female)—will probably be more thoroughly taught in the things of God than the men, who generally will not be found sitting under the instruction of a woman, regardless of how much they may need to hear her words. Yet the men will be considered most qualified to teach and to lead the church.

Men and women in the church also will be denied the benefits of a gender-inclusive pastorate. Pastoral models of competent, caring, and gifted women contribute toward building self-confidence in all women, as well as respect for women in men. Women are generally more comfortable approaching a woman for pastoral care and counseling. Moreover, the opportunity for female pastors to counsel women in the church would provide the best solution yet devised for a problem that evidently has reached epidemic proportions in the church today, namely, the developing of illicit relationships between male pastors and female parishioners.

On a more theological level, illegitimately denying women opportunities for ministry risks quenching the Spirit, which is not something the church can ever afford to do—especially not in these days. Also, when gender is perceived as a factor relevant to the position of pastor, then gender is likely to be perceived as relevant to the nature of God and to one's relationship to God. But when the pastorate is not restricted to males, maleness is not likely to be regarded as an attribute of God, nor godlikeness as characteristic of males. One female bishop observed that, "One of the advantages of being a woman priest is that people tend not to mistake us for God, which they sometimes do with men"![18]

Finally, when a number of people in a church are preoccupied with preventing women from usurping the supposed God-ordained spiritual authority of men, and the church consequently enters into much dispute over who is and who is not sexually qualified for which types of ministry, then the church's focus will not be outward, but inward. It will not be healthy, but spiritually diseased, even as a physically ill person is consumed with ameliorating his ailments and has little energy left over for the rest of the world.

But when all in the church are encouraged to minister in ways suitable to their individual gifts and callings, toward the end of building up the body of Christ and evangelizing a lost world, then the church will have the mark of spiritual health. It will be focused outwardly on ministry, on doing the works of Christ. Believers in such a church will not be caught up in controversy over whether or not one's gender has a unique claim to spiritual authority or a unique obligation to be subordinate, but will simply regard and respect one another, whether male or female, with humility, love, an attitude of submission, and a desire to serve. This is the essence of Christlike character, and it does not come in shades of pink and blue.

Notes

Introduction

1. For more on errors in church history, see Alvin Schmidt, *Veiled and Silenced: How Culture Shaped Sexist Theology* (Macon, Ga.: Mercer University Press, 1989); and Rebecca Merrill Groothuis, *Women Caught in the Conflict: The Culture War Between Traditionalism and Feminism,* chapters 3–4, published by Wipf and Stock, 790 East 11th Ave., Eugene, OR 97401, 541-485-5475.

2. Blaise Pascal, "Preface to the Treatise on the Vacuum," *Great Works of the Western World,* vol. 33 (Chicago: Encyclopedia Britannica, 1952), 358.

Chapter 1: One in Christ and Heirs of God

1. I owe this insight to Richard Mouw.

2. See chapter 5 for discussion of Genesis 1–3. See Mary Stewart Van Leeuwen, *Gender and Grace: Love, Work, and Parenting in a Changing World* (Downers Grove, Ill.: InterVarsity Press, 1990), chapter 2, for how the fall could have affected men and women differently.

3. Craig S. Keener, *Paul, Women, and Wives: Marriage and Women's Ministry in the Letters of Paul* (Peabody, Mass.: Hendrickson Publishers, 1992), 196.

4. See chapters 6 and 7.

5. See the first section of chapter 8 for more on Old Testament women in leadership.

6. See Mary Hayter, *The New Eve in Christ: The Use and Abuse of the Bible in the Debate about Women in the Church* (Grand Rapids, Mich.: William B. Eerdmans Publishing Company, 1987), 66, 68; also, Stanley J. Grenz with Denise Muir Kjesbo, *Women in the Church: A Biblical Theology of Women in Ministry* (Downers Grove, Ill.: InterVarsity Press, 1995), 72.

7. For more on Jesus' interaction with women in light of cultural customs, see Alvin John Schmit, *Veiled and Silenced: How Culture Shaped Sexist Theology* (Macon, Ga.: Mercer University Press, 1989), 92–93, 163–175.

8. Helmut Thielicke, *Sex,* vol. 3 of *Theological Ethics,* trans. John W. Doberstein (Grand Rapids, Mich.: William B. Eerdmans Publishing Co., 1979), 9.

9. W. Ward Gasque, "Response," in *Women, Authority, and the Bible,* ed. Alvera Mickelsen (Downers Grove, Ill.: InterVarsity Press, 1986), 191.

10. For women's status and roles in ancient Greco-Roman and Jewish societies, see Keener, 139–148, 159–166; William Barclay, *The Letters to The Galatians and Ephesians,* 2d ed. (Philadelphia: The Westminster Press, 1958), 200–202; and Grenz, 72–75.

11. See chapters 6–9, especially chapter 7, for further discussion of this concept.

12. Klyne R. Snodgrass, "Galatians 3:28: Conundrum or Solution?" in *Women, Authority, and the Bible,* 179. See also Daniel P. Fuller, "Paul and Galatians 3:28," *TSF Bulletin,* November/December 1985, 9–13.

13. See Keener, 1985–1986.

14. F. F. Bruce, *The Epistle to the Galatians: A Commentary on the Greek Text* (Grand Rapids, Mich.: William B. Eerdmans Publishing Company, 1982), 190.

15. Ibid., 187.

16. See Aida Besancon Spencer, *Beyond the Curse: Women Called to Ministry* (Nashville: Thomas Nelson Publishers, 1985), 65–71.

17. Bruce, 189–190.

18. See, for example, S. Lewis Johnson, "Role Distinctions in the Church: Galatians 3:28," in *Recovering Biblical Manhood and Womanhood: A Response to Evangelical Feminism,* ed. John Piper and Wayne Grudem (Wheaton, Ill.: Crossway Books, 1991), 161.

19. Clarence Boomsma, *Male and Female, One in Christ: New Testament Teaching on Women in Office* (Grand Rapids, Mich.: Baker Book House, 1993), 38.

20. C. S. Lewis, "Priestesses in the Church?" in *God in the Dock: Essays on Theology and Ethics,* ed. Walter Hooper (Grand Rapids, Mich.: William B. Eerdmans Publishing Company, 1970), 239. I critique this idea in chapter 4.

21. Schmidt, 198–199.

22. Snodgrass, 178.

23. Boomsma, 37.

24. Stephen R. Clark, *Man and Woman in Christ* (Ann Arbor, Mich.: Servant Books, 1980), 152.

25. Merrill F. Unger, *The New Unger's Bible Dictionary,* ed. R. K. Harrison (Chicago: Moody Press, 1988), 1262.

26. Eileen Vennum, "Do Male Old Covenant Priests Exclude Female New Covenant Pastors?" *Priscilla Papers* 17, no. 2 (Spring 1993): 7. For more on women and the Old Testament priesthood, see Hayter, 67–77.

27. Vennum, 7.

28. See Bruce Waltke, "Shared Leadership or Male Authority?" *Christianity Today,* 3 October 1986, 13-I. See also Bob Mumford, *Living Happily Ever After* (Old Tappan, N.J.: Revell, 1973), 80; cited in Kari Torjesen Malcolm, *Women at the Crossroads* (Downers Grove, Ill.: InterVarsity Press, 1982), 160. I discuss male headship in chapter 6.

29. Snodgrass, 177.

30. See ibid., 173; and Grenz, 99–100.

31. See chapter 4 for a discussion of this and related issues.

32. Bruce, 190.

33. Gilbert Bilezikian, *Beyond Sex Roles: What the Bible Says About a Woman's Place in Church and Family,* 2d ed. (Grand Rapids, Mich.: Baker Book House, 1986), 277 n.8.

34. Snodgrass, 181.

35. The many ritual requirements of the ceremonial Law are no longer applicable or binding under the new covenant. The Old Testament moral Law, however, embodies universal principles of righteousness, and so continues to apply as a standard for our behavior. See Millard Erickson, *Christian Theology,* one-volume edition (Grand Rapids, Mich.: Baker Book House, 1983, 1984, 1985), 975–78.

36. Wayne Grudem, *Systematic Theology: An Introduction to Biblical Doctrine* (Grand Rapids, Mich.: Zondervan Publishing House, 1994), 458.

37. Johnson, 158.

38. Ibid., 164.

39. Clark, 149.

40. Ibid., 155.

41. H. Wayne House, "Creation and Redemption: A Study of Kingdom Interplay," *Journal of the Evangelical Theological Society* 35 (March 1992): 15.

42. See chapters 6–9 for discussion of these texts.

43. The problems with the "equal in being, different in function" defense of gender hierarchy are discussed in chapter 2.

Chapter 2: Equal in Being, Unequal in Function?

1. Advocates of gender hierarchy appeal not only to texts that speak of women's submission, but also to texts that they take to be speaking of women's submission, but which, properly interpreted, are not. Both types of traditionalist proof texts are discussed in chapters 5–9.

2. For a discussion of these principles of interpretation, see the section "How to Do Biblical Interpretation," in chapter 6. See also Rebecca Merrill Groothuis, *Women Caught in the Conflict: The Culture War Between Traditionalism and Feminism* (Grand Rapids, Mich.: Baker Book House, 1994), 111–15; and Gordon D. Fee and Douglas Stuart, *How to Read the Bible for all Its Worth* (Grand Rapids, Mich.: Zondervan Publishing House, 1982).

3. Wayne Grudem, *Systematic Theology: An Introduction to Biblical Doctrine* (Grand Rapids, Mich.: Zondervan Publishing House, 1994), 459.

4. See Groothuis, chapter 3, for an overview of nineteenth-century classical/evangelical feminism.

5. Richard Mouw, "Ending the Cold War Between Theologians and Laypeople," *Christianity Today,* 18 July 1994, 29.

6. See discussion on this in chapter 3, in the sections "Servant Leadership" and "Unearned, Unaccountable, and God-ordained."

7. See Groothuis, chapter 9.

8. H. Wayne House, *The Role of Women in Ministry Today* (Nashville, Tenn.: Thomas Nelson Publishers, 1990), 19.

9. John Leo, "Let's Try Discriminating for Once," *U.S. News & World Report,* 7 August 1989, 53.

10. See, for example, House, 23–25.

11. John Piper and Wayne Grudem, eds., *Recovering Biblical Manhood and Womanhood: A Response to Evangelical Feminism* (Wheaton, Ill.: Crossway Books, 1991), 64; also xiv, 52–53. See also, Jack Hayford, *A Man's Starting Place: A Study of How Men Become Mature in Christ Through Relationships* (Van Nuys, Calif.: Living Way Ministries, 1992), 15.

12. Piper and Grudem, "An Overview of Central Concerns," *Recovering Biblical Manhood and Womanhood,* 78–79.

13. Raymond C. Ortlund Jr., "Male-Female Equality and Male Headship: Genesis 1–3," in *Recovering Biblical Manhood and Womanhood,* 481 n.32.

14. Millard Erickson, *Christian Theology,* one-volume edition (Grand Rapids, Mich.: Baker Book House, 1983, 1984, 1985), 338; also, 735.

15. See, for example, *Recovering Biblical Manhood and Womanhood,* 103, 128, 457, 540 n.63; and Grudem, *Theology,* 459–60, 251 n.35.

16. Grudem, *Theology,* 251.

17. See the section, "Headship in 1 Corinthians 11:3–16," in chapter 6.

18. Stanley J. Grenz, with Denise Muir Kjesbo, *Women in the Church: A Biblical Theology of Women in Ministry* (Downers Grove, Ill.: InterVarsity Press, 1995), 153.

19. Robert Letham, "The Man-Woman Debate: Theological Comment," *Westminster Theological Journal* 52 (1990): 67.

20. Ibid., 68. Gilbert Bilezikian pointed out this inconsistency in Letham's argument in a lecture given at the 1993 CBE national conference.

21. See *Recovering Biblical Manhood and Womanhood,* 35–36, 60.

22. Letham, 74.

23. Royce Gordon Gruenler, *The Trinity in the Gospel of John: A Thematic Commentary on the Fourth Gospel* (Grand Rapids, Mich.: Baker Book House, 1986), xv.

24. Ibid., xviii.

25. Millard J. Erickson, *God in Three Persons: A Contemporary Interpretation of the Trinity* (Grand Rapids, Mich.: Baker Book House, 1995), 309. Erickson's treatment (which I discovered only after completing the writing of this chapter) is an erudite overview and analysis of the Eastern and Western views of the relative status of the three members of the Trinity.

26. See ibid., 309–10.

27. I owe this insight to Douglas Groothuis.

28. See the final section in chapter 7 for a discussion of how mutual submission renders hierarchy unnecessary in marriage.

29. Ortlund, 104.

30. This observation undercuts the traditionalist effort to wrest from Eve's role as "helper" a God-ordained subordinate position; for the Hebrew word translated "helper" is used most often of God's relationship to his people. See section on "Woman: Man's Helper" in chapter 5.

31. James Henry Hammond, "'Mud-Sill' Speech," in *Slavery Defended: The Views of the Old South,* ed. Eric L. McKitrick (Englewood Cliffs, N.J.: Prentice-Hall, 1963), 122–23.

32. George Fitzhugh, "Sociology for the South," in *Slavery Defended: The Views of the Old South,* 37–38.

33. Charles Hodge, "The Bible Argument on Slavery," in *Cotton is King, and Pro-Slavery Arguments,* ed. E. N. Elliot (Augusta: Pritchard, Abbott and Loomis, 1960; repr. 1968), 863; cited in Klyne R. Snodgrass, "Galatians 3:28: Conundrum or Solution?" in *Women, Authority, and the Bible,* ed. Alvera Mickelsen (Downers Grove, Ill.: InterVarsity Press, 1986), 162.

Chapter 3: Issues in Inequality

1. Raymond C. Ortlund Jr., "Male-Female Equality and Male Headship: Genesis 1–3," in *Recovering Biblical Manhood and Womanhood: A Response to Evangelical Feminism,* ed. John Piper and Wayne Grudem (Wheaton, Ill.: Crossway Books, 1991), 112.

2. Ibid., 481 n.32.

3. See David Neff, "Women in the Confidence Gap," *Christianity Today,* 22 July 1991, 13.

4. John Piper, "A Vision of Biblical Complementarity: Manhood and Womanhood Defined According to the Bible," in *Recovering Biblical Manhood and Womanhood,* 35–36.

5. Ortlund, 99.

6. This was, for example, a key element in the homosexual orientation of men in ancient Greece. See Reay Tannahill, *Sex in History* (New York: Stein and Day, 1980), 85–87.

7. See Josephine Donovan, *Feminist Theory: The Intellectual Traditions of American Feminism,* New Expanded Edition (New York: Continuum, 1992), 161–66.

8. This, in fact, was the testimony of a Christian woman who wrote to me of her joyous experience of discovering the truth of biblical equality.

9. Ortlund, 481 n.32.

10. Ibid., 99.

11. Piper, 35.

12. Elisabeth Elliot, *Let Me Be A Woman: Notes to My Daughter on the Meaning of Womanhood* (Wheaton, Ill.: Tyndale House Publishers, Inc., 1976), 93.

13. Piper, 50.

14. David Neff, "Two Men Don't Make a Right," *Christianity Today,* 19 July 1993, 15.

15. See, for example, John Piper and Wayne Grudem, "An Overview of Central Concerns," in *Recovering Biblical Manhood and Womanhood,* 82–84.

16. For discussions of biblical teaching on homosexuality, see J. Isamu Yamamoto, ed., *The Crisis of Homosexuality,* Christianity Today Series (Wheaton, Ill.: Victor Books, 1990), 131–64; also, John R. W. Stott, *Decisive Issues Facing Christians Today,* rev. enl. ed. of *Involvement* in 2 vols. (Old Tappan, N.J.: Revell, 1990), 336–64.

17. Royce Gordon Gruenler, *The Trinity in the Gospel of John: A Thematic Commentary on the Fourth Gospel* (Grand Rapids, Mich.: Baker Book House, 1986), xv–xvi.

18. Ortlund, 112.

19. Stephen D. Lowe, "Rethinking the Female Status/Function Question: The Jew/Gentile Relationship as Paradigm," *Journal of the Evangelical Theological Society* 34, no. 1 (March 1991): 67.

20. See, for example, Piper and Grudem, 73–74.

21. Ibid., 60, 74, 87.

22. John Knox, *The First Blast of the Trumpet against the Monstrous Regiment of Women* (1558), in *The Political Writings of John Knox: The First Blast of the Trumpet against the Monstrous Regiment of Women and Other Selected Works,* ed. Marvin A. Breslow (Washington: Folger Books, The Folger Shakespeare Library, 1985), 42–43.

23. Nicholas Wolterstorff, "Hearing the Cry," in *Women, Authority, and the Bible,* ed. Alvera Mickelsen (Downers Grove, Ill.: InterVarsity Press, 1986), 290.

24. See chapter 1.

25. See chapters 6 and 7.

26. Wayne Grudem, "Wives Like Sarah, and Husbands Who Honor Them," in *Recovering Biblical Manhood and Womanhood,* 207. James B. Hurley describes the husband's role similarly in *Man and Woman in Biblical Perspective* (Grand Rapids, Mich.: Zondervan Publishing House, 1981), 151.

27. Mutual decision making in marriage is discussed in the final section of chapter 7.

28. John Stuart Mill, introduction to *The Subjection of Women,* ed. Wendell Robert Carr (Cambridge, Mass.: M.I.T. Press, 1970; orig. pub. 1869), xvii.

29. Peter Keely, "Who Speaks for God?" an unpublished paper; quoted in James Alsdurf and Phyllis Alsdurf, *Battered Into Submission: The Tragedy of Wife Abuse in the Christian Home* (Downers Grove, Ill.: InterVarsity Press, 1989), 80. See also final section of chapter 10, especially note 15.

30. Examples of such statements can be found in Jack Hayford, *A Man's Starting Place* (Van Nuys, Calif.: Living Way Ministries, 1992), 14, 20, 48.

31. See Rebecca Merrill Groothuis, *Women Caught in the Conflict: The Culture War Between Traditionalism and Feminism* (Grand Rapids, Mich.: Baker Book House, 1994), 20–23, for a discussion of the difference between the truly traditional view of male authority and that of today's traditionalists.

32. Ortlund, 482 n.50.

33. Ibid., 110.

34. Piper and Grudem, 64.

35. Piper, 37–38.

36. C. S. Lewis, "Priestesses in the Church?" *God in the Dock: Essays on Theology and Ethics,* ed. Walter Hooper (Grand Rapids, Mich.: William B. Eerdmans Publishing Company, 1970), 238.

37. Thomas Howard, "A Note from Antiquity on the Question of Women's Ordination," *Churchman* 92, no. 4 (1978): 323.

38. Elisabeth Elliot, *Let Me Be a Woman: Notes to My Daughter on the Meaning of Womanhood* (Wheaton, Ill.: Tyndale House Publishers, Inc., 1976), 59–64.

39. Larry Crabb, *Men and Women: Enjoying the Difference* (Grand Rapids, Mich.: Zondervan Publishing House, 1991), 132–33.

40. Larry Crabb, *Inside Out* (Colorado Springs, Colo.: Navpress, 1988), 208–9.

41. Crabb, *Men and Women,* 151.

42. Piper and Grudem, 86–87.

43. Emil Brunner, *Man in Revolt: A Christian Anthropology,* trans. Olive Wyon (Philadelphia: The Westminster Press, 1947), 352–53.

44. Ibid., 355.

45. Susan Foh is one such traditionalist; according to Faith Martin, she is the only one. See Faith McBurney Martin, *Call Me Blessed: The Emerging Christian Woman* (Grand Rapids, Mich.: William B. Eerdmans Publishing Co., 1988), 84.

46. See David Basinger, "Gender, Scripture, and Science," *Christian Scholars Review* 17 (1988): 245.

47. Piper, 33–36.

48. Susan Foh, "Why Joanie Can't be Johnny," review of *Recovering Biblical Manhood and Womanhood,* in *Christianity Today,* 8 April 1991, 49–50.

49. Susan T. Foh, *Women and the Word of God: A Response to Biblical Feminism* (Grand Rapids, Mich.: Baker Book House, 1979), 175–76.

50. Quoted in Robert L. Wilken, "The Lives of the Saints and the Pursuit of Virtue," *First Things,* December 1990, 50.

51. Elizabeth A. Morelli, "The Question of Woman's Experience of God," in *Speaking the Christian God: The Holy Trinity and the Challenge of Feminism,* ed. Alvin F. Kimel Jr. (Grand Rapids, Mich.: William B. Eerdmans Publishing Co., 1992), 236.

Chapter 4: Sexuality in God and in the Image of God

1. Donald G. Bloesch, *Is the Bible Sexist? Beyond Feminism and Patriarchalism* (Westchester, Ill.: Crossway Books, 1982), 66.

2. Ibid., 76–77.

3. C. S. Lewis, "Priestesses in the Church," in *God in the Dock: Essays on Theology and Ethics,* ed. Walter Hooper (Grand Rapids, Mich.: William B. Eerdmans Publishing Co., 1970), 237.

4. Ibid., 239.

5. Craig S. Keener, *Paul, Women, and Wives: Marriage and Women's Ministry in the Letters of Paul* (Peabody, Mass.: Hendrickson Publishers, 1992), 110. See also Nancy Tuana, *The Less Noble Sex: Scientific, Religious, and Philosophical Conceptions of Woman's Nature* (Bloomington, Ind.: Indiana University Press, 1993), 57–58.

6. Lewis, 237.

7. Many biblical references to feminine imagery for God are discussed in Aida Besancon Spencer, *Beyond the Curse: Women Called to Ministry* (Nashville, Tenn.: Thomas Nelson, 1985), 121–31.

8. See Aida Besancon Spencer, et al., *The Goddess Revival* (Grand Rapids, Mich.: Baker Book House, 1995), 112–13.

9. J. I. Packer and Thomas Howard, *Christianity: The True Humanism* (Waco, Tex.: Word Books, 1985), 143.

10. Werner Neuer, *Man and Woman in Christian Perspective* (Wheaton, Ill.: Crossway Books, 1991), 64.

11. Ibid., 152.

12. Ibid., 155.

13. Millard J. Erickson, *God in Three Persons: A Contemporary Interpretation of the Trinity* (Grand Rapids, Mich.: Baker Books, 1995), 301.

14. See Mary Stewart Van Leeuwen, et al., *After Eden: Facing the Challenge of Gender Reconciliation* (Grand Rapids, Mich.: William B. Eerdmans Publishing Co., 1993), 163.

15. Mary Hayter, *The New Eve in Christ: The Use and Abuse of the Bible in the Debate about Women in the Church* (Grand Rapids, Mich.: William B. Eerdmans Publishing Co., 1987), 34.

16. Neuer, 155–56.

17. Ibid., 158, 160–62.

18. Ibid., 162.

19. See John Frame, "Men and Women in the Image of God," in *Recovering Biblical Manhood and Womanhood: A Response to Evangelical Feminism,* ed. John Piper and Wayne Grudem (Wheaton, Ill.: Crossway Books, 1991), 229–30; and James B. Hurley, *Man and Woman in Biblical Perspective* (Grand Rapids, Mich.: Zondervan Publishing House, 1981), 173.

20. Faith Martin, "Mystical Masculinity: The New Question Facing Women," *Priscilla Papers* 6, no. 4 (Fall 1992): 5.

21. Faith Martin, *Call Me Blessed: The Emerging Christian Woman* (Grand Rapids, Mich.: William B. Eerdmans Publishing Co., 1988), 104.

22. Hayter, 41.

23. Martin, "Mystical Masculinity," 6. For excellent and enlightening discussions of God and gender, see Hayter, chapters 1 and 2; Martin, *Call Me Blessed,* 98–105; Martin, "Mystical Masculinity," 1–7.

24. Mary J. Evans, *Woman in the Bible: An Overview of all the Crucial Passages on Women's Roles* (Downers Grove, Ill.: InterVarsity Press, 1983), 108. The issue of the maleness of Christ and the priesthood will be discussed later in this chapter.

25. Carl F. H. Henry, *God, Revelation, and Authority,* vol. 5 (Waco, Tex.: Word Books Publisher, 1982), 159.

26. Spencer, *Goddess Revival,* 121–26.

27. Hayter, 14–15.

28. Alister E. McGrath, *Intellectuals Don't Need God and Other Modern Myths* (Grand Rapids, Mich.: Zondervan Publishing House, 1993), 174. See also Alister E. McGrath, *Christian Theology: An Introduction* (Cambridge, Mass.: Blackwell, 1994), 135, 205–207.

29. According to ancient cultures, this would make God more like a father than a mother, for mothers were not recognized as contributing to the genetic makeup of their offspring.

30. See Spencer, *Goddess Revival,* 119.

31. See ibid., 87; and Gary W. Deddo, "Speaking of God," *Religious and Theological Studies Fellowship Bulletin,* April/May 1995, 12.

32. Tikva Frymer-Kensky, *In the Wake of the Goddesses: Women, Culture, and the Biblical Transformation of Pagan Myth* (New York: Fawcett Columbine, 1992), 188.

33. Hayter, 18. Note that this perspective provides a corrective to Elizabeth Achtemeier's contention that pantheism follows from goddess worship. See Elizabeth Achtemeier, "Exchanging God for 'No Gods': A Discussion of Female Language for God," in *Speaking the Christian God: The Holy Trinity and the Challenge of Feminism,* ed. Alvin F. Kimel Jr. (Grand Rapids, Mich.: William B. Eerdmans Publishing Co., 1992), 8–9. It is not simply the concept of a goddess that entails a creator/creature conflation (as Achtemeier maintains), but the concept of a deity that is in any sense sexual.

34. Thomas Howard, "A Note from Antiquity on the Question of Women's Ordination," *Churchman* 92, no. 4 (1978): 323.

35. Cynthia Eller, *Living in the Lap of the Goddess* (New York, N.Y.: The Crossroad Publishing Co., 1993), 52.

36. Susan Foh, *Women and the Word of God: A Response to Biblical Feminism* (Grand Rapids, Mich.: Baker Book House, 1980), 177.

37. Michael Novak, "Women, Ordination, and Angels," *First Things,* April 1993, 26. Although the Anglican church now ordains women as priests, its traditional theological rationale for *not* ordaining women follows along lines similar to Catholic thought—as seen in J. I. Packer's defense of an all-male presbytery, discussed later in this chapter.

38. Sarah M. Grimke, *Letters on the Equality of the Sexes and the Condition of Woman* (1838; repr., New York: Burt Franklin, 1970), 98; quoted in Josephine Donovan, *Feminist Theory: The Intellectual Traditions of American Feminism,* New Expanded Edition (New York: Continuum, 1992), 16. Emphasis in the original.

39. Wayne Grudem does offer a chapter-length defense of male authority in *Systematic Theology: An Introduction to Biblical Doctrine* (Grand Rapids, Mich.: Zondervan Publishing House, 1994), 454–74. Absent from his largely exegetical treatment, however, are the theological tenets that seem clearly to be entailed by the doctrine of male hierarchy (see above), and which high church traditions have considered essential to a theological defense of a male-only clergy. Grudem's theological construct is based primarily on the "equal in being, different in function" concept, as illustrated and justified by the subordination of Christ to God (which I critique in chapter 2); he also makes extensive use of the traditionalist interpretation of Genesis 1–3 (which I critique in chapter 5).

40. J. I. Packer, "Let's Stop Making Women Presbyters," *Christianity Today,* 11 February 1991, 13–21.

41. For an explanation of why no women served as priests in the Old Testament, see Hayter, 63–77.

42. Gilbert Bilezikian, *Beyond Sex Roles: What the Bible Says About a Woman's Place in Church and Family,* 2d ed. (Grand Rapids, Mich.: Baker Book House, 1986), 69.

43. For a discussion of female prophets in the Bible, see the beginning of chapter 8.

44. Paul K. Jewett, *Man as Male and Female* (Grand Rapids, Mich.: William B. Eerdmans Publishing Co., 1975), 164.

45. See Hayter, 52; see also Stanley J. Grenz with Denise Muir Kjesbo, *Women in the Church: A Biblical Theology of Women in Ministry* (Downers Grove, Ill.: InterVarsity Press, 1995), 201–5.

46. Hayter, 55.

47. Ibid., 56.

48. See Lewis, 237, for a statement of this view.

49. The traditional theological argument for male priests does not stand or fall on this question of the separability of being and function. Rather, the argument founders primarily on its premises that maleness is essential to who Christ is as Christ, and that the priest (or pastor) serves as an icon, a literal symbol or representation, of Christ.

50. Packer, 20.

51. Cornelius Plantinga Jr., Letter to the Editor, *Christianity Today,* 29 April 1991, 8.

52. Ruth A. Tucker, *Women in the Maze: Questions and Answers on Biblical Equality* (Downers Grove, Ill.: InterVarsity Press, 1992), 26.

53. Jewett, 168.

54. See Alvin John Schmidt, *Veiled and Silenced: How Culture Shapes Sexist Theology* (Macon, Ga.: Mercer University Press, 1989), 166–68.

55. See Richard and Catherine Kroeger, "Why Were There No Women Apostles?" CBE reprint; originally published in *Equity* (1982): 10–12.

56. Millard Erickson, *The Word Became Flesh: An Incarnational Christology* (Grand Rapids, Mich.: Baker Book House, 1991), 590.

57. See the section on "The Old Covenant Versus the New" in chapter 1.

58. See Grenz, 212.

59. Erickson, *The Word Became Flesh,* 593.

60. Alister McGrath, "In What Way Can Jesus Be a Moral Example for Christians?" *Journal of the Evangelical Theological Society* 34, no. 3 (September 1991): 295.

61. Hayter, 55.

62. Grenz, 206. For more on the New Testament emphasis on Jesus' humanity over his maleness, see Spencer, *Goddess Revival,* 99–101.

63. Erickson, *The Word Became Flesh,* 582.

64. Ibid., 581–82.

65. In more general, less theological contexts, there is also a growing tendency to speak of masculinity as though it were a distinctly Christlike attribute. In fact, the idea that Christ is the perfect model of masculinity has become something of a slogan for the Christian men's movement. But if masculinity is understood to be the manly behavior that sets men apart from women—and which, therefore, is inappropriate for women—and if Christ serves as a model for this sort of behavior, then women are constitutionally incapable of emulating Christ to the degree that men are able to do. In other words, if Christian men are like Christ not merely because they are Christians, but also because they are men, then men are simply more Christlike than women. Many teachers and writers on men's issues seem unaware that, biblically, Christ is as much of a model and example for women as for men, and that there is *nothing* in Christ's behavior or character that is appropriate only for men to emulate. For a critique of the Promise Keepers' movement, see Rebecca Merrill Groothuis and Douglas Groothuis, "Women Keep Promises Too! Or, the Christian Life is for Both Men and Women," *Perspectives* 10, no. 7 (August/September 1995): 19–23.

66. Packer, 21.

67. Ibid., 20.

68. Ibid., 21.

69. See chapter 2 for a critique of the being/function distinction with respect to women's subordination.

70. These concepts are discussed at more length in the section, "The Old Covenant Versus the New," in chapter 1.

71. The "spiritual leadership" of the husband in the traditionalist agenda is discussed and critiqued in the sections, "Servant Leadership" and "Unearned, Unaccountable, and God-ordained," in chapter 3.

Chapter 5: In the Beginning

1. These New Testament texts are discussed in chapters 6–9.

2. The Danvers Statement, in *Recovering Biblical Manhood and Womanhood: A Response to Evangelical Feminism,* ed. John Piper and Wayne Grudem (Wheaton, Ill.: Crossway Books, 1991), 469.

3. John Piper, "A Vision of Biblical Complementarity: Manhood and Womanhood Defined According to the Bible," in *Recovering Biblical Manhood and Womanhood,* 35, 477 n.25.

4. See the section on "How to do Biblical Interpretation" in chapter 6.

5. I am indebted to Robert Hubbard for this insight on the text.

6. Raymond C. Ortlund Jr., "Male-Female Equality and Male Headship: Genesis 1–3," in *Recovering Biblical Manhood and Womanhood,* 98.

7. Ibid.

8. See the discussion of headship in chapter 6.

9. Donald Joy, *Lovers: Whatever Happened to Eden?* (Waco, Tex.: Word Books, 1987), 27–37.

10. Ibid., 37.

11. Donald Joy, "Toward a Symbolic Revival: Creation Revisited," *The Asbury Seminarian* 4, no. 2 (Winter 1985): 11. This is not Joy's view, but his description of the traditional view.

12. Ortlund, 98.

13. See chapter 2 on the logical problems with the "equal but subordinate" approach.

14. See Faith Martin, *Call Me Blessed: The Emerging Christian Woman* (Grand Rapids, Mich.: William B. Eerdmans Publishing Co., 1988), 18–27, 80–84.

15. Augustine, *The Trinity,* trans. Stephen McKenna, *The Fathers of the Church,* vol. 45 (Washington D.C.: Catholic University of America Press, 1963), 352.

16. Abraham Kuyper, *Women of the Old Testament,* 2d ed. (Grand Rapids, Mich.: Zondervan Publishing House, 1936), 5.

17. See the section, "Adam Was Formed First," in chapter 9 for a response to the argument for male authority from the ancient patriarchal custom of primogeniture.

18. I owe this observation to Robert Hubbard.

19. Roger Nicole, lecture entitled, "In the Beginning there was Equality." Audio tape available from CBE.

20. Ortlund, 102, 481 n.26.

21. Joy Elasky Fleming with J. Robin Maxson, *Man and Woman in Biblical Unity: Theology From Genesis 2–3* (Saint Paul, Minn.: Christians for Biblical Equality, 1993), 14.

22. See the section on 1 Corinthians 11:3–16 in chapter 6.

23. Aida Besancon Spencer, *Beyond the Curse: Women Called to Ministry* (Nashville, Tenn: Thomas Nelson Publishers, 1985), 28.

24. Millard J. Erickson, *Christian Theology,* one-volume edition (Grand Rapids, Mich.: Baker Book House, 1985), 546.

25. Spencer, 27.

26. Ibid., 26.

27. John Piper and Wayne Grudem, "An Overview of Central Concerns: Questions and Answers," in *Recovering Biblical Manhood and Womanhood,* 87. Piper and Grudem seem to have confused the egalitarian argument regarding "helper" with the strange notion—held by no one that I know of—that because the woman is a helper she is *like* God.

28. See Nancy Tuana, *The Less Noble Sex: Scientific, Religious, and Philosophical Conceptions of Women's Nature* (Bloomington, Ind.: Indiana University Press, 1993); and Page duBois, *Centaurs and Amazons: Women and the Pre-History of the Great Chain of Being* (Ann Arbor, Mich.: The University of Michigan Press, 1982).

29. Piper and Grudem, 87.

30. Ortlund, 104.

31. Wayne Grudem, *Systematic Theology: An Introduction to Biblical Doctrine* (Grand Rapids, Mich.: Zondervan Publishing House, 1994), 461–62.

32. Gilbert Bilezikian, *Beyond Sex Roles: What the Bible Says About a Woman's Place in Church and Family,* 2d ed. (Grand Rapids, Mich.: Baker Book House, 1986), 40–41.

33. Ibid., 41.

34. Ibid., 34.

35. Ortlund, 103.

36. Anne Atkins, *Split Image: Male and Female After God's Likeness* (Grand Rapids, Mich.: William B. Eerdmans Publishing Co., 1987), 20–21; in the reference to the meaning of "cleaving," Atkins cites Mary J. Evans, *Woman in the Bible* (Paternoster Press, 1983), 17.

37. See Ortlund, 107–8.

38. Walter C. Kaiser Jr., *Hard Sayings of the Old Testament* (Downers Grove, Ill.: InterVarsity Press, 1988), 35.

39. Spencer, 36.

40. Kaiser, 34–35.

41. Mary Stewart Van Leeuwen, *Gender and Grace: Love, Work, and Parenting in a Changing World* (Downers Grove, Ill.: InterVarsity Press, 1990), 47. The following represents a slightly different slant on Van Leeuwen's discussion.

42. See Robert D. Culver, "Let Your Women Keep Silence," in *Women in Ministry*, 107–108; and Bilezikian, 264–66 n.12. This interpretation apparently was devised originally by Susan Foh, who sets it forth in Susan T. Foh, "The Head of the Woman is the Man," in *Women in Ministry: Four Views*, ed. Bonnidell Clouse and Robert G. Clouse (Downers Grove, Ill.: InterVarsity Press, 1989), 74–75; and elsewhere.

43. Ortlund, 109.

44. See Faith Martin, "A Response to *Recovering Biblical Manhood and Womanhood*," presented at the Conference for Women, Beaver Falls, Pennsylvania, February 27, 1993. Available from CBE.

45. Bilezikian, 266.

46. Spencer, 30–31.

47. See Bilezikian, 42.

48. Ortlund, 482 n.50.

49. Ortlund, 109.

50. Danvers Statement, in *Recovering Biblical Manhood and Womanhood*, 470.

Chapter 6: "The Husband Is the Head of the Wife"

1. An excellent place to begin learning about the cultural settings of New Testament texts is in Craig S. Keener, *The IVP Bible Background Commentary: New Testament* (Downers Grove, Ill.: InterVarsity Press, 1993).

2. Mark Noll, *Between Faith and Criticism: Evangelicals, Scholarship, and the Bible in America*, 2d ed. (Grand Rapids, Mich.: Baker Book House, 1991), 58–59.

3. Mark Noll, *The Scandal of the Evangelical Mind* (Grand Rapids, Mich.: William B. Eerdmans Publishing Co., 1994), 133.

4. See ibid., 127.

5. Gordon D. Fee and Douglas Stuart, *How to Read the Bible For All Its Worth* (Grand Rapids, Mich.: Zondervan Publishing House, 1982), 67.

6. Craig S. Keener, *Paul, Women, and Wives: Marriage and Women's Ministry in the Letters of Paul* (Peabody, Mass: Hendrickson Publishers, 1992), 226.

7. Fee and Stuart, 66.

8. I owe this insight to Craig Keener. For a discussion of women in the Bible with leadership ministries, see chapter 8.

9. See Fee and Stuart, 65–70, for a more extended discussion on how to distinguish between that which is culturally relative and that which is universally normative in the Bible.

10. See Rebecca Merrill Groothuis, *Women Caught in the Conflict: The Culture War Between Traditionalism and Feminism* (Grand Rapids, Mich.: Baker Book House, 1994), chapter 3.

11. This is discussed in more detail in the section, "The Old Covenant Versus the New," in chapter 1.

12. James Davison Hunter, *Evangelicalism: The Coming Generation* (Chicago: The University of Chicago Press, 1987), 103.

13. For ancient Greek understandings of the "head" metaphor, see Catherine Clark Kroeger, "The Classical Concept of Head as 'Source,'" Appendix III in Gretchen Gaebelein Hull, *Equal to Serve: Women and Men in the Church and Home* (Old Tappan, N.J.: Fleming H. Revell, 1987), 267–83; Gilbert Bilezikian, *Beyond Sex Roles: What the Bible Says About a Woman's Place in Church and Family*, 2d ed. (Grand Rapids, Mich.: Baker Book House, 1986), Appendix, 215–52;

C. C. Kroeger, "Head," in *Dictionary of Paul and His Letters,* ed. Gerald F. Hawthorne, et al. (Downers Grove, Ill.: InterVarsity Press, 1993), 375–77; Keener, *Paul, Women, and Wives,* 32–34; and Gordon D. Fee, *The First Epistle to the Corinthians,* New International Commentary on the New Testament (Grand Rapids, Mich.: William B. Eerdmans Publishing Co., 1987), 501–5. See also Mary J. Evans, *Woman in the Bible* (Downers Grove, Ill.: InterVarsity Press, 1983), 65; S. Scott Bartchy, "Power, Submission, and Sexual Identity Among the Early Christians," in *Essays on New Testament Christianity: A Festschrift in Honor of Dean E. Walker,* ed. C. Robert Wetzel (Cincinnati: Standard Publishing, 1978), 79; and Aida Besancon Spencer, *Beyond the Curse: Women Called to Ministry* (Nashville, Tenn.: Thomas Nelson Publishers, 1985), 104 n.14. For a review of the literature on *kephale,* see David M. Scholer, "The Evangelical Debate Over Biblical Headship," in *Women, Abuse, and the Bible: How Scripture Can Be Used to Hurt or to Heal,* ed. Catherine Clark Kroeger and James R. Beck (Grand Rapids, Mich.: Baker Book House, 1996), 40–44.

14. Henry George Liddell and Robert Scott, *A Greek-English Lexicon,* revised and augmented throughout by Sir Henry Stuart Jones with the assistance of Roderick McKenzie (Oxford: Clarendon Press, 1940; with a supplement, 1968), 945.

15. Fee, 502–3.

16. See Keener, *Paul, Women, and Wives,* 32.

17. Ibid., 168.

18. I owe this insight in part to Sulia Mason.

19. "Authoritarian" refers to an authority that requires complete obedience, is centered in one person, and is not accountable to those whom the person governs. In this sense, it is unqualified, unrestricted, and absolute. The authority traditionally accorded a husband over his family is just such an authority. This, at root, is what is still advocated by traditionalists, although the force of it is mitigated by talk of husbandly consideration and respect. See the sections, "Servant Leadership" and "Unearned, Unaccountable, and God-ordained," in chapter 3 for more on this.

20. See Robert W. Wall, "Wifely Submission in the Context of Ephesians," *Christian Scholars Review* 17 (1988): 282.

21. Mutual submission in marriage is discussed in the following chapter.

22. Aida Besancon Spencer, "From Poet to Judge: What Does Ephesians 5 Teach About Male-Female Roles?" *Priscilla Papers* 4, no. 3 (Summer 1990): 13–14.

23. Paul E. Billheimer, *Destined for the Throne: A New Look at the Bride of Christ* (Fort Washington, Penn.: Christian Literature Crusade, 1976), 27, 31 n.9.

24. I owe this insight to Douglas Groothuis.

25. See the section, "He Will Rule over You," in chapter 5.

26. Eugene H. Peterson, *The Message: The New Testament in Contemporary English* (Colorado Springs, Colo.: Navpress, 1993), 409.

27. See the discussion on "Servant Leadership" in chapter 3 for more on this.

28. Fee, 492.

29. Bilezikian, 137–39.

30. See Kroeger, "Classical Concept," 268–69, 276–79, 283; Kroeger, "Head," 377; and Fee, 504 n.48.

31. See section on "Functional Subordination and the Godhead" in chapter 2 for more on this. See also "Subordinationism" in *Evangelical Dictionary of Theology,* ed. Walter A. Elwell (Grand Rapids, Mich.: Baker Book House, 1986), 1058; Bilezikian, 278–80 n.16; and Gilbert Bilezikian, "Subordination in the Godhead," a lecture given at the CBE National Conference, August 1993, available from Christians for Biblical Equality.

32. The same Greek word can be translated either "woman" or "wife," and likewise the same word is used for either "man" or "husband." In 1 Cor. 11:3 the words are usually translated "man" and "woman," but often interpreted to mean "husband" and "wife."

33. Peterson, 354.

34. Keener, *Paul, Women, and Wives,* 38; Fee, 502; and Stanley J. Grenz with Denise Muir Kjesbo, *Women in the Church: A Biblical Theology of Women in Ministry* (Downers Grove, Ill.: InterVarsity Press, 1995), 112–13.

35. Fee, 518–23.

36. See ibid., 522–24.

37. Bartchy, 59.

38. Keener, *Paul, Women, and Wives,* 28–30.

39. See Bizhan Torabi, "Veil of Darkness Descends on Iran's Women," *Rocky Mountain News,* 4 August 1995.

40. Katherine M. Haubert, *Women as Leaders: Accepting the Challenge of Scripture* (Monrovia, Calif.: Marc, 1993), 54–55; and Fee, 510–12.

41. Keener, *Paul, Women, and Wives,* 37.

42. Fee, 517.

Chapter 7: Marriage and Mutual Submission

1. Gerhard Kittel, *Theological Dictionary of the New Testament,* vol. 8, ed. Gerhard Friedrich, trans. and ed. Geoffrey W. Bromiley (Grand Rapids, Mich.: William B. Eerdmans Publishing Co., 1972), 39–42; and Mary J. Evans, *Woman in the Bible* (Downers Grove, Ill.: InterVarsity Press, 1983), 67–68.

2. Kittel, 45.

3. C. E. B. Cranfield, *A Critical and Exegetical Commentary on The Epistle to the Romans* (Edinburgh: T. & T. Clark Limited, 1979), 660–62.

4. Craig S. Keener, *Paul, Women, and Wives: Marriage and Women's Ministry in the Letters of Paul* (Peabody, Mass.: Hendrickson Publishers, 1992), 168. See also Cranfield, 661; and Kittel, 40.

5. Keener, 167.

6. Walter A. Elwell, ed., *Evangelical Commentary on the Bible* (Grand Rapids, Mich.: Baker Book House, 1989), 1031.

7. See Wayne Grudem, "Wives Like Sarah, and the Husbands Who Honor Them: 1 Peter 3:1–7," in *Recovering Biblical Manhood and Womanhood: A Response to Evangelical Feminism,* ed. John Piper and Wayne Grudem (Wheaton, Ill.: Crossway Books, 1991), 199.

8. Walter L. Liefeld, commentator for Ephesians, in *The NIV Study Bible,* ed. Kenneth L. Barker (Grand Rapids, Mich.: Zondervan Bible Publishers, 1985), 1798.

9. Keener, 158.

10. Cranfield, 661–62.

11. Grudem, 199.

12. Keener, 167.

13. Ibid., 157.

14. Liefeld, 1798.

15. Keener, 162, 165.

16. Ibid., 157.

17. See Katherine M. Haubert, *Women as Leaders: Accepting the Challenge of Scripture* (Monrovia, Calif.: Marc, 1993), 76.

18. See Craig S. Keener, *The IVP Bible Background Commentary: New Testament* (Downers Grove, Ill.: InterVarsity Press, 1993), 715.

19. William Barclay, *The Letters of James and Peter,* 2d ed. (Philadelphia: The Westminster Press, 1960), 258–59. In Barclay, "make a decision" read "take a decision," which I changed for the sake of clarity.

20. Keener, *The IVP Bible Background Commentary: New Testament,* 716.

21. Evans, 117.

22. Peter H. Davids, *More Hard Sayings of the New Testament* (Downers Grove, Ill.: InterVarsity Press, 1991), 159 n.1.

23. Keener, *The IVP Bible Background Commentary: New Testament,* 716.

24. Millard J. Erickson, *Christian Theology* (Grand Rapids, Mich.: Baker Book House, 1985), 547.

25. Lee Anna Starr, *The Bible Status of Woman* (1926; repr., Zarephath, N.J.: Pillar of Fire, 1955), 222–23.

26. J. Chrysostom, *Homilies on the Epistles to the Corinthians,* 155; cited in Evans, 119.

27. Keener, *Paul, Women, and Wives,* 211 n.1.

28. Evans, 120.

29. Barclay, 265.

30. Starr, 216.

31. See Keener, *Paul, Women, and Wives,* chapter 6, for a discussion of the analogy between slavery and male authority in marriage.

32. See, for example, John Piper and Wayne Grudem, "An Overview of Central Concerns: Questions and Answers," in *Recovering Biblical Manhood and Womanhood,* 65–66.

33. James Alsdurf and Phyllis Alsdurf, *Battered into Submission: The Tragedy of Wife Abuse in the Christian Home* (Downers Grove, Ill.: InterVarsity Press, 1989), 88.

34. James B. Hurley, *Man and Woman in Biblical Perspective* (Grand Rapids, Mich.: Zondervan Publishing House, 1981), 153–54.

35. Grudem, 201–2.

36. Ibid., 501 n.13.

37. Thankfully, some traditionalists do make it clear that the best course of action for an abused wife often includes spearating from the abusive husband (even though this approach is, strictly speaking, inconsistent with a traditionalist interpretation of 1 Peter 2–3). James Dobson's Focus on the Family, for example, offers some very helpful and sensible advice in its information sheet on spouse abuse. A booklet from Radio Bible Class, *When Violence Comes Home,* is another example.

38. Craig S. Keener, *. . . And Marries Another: Divorce and Remarriage in the Teaching of the New Testament* (Peabody, Mass.: Hendrickson Publishers, 1991), 106.

39. Keener, *IVP Bible Background Commentary: New Testament,* 716.

40. See Keener, *Paul, Women, and Wives,* 134–35.

41. Gordon D. Fee and Douglas Stuart, *How to Read the Bible For All Its Worth* (Grand Rapids, Mich.: Zondervan Publishing House, 1982), 68.

42. See Aida Besancon Spencer, "From Poet to Judge: What Does Ephesians 5 Teach About Male-Female Roles?" *Priscilla Papers* 4, no. 3 (Summer 1990): 15.

43. James Zumwalt, "Being Tested Made Us Stronger," *Parade Magazine,* 5 June 1994, 5.

44. Gretchen Gaebelein Hull, *Equal to Serve: Women and Men in the Church and Home* (Old Tappan, N.J.: Fleming H. Revell Company, 1987), 98.

45. "20/20" television program, ABC-TV, November 1, 1991.

46. Robertson McQuilkin, "Living by Vows," *Christianity Today,* 8 October 1990, 40.

47. James Houston, *The Heart's Desire: A Guide to Personal Fulfillment* (Batavia, Ill.: Lion, 1992), 82.

48. For more on mutual submission in marriage, see Jack O. Balswick and Judith K. Balswick, *The Family: A Christian Perspective of the Contemporary Home* (Grand Rapids, Mich.: Baker Book House, 1989), chapter 5; and Patricia Gundry, *Heirs Together: Mutual Submission in Marriage* (Grand Rapids, Mich.: Zondervan Publishing House, 1980).

Chapter 8: The Bible and Women in Leadership

1. Aida Besancon Spencer, *Beyond the Curse: Women Called to Ministry* (Nashville, Tenn.: Thomas Nelson Publishers, 1985), 99–100.

2. John Piper and Wayne Grudem, "An Overview of Central Concerns: Questions and Answers," in *Recovering Biblical Manhood and Womanhood: A Response to Evangelical Feminism,* ed. John Piper and Wayne Grudem (Wheaton, Ill.: Crossway Books, 1991), 72.

3. Thomas R. Schreiner, "The Valuable Ministries of Women in the Context of Male Leadership: A Survey of Old and New Testament Examples and Teaching," in *Recovering Biblical Manhood and Womanhood,* 216.

4. See the section later in this chapter on the traditionalist hierarchy of spiritual authority.

5. Stanley Grenz with Denise Muir Kjesbo, *Women in the Church: A Biblical Theology of Women in Ministry* (Downers Grove, Ill.: InterVarsity Press, 1995), 238 n.10.

6. Merrill F. Unger, *The New Unger's Bible Dictionary,* ed. R. K. Harrison (Chicago: Moody Press, 1988), 724.

7. See John Piper and Wayne Grudem, ed., *Recovering Biblical Manhood and Womanhood,* 72, 216, 275.

8. See Craig S. Keener, *Paul, Women, and Wives: Marriage and Women's Ministry in the Letters of Paul* (Peabody, Mass.: Hendrickson Publishers, 1992), 244–45.

9. S. Scott Bartchy, "Power, Submission, and Sexual Identity Among the Early Christians," in *Essays on New Testament Christianity: A Festschrift in Honor of Dean E. Walker,* ed. C. Robert Wetzel (Cincinnati: Standard Publishing, 1978), 62.

10. Keener, 28–31. See chapter 6, where this text is discussed.

11. Walter C. Kaiser, *Toward An Exegetical Theology: Biblical Exegesis for Preaching and Teaching* (Grand Rapids, Mich.: Baker Book House, 1983), 119. David M. Scholer, "1 Timothy 2:9–15 and the Place of Women in the Church's Ministry," in *Women, Authority, and the Bible,* ed. Alvera Mickelsen (Downers Grove, Ill.: InterVarsity Press, 1986), 207.

12. Keener, 241.

13. John Chrystostom, *Homily on the Epistle of St. Paul the Apostle to the Romans* XXXI; quoted in Spencer, 101.

14. See Spencer, 101; Kevin Giles, *Patterns of Ministry Among the First Christians* (Melbourne, Australia: Collins Dove, 1989), 167–68; and Gilbert Bilezikian, *Beyond Sex Roles: What the Bible Says About a Woman's Place in Church and Family,* 2d ed. (Grand Rapids, Mich.: Baker Book House, 1986), 301 n.54.

15. Grenz, 94–95; Keener, 242.

16. Keener, 242.

17. Piper and Grudem, 80–81.

18. Grenz, 93.

19. Although Piper and Grudem seem to say that Paul was one of the Twelve, this was not the case. Matthias (Acts 1:15–26), not Paul, replaced Judas as one of the Twelve.

20. The above understanding of NT apostles is taken from Paul W. Barnett, "Apostle," in *Dictionary of Paul and His Letters,* ed. Gerald F. Hawthorne, et al. (Downers Grove, Ill.: InterVarsity Press, 1993), 47–48.

21. Katherine M. Haubert, *Women as Leaders: Accepting the Challenge of Scripture* (Monrovia, Calif.: Marc, 1993), 72, 93–94 n.144.

22. Grenz, 88–89.

23. Keener, 238–39.

24. Mary J. Evans, *Woman in the Bible: An Overview of all the Crucial Passages on Women's Roles* (Downers Grove, Ill.: InterVarsity Press, 1983), 125.

25. Keener, 240; Spencer, 113–17.

26. Spencer, 107.

27. Richard and Catherine Kroeger, *Women Elders . . . Sinners or Servants?* (New York: Council on Women and the Church, 1981), 11, 9.

28. Keener, 239; Spencer, 112.

29. Spencer, 109–11; Grenz, 91–92.

30. Spencer, 112.

31. Haubert, 75.

32. Kroeger and Kroeger, 9–10; Grenz, 39–40.

33. Keener, 113, 248.

34. For further discussion of the biblical accounts of women in ministry and leadership, see Grenz, 63–97.

35. Susan T. Foh, "A Male Leadership View," *Women in Ministry: Four Views,* ed. Bonnidell Clouse and Robert G. Clouse (Downers Grove, Ill.: InterVarsity Press, 1989), 93.

36. D. A. Carson, "'Silent in the Churches': On the Role of Women in 1 Corinthians 14:33b–36," in *Recovering Biblical Manhood and Womanhood,* 153.

37. Schreiner, 217.

38. See Grenz, 213–18.

39. W. Ward Gasque and Laurel Gasque, "F. F. Bruce: A Mind for What Matters: A Conversation With a Pioneer of Evangelical Biblical Scholarship," *Christianity Today,* 7 April 1989, 24–25.

40. See H. Wayne House, *The Role of Women in Ministry Today* (Nashville, Tenn.: Thomas Nelson Publishers, 1990), 39, 128; and Carson, 140–53.

41. See, for example, Piper and Grudem, 70; and Carson, 151–53.

42. Piper and Grudem, 71.

43. Keener, 72.

44. See ibid., 81–82.

45. Grenz, 123.

46. Keener, 80–86.

47. Ibid., 87.

48. Haubert, 62–63; Grenz, 119.

49. Keener, 88.

50. Walter C. Kaiser Jr., *Hard Sayings of the Old Testament* (Downers Grove, Ill.: InterVarsity Press, 1988), 36; Kaiser, *Exegetical Theology,* 76–77.

51. Gordon D. Fee, *The First Epistle to the Corinthians,* New International Commentary on the New Testament (Grand Rapids, Mich.: William B. Eerdmans Publishing Co., 1987), 699.

52. Ibid., 701.

53. Ibid., 705. Fee also notes that marginal glosses are well documented elsewhere in the New Testament (e.g., John 5:3b–4; 1 John 5:7). For a more recent defense of this position, see Gordon D. Fee, *God's Empowering Presence: The Holy Spirit in the Letters of Paul* (Peabody, Mass.: Hendrickson Publishers, 1994), 272–81.

54. Craig S. Keener, *The IVP Bible Background Commentary: New Testament* (Downers Grove, Ill.: InterVarsity Press, 1993), 612. See also "The Husband of One Wife?" *Priscilla Papers* 4, no. 2 (Spring 1990): 13–14, for documentation of the prevalence of polygamy in the world of the New Testament.

55. Keener, *The IVP Bible Background Commentary: New Testament,* 612, 635.

56. Scholer, 198.

57. Keener, *Paul, Women, and Wives,* 110.

58. Bilezikian, 187–88.

59. Spencer, 94.

60. Kroeger and Kroeger, 9.

61. Jan Huffaker, "Tongue-in-Cheek Department," *Mutuality,* May 1995, 6.

62. See F. F. Bruce, *The Hard Sayings of Jesus* (Downers Grove, Ill.: InterVarsity Press, 1983), 120.

Chapter 9: "I Do Not Permit a Woman . . ."

1. David M. Scholer, "1 Timothy 2:9–15 and the Place of Women in the Church's Ministry," in Alvera Mickelsen, ed., *Women, Authority, and the Bible* (Downers Grove, Ill.: InterVarsity Press, 1986), 206 n.38.

2. Ibid., 213.

3. See chapters 1–4 for a development of this position.

4. Douglas Moo, "What Does It Mean Not to Teach or Have Authority Over Men? 1 Timothy 2:11–15," in *Recovering Biblical Manhood and Womanhood: A Response to Evangelical Feminism,* ed. John Piper and Wayne Grudem (Wheaton, Ill.: Crossway Books, 1991), 189.

5. Craig S. Keener, *Paul, Women, and Wives: Marriage and Women's Ministry in the Letters of Paul* (Peabody, Mass.: Hendrickson Publishers, 1992), 112.

6. Ibid.

7. See Scholer, 203; and Gordon D. Fee, "Issues in Evangelical Hermeneutics, Part III: The Great Watershed—Intentionality and Particularity/Eternality: 1 Timothy 2:8–15 as a Test Case," *Crux* XXVI, no. 4 (December 1990): 32. Fee's excellent article also appears in Gordon D. Fee, *Gospel and Spirit: Issues in New Testament Hermeneutics* (Peabody, Mass.: Hendrickson Publishers, 1991), 52–65.

8. Fee, 32.

9. Ibid., 34.

10. Ibid., 37 n.11.

11. Keener, 108.

12. Aida Besancon Spencer, *Beyond the Curse: Women Called to Ministry* (Nashville, Tenn.: Thomas Nelson Publishers, 1985), 77.

13. Keener, 111–12.

14. Fee, 32.

15. David M. Scholer, "The Evangelical Debate Over Biblical 'Headship,'" in *Women, Abuse, and the Bible: How Scripture Can Be Used to Hurt or to Heal,* ed. Catherine Clark Kroeger and James R. Beck (Grand Rapids, Mich.: Baker Book House, 1996), 46.

16. Ronald W. Pierce, "Evangelicals and Gender Roles in the 1900s: 1 Tim. 2:8–15: A Test Case," *Journal of the Evangelical Theological Society* 36, no. 3 (September 1993): 349.

17. See Scholer, "Headship," 46, 49–50.

18. Richard Clark Kroeger and Catherine Clark Kroeger, *I Suffer Not a Woman: Rethinking 1 Timothy 2:11–15 in Light of Ancient Evidence* (Grand Rapids, Mich.: Baker Book House, 1992), 103.

19. Gilbert Bilezikian, *Beyond Sex Roles: What the Bible Says About a Woman's Place in Church and Family,* 2d ed. (Grand Rapids, Mich.: Baker Book House, 1986), 174.

20. Don Williams, *The Apostle Paul and Women in the Church* (Van Nuys, Calif.: BIM Publishing Co., 1977), 112.

21. Walter C. Kaiser, *Toward an Exegetical Theology: Biblical Exegesis for Preaching and Teaching* (Grand Rapids, Mich.: Baker Book House, 1983), 119–20.

22. See Keener, 117; and Mary J. Evans, *Woman in the Bible* (Downers Grove, Ill.: InterVarsity Press, 1983), 104.

23. Kroeger and Kroeger, 117–25.

24. John Calvin, *Pastoral Epistles,* trans. Rev. William Pringle (Grand Rapids, Mich.: Eerdmans, 1959), 68.

25. Ibid., 69.

26. Evans, 104.

27. See chapter 5 for a discussion of the Genesis creation account.

28. John Piper and Wayne Grudem, "An Overview of Central Concerns: Questions and Answers," in *Recovering Biblical Manhood and Womanhood,* 81; emphasis mine.

29 Wayne Grudem, *Systematic Theology: An Introduction to Biblical Doctrine* (Grand Rapids, Mich.: Zondervan Publishing House, 1994), 461.

30. Craig L. Blomberg, "Not Beyond What is Written: A Review of Aida Spencer's *Beyond the Curse: Women Called to Ministry,*" *Criswell Theological Review* 2.2 (1988): 414. Other efforts to invoke the custom of primogeniture in defense of a traditional interpretation of this text include James B. Hurley, *Man and Woman in Biblical Perspective* (Grand Rapids, Mich.: Zondervan Publishing House, 1981), 207–8; and Piper and Grudem, 81.

31. Blomberg, 407. Blomberg does offer other reasons why the creation order "hints" at woman's "functional subordination" to man, namely, that the woman was created to be man's helper, and that the man named the woman. See chapter 5 for a response to these arguments.

32. This observation was suggested in part by Joan Tyvoll, in her paper, "A Theological Analysis of Hierarchicalism" (audio tape of lecture available through CBE).

33. See Bilezikian, 257.

34. See Spencer, 88–89; and Evans, 104.

35. Fee, 34.

36. Bilezikian, 180.

37. Evans, 104; see, for example, Walter Martin, *The Kingdom of the Cults,* rev. ed. (Minneapolis: Bethany House Publishers, 1985), 250.

38. Blomberg, 413–14.

39. Moo, 190.

40. See section on "The Man's Sin of Obedience" in chapter 5.

41. Moo, 190.

42. Hurley, 216.

43. I owe this insight to Douglas Groothuis.

44. See chapters 2 and 3 for a discussion of the correlation between inferiority in being and inferiority in function in the traditionalist subordination of women.

45. Spencer, 92.

46. Fee, 34.

47. Scholer, "1 Timothy 2:9–15," 197.

48. Ibid., 199.

49. Keener, 119–20.

50. Ibid., 119.

51. Ibid., 119–20.

52. Ibid., 117.

53. Spencer, 92–93.

54. Mark D. Roberts, "Woman Shall Be Saved: A Closer Look at 1 Timothy 2:15," *TSF Bulletin,* November/December 1981, 6.

55. Ibid., 7.

56. Kroeger and Kroeger, 176.

57. Scholer, "1 Timothy 2:9–15," 196.

Chapter 10: Ending the Stalemate

1. Chapters 2 and 3 discuss the problems entailed by using this concept in support of the traditionalist case.

2. The theological case for equality is made in chapters 1–4.

3. David Basinger, "Gender Roles, Scripture, and Science: Some Clarifications," *Christian Scholars Review* 17 (1988): 247.

4. J. P. Moreland, *Scaling the Secular City: A Defense of Christianity* (Grand Rapids, Mich.: Baker Book House, 1987), 214–20. Moreland goes so far as to say that a scientific interpretation that is strongly attested should be preferred even if the exegetical case is *less* plausible for it than for the alternative view, as he believes to be the case with progressive creationism versus young earth creationism. (However, others believe the exegetical case for progressive creationism is as strong or stronger than the case for a young earth. See Hugh Ross, *Creation and Time* [Colorado Springs, Colo.: Navpress, 1994], especially chapters 2, 5, 6.) It seems that although Moreland's principle may prove true in some cases, accepting a less plausible exegetical argument should be done with considerable caution. At any rate, such caution is not called for in applying this principle to the gender debate, for the exegetical case for equality is at least as plausible as the case for hierarchy.

5. See Basinger for a carefully argued presentation of this line of thought with respect to gender roles.

6. Gregg Johnson, "The Biological Basis for Gender-Specific Behavior," in *Recovering Biblical Manhood and Womanhood: A Response to Evangelical Feminism,* ed. John Piper and Wayne Grudem (Wheaton, Ill.: Crossway Books, 1991), 289.

7. Ibid.

8. Lisa Sowle Cahill, *Between the Sexes: Foundations of a Christian Ethics of Sexuality* (Philadelphia: Fortress Press, 1985), 91.

9. See Gina Kolata, "Men and Women Use Brain Differently," *New York Times,* 16 February 1995, 1. See also John Leo, "Sex: It's All in Your Brain," *U.S. News & World Report,* 27 February 1995, 22.

10. Tom Hess, "ABC News Breaks New Ground Again," *Focus on the Family Citizen,* 20 March 1995, 12.

11. John Stossel, "Boys and Girls Are Different," ABC-TV, 1 February 1995.

12. Alice H. Eagly, "The Science and Politics of Comparing Women and Men," *American Psychologist* 50, no. 3 (March 1995): 150–51.

13. Craig S. Keener, *Paul, Women, and Wives: Marriage and Women's Ministry in the Letters of Paul* (Peabody, Mass.: Hendrickson Publishers, 1992), 227–28.

14. See Mary Stewart Van Leeuwen, *Gender and Grace: Love, Work, and Parenting in a Changing World* (Downers Grove, Ill.: InterVarsity Press, 1990), 150–63, 170–71.

15. See Rebecca Merrill Groothuis, *Women Caught in the Conflict: The Culture War Between Traditionalism and Feminism* (Grand Rapids, Mich.: Baker Book House, 1994) for an in-depth refutation of the "slippery slope" view of evangelical feminism.

16. See the final section of chapter 7 for a description of egalitarian marriage.

17. Carolyn Holderread Heggen, *Sexual Abuse in Christian Homes and Churches* (Scottdale, Pa.: Herald Press, 1993), 73–74. See also Groothuis, *Women Caught,* 25–26; Heggen, chapter 5; James Alsdurf and Phyllis Alsdurf, *Battered into Submission: The Tragedy of Wife Abuse in the Christian Home* (Downers Grove, Ill.: InterVarsity Press, 1989), chapter 6; Florence Littauer, *Wake Up, Women! Submission Doesn't Mean Stupidity* (Dallas: Word Publishing, 1994), chapter 6.

18. Penelope Jamieson, Bishop of Dunedin, New Zealand, in the *Church of England Newspaper,* 20 November 1992; quoted in *Christianity Today,* 17 May 1993, 47.

For Further Reading

General

Gundry, Patricia. *Woman Be Free! The Clear Message of Scripture*. Grand Rapids, Mich.: Zondervan Publishing House, 1977. 112 pp. A concise, classic exposition of the biblical case for women's equality.

Hagen, June Steffensen, ed. *Gender Matters: Women's Studies for the Christian Community*. Grand Rapids, Mich.: Zondervan Publishing House, 1990. 304 pp. A collection of essays, mostly by college professors, giving a Christian feminist perspective on various areas of academic study.

Hull, Gretchen Gaebelein. *Equal to Serve: Women and Men in the Church and Home*. Old Tappan, N.J.: Fleming H. Revell Co., 1987. 302 pp. Describes biblical feminism as the belief that women and men should have equal opportunity to serve in both church and society; this is contrasted with the secular feminist emphasis on equal rights and the traditionalist emphasis on prescribed roles.

Malcolm, Kari Torjesen. *Women at the Crossroads: A Path Beyond Feminism and Traditionalism*. Downers Grove, Ill.: InterVarsity Press, 1982. 215 pp. This book gently points the reader toward a biblical balance between two cultural extremes. Especially valuable for its insight into women's roles throughout church history and its personalized approach encouraging women to make Christ their first love.

Martin, Faith McBurney. *Call Me Blessed: The Emerging Christian Woman*. Grand Rapids, Mich.: William B. Eerdmans Publishing Co., 1988. 180 pp. A gold mine of insight and information ranging over many aspects of the gender issue, including biblical and church history, theology, and biblical studies.

Sayers, Dorothy L. *Are Women Human?* Introduction by Mary McDermott Shideler. Grand Rapids, Mich.: William B. Eerdmans Publishing Co., 1971. 47 pp. A reprint of Dorothy L. Sayers' two lectures on the subject of womanhood and the difference it does and does not make. Trenchant, witty, and thoroughly delightful to read.

Storkey, Elaine. *Contributions to Christian Feminism*. London: Christian Impact, 1995. 102 pp. A collection of thought-provoking essays and lectures, offering theological and sociological reflections on Christianity and feminism.

Tucker, Ruth A. *Women in the Maze: Questions and Answers on Biblical Equality*. Downers Grove, Ill.: InterVarsity Press, 1992. 276 pp. A clear and readable response to questions frequently asked concerning the gender of God, the significance for women of the creation and fall, the Old Testament and Jewish culture, the New Testament and women, the role of women in church history, and issues relating to feminism in contemporary society.

History and Social Science

Bendroth, Margaret Lamberts. *Fundamentalism and Gender: 1875 to the Present.* New Haven: Yale University Press, 1993. 179 pp. A well-researched account of the different phases fundamentalism has gone through with respect to gender roles, from 1875 to the present. Provides historical background essential to understanding fundamentalist and evangelical teaching on gender issues today.

Brown, Ann. *Apology to Women: Christian Images of the Female Sex.* Leicester, England: InterVarsity, 1991. 192 pp. An overview of how women have been perceived throughout church history, with an emphasis on traditional Christian art and literature.

Cook, Kaye V., and Lance L. Lee. *Man and Woman, Alone and Together: Gender Roles, Identity, and Intimacy in a Changing Culture.* Wheaton, Ill.: Victor Books, 1992. 288 pp. A self-help approach by two psychologists, encouraging men and women to adopt the values of flexibility, tolerance, respect, and responsibility in their relations with one another.

DeBerg, Betty A. *Ungodly Women: Gender and the First Wave of American Fundamentalism.* Minneapolis: Fortress Press, 1990. 165 pp. Analyzes the roots and character of fundamentalism in light of the gender-role ideology in church and society in the United States between 1880 and 1930. Shows how the fundamentalist view of gender was integral to fundamentalist theology, and reveals the social origins of much of the traditionalist gender ideology in the church today.

Groothuis, Rebecca Merrill. *Women Caught in the Conflict: The Culture War Between Traditionalism and Feminism.* Grand Rapids, Mich.: Baker Book House, 1994. 249 pp. Compares and contrasts evangelical feminism and traditionalism, placing these views within the context of previous and present cultural perspectives on gender roles. Offers a thorough refutation of the common traditionalist charge that biblical egalitarians are on a slippery slope that leads inexorably to the pagan and secular excesses of contemporary radical feminism.

Hassey, Janette. *No Time for Silence: Evangelical Women in Public Ministry Around the Turn of the Century.* Grand Rapids, Mich.: Zondervan Publishing House, 1986. 254 pp. A valuable, eye-opening, historically documented account of the evangelical support for women in preaching and teaching ministries a century ago in the United States.

Hubbard, M. Gay. *Women: The Misunderstood Majority.* Contemporary Christian Counseling series. Irving, Tex.: Word, 1992. 274 pp. Written primarily for counselors by a psychologist, this book helps people "understand women" without the cultural mythology that tends to pervade traditional treatments of women's psychology; it also deals with gender research and the significance of sex differences.

Schmidt, Alvin John. *Veiled and Silenced: How Culture Shaped Sexist Theology.* Macon, Ga.: Mercer Univ. Press, 1989. 238 pp. An exposition of how theologians throughout church history have been influenced by the sexist beliefs of secular culture.

Storkey, Elaine. *What's Right with Feminism.* Grand Rapids, Mich.: William B. Eerdmans Publishing Co., 1985. 186 pp. An overview and critique—from a Christian perspective—of the history and beliefs of some of the major schools of feminist thought. The book concludes by making a biblical, historical, and sociological case for evangelical feminism.

Van Leeuwen, Mary Stewart. *Gender and Grace: Love, Work, and Parenting in a Changing World.* Downers Grove, Ill.: InterVarsity Press, 1990. 278 pp. A Christian psychologist's analyses and insights concerning gender differences and gender roles. An excellent, well-informed, and even-handed treatment of the subject.

Van Leeuwen, Mary Stewart, Annelies Knoppers, Margaret L. Koch, Douglas J. Schuurman, and Helen M. Sterk. *After Eden: Facing the Challenge of Gender Reconciliation.* Grand Rapids, Mich.: William B. Eerdmans Publishing Co., 1993. 651 pp. Written by a team of scholars from the Reformed tradition, this volume ranges widely over historical, cultural, theological, sociological, and anthropological considerations related to the gender issue. While there is much to value here in information and insights, I do take issue with some of the authors' more "liberal" leanings, both political and theological.

Biblical and Theological Studies

Bilezikian, Gilbert. *Beyond Sex Roles: What the Bible Says About a Woman's Place in Church and Family.* 2d ed. Grand Rapids, Mich.: Baker Book House, 1986. 340 pp. Develops a case for biblical equality by looking at the teaching of the entire Bible, not just the proof texts usually employed in the debate. Includes an Appendix responding to Wayne Grudem's study of the meaning of the Greek term for "head" *(kephale)*.

Boomsma, Clarence. *Male and Female, One in Christ: New Testament Teaching on Women in Church Office.* Grand Rapids, Mich.: Baker Book House, 1993. 105 pp. A brief but thoughtfully presented biblical case for women's ordination, by a Christian Reformed pastor. His comments also shed light on the recent upheavals in that denomination over this issue.

Evans, Mary J. *Woman in the Bible: An Overview of All the Crucial Passages on Women's Roles.* Downers Grove, Ill.: InterVarsity Press, 1984. 160 pp. A well-informed study of biblical passages related to gender roles, interjected with valuable background information on the cultural practices of Old and New Testament times.

Grenz, Stanley J., with Denise Muir Kjesbo. *Women in the Church: A Biblical Theology of Women in Ministry.* Downers Grove, Ill.: InterVarsity Press, 1995. 284 pp. A theological, biblical, and historical case for the equal partnership of women and men in all areas of ministry. The final two chapters on the nature of the priesthood and the ordained ministry are especially helpful.

Haubert, Katherine M. *Women as Leaders: Accepting the Challenge of Scripture.* Monrovia, Calif.: MARC, 1993. 101 pp. A brief but helpful response to the primary questions at issue in the debate over women serving in ministerial leadership positions.

Hayter, Mary. *The New Eve in Christ: The Use and Abuse of the Bible in the Debate about Women in the Church.* Grand Rapids, Mich.: William B. Eerdmans Publishing Co., 1987. 190 pp. Written by an Anglican scholar, this book offers insightful and persuasive arguments against the traditional, high-church teaching on the theological necessity of an all-male priesthood.

Keener, Craig S. *Paul, Women and Wives: Marriage and Women's Ministry in the Letters of Paul.* Peabody, Mass.: Hendrickson, 1992. 350 pp. This carefully argued treatment of the Pauline texts on women is notable for the author's in-depth knowledge of the cultural conditions within which Paul was writing and the significance of such for determining Paul's intended meaning in these passages.

Kimel, Alvin F., Jr., ed. *Speaking the Christian God: The Holy Trinity and the Challenge of Feminism.* Grand Rapids, Mich.: William B. Eerdmans Publishing Co., 1992. 337 pp. A critical and scholarly response to recent efforts of theologically liberal feminists to reject biblical descriptions of God in favor of woman-centered, feminized redescriptions. Some essays are better than others.

Kroeger, Catherine Clark, Mary Evans, and Elaine Storkey, eds. *Study Bible for Women: The New Testament.* Grand Rapids, Mich.: Baker Book House, 1995. 599 pp. NRSV translation of the New Testament with commentary and articles by evangelical women, most of whom are biblical scholars. Addresses general biblical topics, as well as issues particularly pertinent to women, from a perspective of biblical equality. Attempts to redress the imbalance in traditional, male-centered biblical commentary.

Kroeger, Richard Clark, and Catherine Clark Kroeger. *I Suffer Not a Woman: Rethinking 1 Timothy 2:11–15 in Light of Ancient Evidence.* Grand Rapids, Mich.: Baker Book House, 1992. 253 pp. Offers new insights and evidence concerning the cultural context of 1 Timothy and its bearing on the meaning of the passage traditionally understood to deny women the opportunity to teach or exercise authority over men in the church.

Mickelsen, Alvera, ed. *Women, Authority and the Bible*. Downers Grove, Ill.: InterVarsity Press, 1986. 304 pp. A compilation of addresses presented at the Evangelical Colloquium on Women and the Bible, October 1984, concerning issues central to the biblical understanding of women's roles in the church and home. A helpful overview of scholarship on the subject.

Spencer, Aida Besancon. *Beyond the Curse: Women Called to Ministry*. Nashville, Tenn.: Thomas Nelson, 1985. 223 pp. An insightful study of Genesis 1–3 and New Testament texts relevant to women in ministry. Includes an Afterword by the author's husband on the practical realities of a marriage of equality.

Spencer, Aida Besancon, Donna F. G. Hailson, Catherine Clark Kroeger, and William David Spencer. *The Goddess Revival*. Grand Rapids, Mich.: Baker Book House, 1995. 304 pp. Chock full of helpful information on the nature of the biblical God as contrasted with the nature of pagan and neopagan gods and goddesses. This book tells the truth that needs to be heard by those interested or involved in radical feminist spirituality.

Marriage and Vocation

Adeney, Miriam. *A Time for Risking: Priorities for Women*. Portland, Ore.: Multnomah, 1987. 182 pp. An encouragement to women to say "yes" to what really matters, to risk pouring out their energies for the kingdom of God and not to be limited by conventional, cultural expectations of the woman's role.

Flynn, Leslie B. *My Daughter a Preacher!?!* 1996. Available from Leslie B. Flynn, 32 Highview Ave., Nanuet, NY 10954. 158 pp. A brief but intriguing account of a Conservative Baptist pastor's journey from an unreflective traditionalism to an appreciation of the Bible's support for women (such as his own daughter) whom God calls to pastoral ministry.

Gundry, Patricia. *Heirs Together: Mutual Submission in Marriage*. Grand Rapids, Mich.: Zondervan Publishing House, 1980. 192 pp. A well-balanced and well-reasoned case for a mutuality and equality in marriage that is biblical, sensible, and workable.

Gundry, Patricia. *Neither Slave Nor Free: Helping Women Answer the Call to Church Leadership*. San Francisco: Harper & Row, Publishers, 1987. 150 pp. An articulation of, and response to, the problems facing women in the church who are called to leadership ministry. Practical, readable, and realistic.

Littauer, Florence. *Wake Up, Women! Submission Doesn't Mean Stupidity*. Dallas: Word Publishing, 1994. 205 pp. Offers simple yet sensible counsel that should be heeded by every woman enmeshed in traditionalist gender ideology. In an easily readable, conversational style, the author discusses problem areas specifically pertinent to women's lives, including abuse within marriage. Stops short of being "feminist" and so would be acceptable to any woman, regardless of her position on gender roles.

Shenk, Sara Wenger. *And Then There Were Three: An Ode to Parenthood*. Scottsdale, Penn.: Herald Press, 1985. 219 pp. A Christian feminist's wise yet realistic reflections on marriage and motherhood, and the ultimate value of family relationships.

Wang, Bee-Lan C., and Richard J. Stellway. *Should You Be the Working Mom? A Guide for Making the Decision and Living with the Results*. Elgin, Ill.: David C. Cook, 1987. 173 pp. A thoughtful yet practical treatment of the issue of employment for mothers, written by an educator and a sociologist.

Wright, Linda Raney. *A Cord of Three Strands: Exploring Women's and Men's Roles in Marriage, Family and Church*. Old Tappan, N.J.: Fleming H. Revell Co., 1987. 256 pp. A very readable, evenhanded explanation of biblical equality with respect to both marriage and ministry.

Subject Index

Scripture Index

271